Tax Planning for Real Estate Investors

James B. Kau and **C. F. Sirmans** are associate professors in the Department of Real Estate and Legal Studies at the University of Georgia, Athens, Georgia.

Tax Planning for Real Estate Investors

JAMES B. KAU

C. F. SIRMANS

A SPECTRUM BOOK

Prentice-Hall, Inc., Englewood Cliffs, New Jersey 07632

Library of Congress Cataloging in Publication Data

Kau, James B
   Tax planning for real estate investors.

   (A Spectrum Book)
   Bibliography: p.
   Includes index.
   1. Real estate investment—Taxation—United
States.   2. Real property and taxation—United
States.   I. Sirmans, C. F., joint author.
II. Title.

KF6535.K36   343.7305'46   80-3
ISBN 0-13-885145-X
ISBN 0-13-885137-9 pbk.

10   9   8   7   6   5   4   3   2   1

Editorial/production supervision
and interior design by Eric Newman
Manufacturing buyer: Barbara A. Frick

Prentice-Hall International, Inc., *London*
Prentice-Hall of Australia Pty. Limited, *Sydney*
Prentice-Hall of Canada, Ltd., *Toronto*
Prentice-Hall of India Private Limited, *New Delhi*
Prentice-Hall of Japan, Inc., *Tokyo*
Prentice-Hall of Southeast Asia Pte. Ltd., *Singapore*
Whitehall Books Limited, *Wellington, New Zealand*

Contents

II.   BUSINESS ORGANIZATIONS AND TAX CONSIDERATIONS, 25

III.   TAXATION AND OPERATIONS, 67

IV.   TAXATION AND DISPOSITION, 131

V.   APPLYING THE AFTER-TAX INVESTMENT PROCESS, 169

Preface

What is a tax shelter? How does a tax shelter work? How can real estate serve as a tax shelter? How does taxation influence the acquisition, operation, and disposition of a real estate investment? How can the taxes from real estate investing be kept at a minimum? How can advantage be taken of real estate tax-shelter opportunities? These are some of the questions to be dealt with in this book.

Real estate as an investment medium continues to be attractive. This book is written both for investors and for real estate professionals, such as brokers, salespersons, appraisers, and lending officers, who have not had experience with analyzing tax impacts on real estate investments. Its purpose is *not* to make the reader a tax expert but rather to provide the investor with techniques for understanding and making effective decisions concerning the impact of taxation on real estate investment analysis.

The decision to invest in an apartment building, an office building, a shopping center, or any other type of real estate investment is one that should be made by an investor only after careful consideration and an informed forecast of the probabilities of success. Investing is by definition the sacrificing of *certain* outflows for *uncertain* inflows. There are risks that must be taken. Decisions are based on a forecast of the *expected* outcomes. In the case of real estate investments, the investor commits some of his or her money, called *equity*, in exchange for the cash inflows that the project is expected to generate. Obviously, there exists the probability that the investment will generate smaller or greater cash inflows than the investor expects.

The investor must carefully consider all of the factors influencing the real estate investment and its projected returns. Income taxes are one of the key factors influencing the investment decision, since they reduce (or—in some cases—increase, as we shall see later) the cash flow generated by a real estate investment. This book is based on the premise that the investor is interested in the "cash flow"—the amount of income remaining after all expenses have been met. One of the largest expenses may be the taxes.

The investor must be careful, however, not to let the pursuit of an income tax shelter and the availability of highly leveraged investments override considerations of economic soundness. Does the project make sense from a market perspective? Is there a demand for the services provided by the project, such as housing or office space? Is there an under- or an oversupply of competing projects? Although the influence of taxes is great in the real estate investment decision, taxes are only one of the factors to be considered.

The specific aims of this book are:

1. To acquaint the reader with how real estate taxes enter into real estate investment decision-making, and
2. To introduce the basic principles of taxation of real estate investments, including the Tax Reform Act of 1978, so that tax planning can take place before acquisition, during operation, and at the time of disposition of the investment.

Investors who buy real estate solely for tax shelters should first explore the available "exits." Although the tax aspects are attractive in the early life of the investment, they can't last forever. As the shelter ages, these deductions decline, often to the point where the investment is producing a negative cash flow for which there is only one cure—more cash. An investor who can't come up with outside financing will have to invest more equity. There may be no easy exit from a "leaking" tax shelter. The investor must face these possibilities *before* the investment is made and not be misled by the short-term benefits. To correctly analyze an investment opportunity, the investor should apply the total investment-analysis process outlined in Chapter 1.

AN OVERVIEW OF THE BOOK

This book is divided into five major parts. Part 1, "Taxation and Real Estate Investing," examines the basic principles of the impact of taxation on real estate investment decision-making. Chapter 1 outlines in detail the real estate investment process. Chapter 2 discusses the basic workings of a tax shelter. Since the investment process we outline is designed to be applicable to any type of real estate investment, the real estate investor can, by following the steps in this process, consider the factors necessary to arriving at a sound investment decision.

Part 2, "Business Organizations and Tax Considerations," examines the techniques for acquiring and holding title to real estate investments. Since each of the forms of ownership have different tax consequences, we describe the basic structure of each form of ownership and discuss the factors that the investor should consider in selecting the appropriate form. Chapter 3 describes partnerships, corporations, syndicates, and other forms of ownership. Chapter 4 discusses the formation of the various types of business entities for real estate investing. Particular attention is paid to the partnership form as it is the most common in real estate investing.

Part 3, "Taxation and Operations," discusses the impact of taxes on the operation of a real estate investment. The three major areas of concern in operating a real estate investment are operating expenses, financing expenses, and taxation expenses. Chapter 5 outlines the interrelationship between operating expenses and taxes. Chapter 6 discusses the impact of financing decisions on the annual cash flow. Chapter 7 discusses forecasting the after-tax cash flows from a real estate investment. This chapter also provides a detailed example of how to set up the expected-annual-cash-flow statement for a real estate investment.

When making a real estate investment, the investor must plan ahead for the expected tax consequences of its disposition. Part 4, "Taxation and Disposition," examines the influences of taxes on the disposition of a real estate investment. The most common form of disposition is the sale of an investment, which is discussed in Chapter 8. Chapter 9 outlines some alternate methods of disposition, primarily deferred-payment sales and real estate exchanges.

Part 5, "Applying the After-Tax Investment Process," brings together the discussion of tax planning for a real estate investor by providing a detailed apartment-investment example of how to make the real estate investment decision on an after-tax basis. This example provides a summary of the investment process outlined in this book. The reader should carefully study Chapters 1 through 9 before proceeding to Chapter 10.

Tax Planning for Real Estate Investors

I

Taxation and Real Estate Investing

How do taxes affect the real estate investment process? This is the major question addressed in Part 1.

Real estate investing is the commitment of certain cash outflows to uncertain cash inflows. The investment decision is based on expectations regarding the inflows. The investor obviously faces the risk that an investment will generate larger or smaller cash flows than expected. Part 1 outlines the basic principles for understanding the role of income taxation in forecasting cash flows for real estate investment decision making.

Chapter 1 describes the various steps in the real estate investment process. Real estate investment analysis involves the careful consideration of many factors. The investor should follow the steps outlined in Chapter 1 in analyzing any type of real estate investment. As will be seen, taxes are one of the key factors that enter into this analysis.

Following a brief history of the income tax in the United States, Chapter 2 provides a discussion of the basic principles of tax shelter analysis, addressing such questions as: What is a tax shelter? What is tax planning? How does the use of borrowed funds (leverage) influence taxes?

1

1

The Role of Taxation in Real Estate Investment Analysis

INTRODUCTION

It has been observed that it probably requires more knowledge, skill, and judgment to achieve success in real estate investment than in any other field of investment. One important reason is that while most investors are well aware of taxes, they fail to understand their importance in investment analysis. This chapter introduces a systematic process which the investor can follow to make real estate investment decisions. The investment decision is viewed from the standpoint of the equity investor. By examining the entire process, the reader will see the important influence of taxation in real estate investment analysis. As will be seen, the real estate investment process also involves a number of other nontax contingencies on which the success of a project depends.

The most important tax for real estate investment decision making is the federal income tax. While the gift and estate taxes are relevant, they will be ignored in large part. Changes in tax rates and provisions occur from year to year. Current regulations should be consulted when preparing tax returns or considering an investment.

Taxation should not be regarded as an absolute evil. It normally benefits some at the expense of others. The purpose of this book is to indicate how the investor can benefit from tax laws. Taxes have complex impacts on investment results (rate of return), investment decisions, and the price which an investor can pay for a real estate investment. We provide a general framework for understanding these impacts, but we don't expect the reader to become an income tax expert.

TAX CLASSIFICATIONS OF REAL ESTATE HOLDINGS

Income from a real estate investment comes from two sources: (1) income during the period of ownership, and (2) income from the sale of the investment. These two types of income are treated differently for tax purposes. The former is taxed as ordinary income while the latter is treated as a capital gain (or loss) if certain requirements are met.

For tax purposes, real estate can be classified into four types of holdings. It is important for the taxpayer to understand these classifications, since the tax laws and regulations differ with each.

1. Real estate held for sale to customers
2. Real estate held as a personal residence
3. Real estate held for use in a trade or business
4. Real estate held for the production of income or investment

Each of these categories is treated somewhat differently for tax purposes. The difference in treatment is due to the character of the property in the hands of the owner. The controlling factor in determining tax treatment is the use to which the owner is putting the property.

This book is concerned primarily with income-producing real estate investments. This includes property held for both current income production as well as capital growth through an increase in real estate prices. All expenses of management and operation are deductible for tax purposes. Likewise, the owner of improved income-producing property is permitted to deduct an allowance for depreciation. Gains and losses on the sale or exchange of such property are taxed as a capital transaction. These might be short or long term, depending upon the period of ownership. If losses are incurred on the sale of such property, these are treated as capital losses. Finally, the owner of such property has the privilege of utilizing the tax-free exchange provisions of the tax laws. All of these aspects will be discussed in detail in later chapters.

Almost all real estate investments, such as apartment buildings or office buildings owned and operated by a taxpayer, are classified as held for trade or business rather than as falling under the IRS definition of investment real estate. The two key exceptions that are classified as investment property by the IRS are net leased property and undeveloped land. The distinction between investment real estate and property held for trade or business is important for the deduction of interest. In general, interest is deductible. But property classified as being held for investment purposes has a limitation on the amount of investment interest that is deductible.

Rental property is generally considered an investment property if the property is rented under a net lease arrangement. The determination of whether or not a property is rented under a net lease is made each year. A lease is considered a net lease if any of the following conditions are met:

1. Business deductions with respect to the leased property are less than 15 percent of the rental income from the property.
2. The taxpayer is guaranteed a specific return.
3. The taxpayer is guaranteed, in whole or in part, against loss of income.

A second major type of property that will ordinarily be classified for tax purposes as investment real estate is raw land held for speculation. Interest on loans used to finance such land may be subject to the excess interest limitation. The investor must be careful in investing in raw land. Suppose an investor acquired land intending to build an apartment building? He or she may have a hard time proving that it is not *investment property* in the tax sense of the term. The current law limits interest on investment indebtedness to $10,000 per year plus the net income from the investment.

The key tax aspects of property held for trade or business, as pointed out in Table 1-1, are:

1. Owner is entitled to deduct all expenses of managing and operating the property.
2. Owner of improved property is allowed a deduction for depreciation.
3. Owner is allowed to treat long-term gains and losses realized on the sale or exchange of such property as capital transactions and thus subject to capital gains taxation.
4. Owner is allowed to utilize the tax-free exchange provisions of the tax law.

Table 1-1 outlines some of the important characteristics of each type of real estate holding. As can be seen in the table, real estate held for trade or business receives the most favorable tax treatment.

THE REAL ESTATE INVESTMENT PROCESS

Any successful real estate investment requires a careful analysis of the numerous contingencies on which the decision depends. Figure 1-1 provides an overview of the real estate investment process. This process consists of five basic steps:

1. Identify the objectives, goals, and constraints of the investor.
2. Analyze the investment environment and market conditions.

TABLE 1-1. Characteristics of Real Estate Holdings

Type of Holding	Characteristic					
	Depreciation Allowance	Treatment of Gain	Treatment of Loss	Repair, Maintance Deduction	Property Tax Deduction	Interest Deduction
1. Personal residence	No	Capital gain	Loss not deductible	No	Yes	Yes
2. For sale to customers	No	Ordinary income	Ordinary loss	Yes	Yes	Yes
3. Trade or business	Yes	Capital gain (Section 1231)	Deductible (can be carried forward or backward)	Yes	Yes	Yes
4. Investment	Yes	Capital gain	Deductible	Yes	Yes	Limited

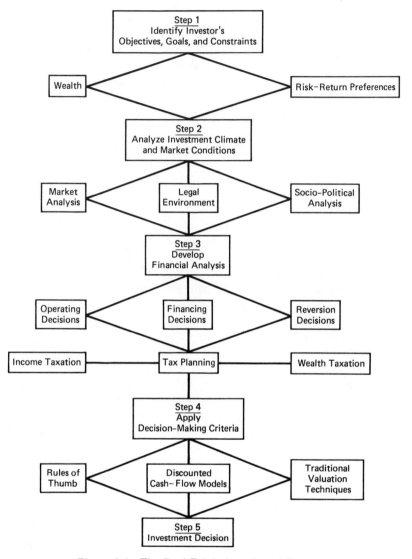

Figure 1-1. The Real Estate Investment Process.

3. Develop the financial analysis by forecasting cash flows from the project and the costs of investing.
4. Apply the decision-making criteria which will convert the expected benefits (cash flows) into a value estimate for the investor.
5. Make the investment decision.

This investment process can be applied to any type of income-producing real estate asset, both existing properties as well as proposed developments. It is simply an orderly procedure which the analyst can follow in considering the impact of the various contingencies that influence the feasibility of the investment. Novices to real estate investment will find the process helpful in avoiding many of the pitfalls of investing. The analysis may be terminated with any step that obviates those that follow. A real estate investment may be considered feasible when analysis indicates that there is a reasonable likelihood of satisfying the investor's objectives.

There are four major participants in a real estate investment. These are the equity investor, the mortgage lender, the user of the space and services provided, and the government—including federal, state, and local levels. All of these participants place constraints on the feasibility of a project. The analyst must consider the constraints of all four participants.

Since most projects are financed with some borrowed funds, the investment must meet the criteria of the lender. The user of the project creates the demand for the project. The government is involved at all levels, particularly at the federal with income taxation and at the local with property taxation, zoning, and other land-use constraints. The equity investor, as the ultimate decision maker in an investment, is the participant whose viewpoint is taken throughout this book.

Let us now examine each of the five steps in more detail.

Step 1: The analyst must identify the investor's objectives, goals, and constraints—the criteria which an investment project must satisfy in order to be a viable alternative. Investors have different objectives and constraints. Some, for example, are restricted by laws and regulations (insurance companies, REITs); some in high income tax brackets are interested in highly tax-sheltered investments; some seek fixed-income, secured-debt positions (by legal restrictions or choice); some investors are making a "one-shot" investment while others are in the investment market on a continuing basis; some are interested in highly leveraged, speculative equity positions; some prefer real estate–oriented investments while others consider real estate as only one alternative.

Step 2: The analyst must research the overall investment climate and the market conditions affecting the investment. This step in the investment process involves three distinct areas of analysis: market environment, legal environment, and sociopolitical environment.

Market analysis is concerned with understanding the supply and demand forces that influence feasibility of a particular investment. Market analysis must take into account these forces at the national, regional, and local levels. The analyst must remember that the demand for real estate is derived from the demand for the goods and services that it provides. For example, the demand for residential properties is derived from the demand for housing services; the demand for shopping centers is derived from the demand for retail goods, such as shoes and clothes, which the stores will provide; the demand for office buildings is derived from the demand for professional services, such as those provided by dentists' and doctors' offices.

Real estate investors often believe that the real estate itself has an intrinsic value. What is valued, however, are the services that a real estate investment provides. The lesson for the investor is thus to analyze the correct source of demand. If the investor knows six dentists who are in need of an office building, the task is much easier. All that is necessary is to determine the characteristics that they demand in an office. If the investor does not know his or her clients, the analyst might infer that there is a demand for office buildings because of increases in aggregate statistics, such as population, income, and employment. Obviously, the latter situation entails substantially more uncertainty that the former. Often the analyst is forced to this *secondary data*, as opposed to *primary data*, to infer demand conditions.

The real estate market is divided into many submarkets which can be delineated in different ways: for example, the residential market, the industrial market, the commercial market, and the vacant land market. Obviously even these broad groups can be further subdivided into other subgroups. The residential submarket, for example, can be divided into owner-occupied and renter-occupied subgroups. Even these subgroups are often too broad and must be further subdivided. The market can also be delineated by size of project, by location, or by type of structure.

Often, the investor fails to identify the appropriate market in which an investment is competing. Another common error in investment analysis is the failure to consider both sides of the market. Often the analyst will analyze only the demand side, for example, while ignoring supply considerations. The *analyst must identify the appropriate submarket in which a real estate investment is competing or will compete (in the case of a proposed development) and identify the supply and demand influences operating in that market.*

Market analysis is concerned with a reduction of aggregate data, such as population, employment, and income totals, to factors that are relevant to a particular project. It deals with factors that are, to a great extent, beyond the control of the buyer.

One of the purposes of market analysis is the identification of the users of the services provided by the investment. Their characteristics and preferences must be carefully analyzed to appropriately identify the demand for any given real estate project. If the analyist is able to identify potential customers, the need for aggregate data declines in importance.

The analyst must also carefully analyze the legal environment of an investment project. Legal constraints are often imposed not only on the investment itself but also on the investor and the potential tenant of the investment project. Factors such as appropriate form of ownership, zoning, and other land-use constraints, as well as private limitations, such as deed restriction and lease contracts, must be considered by the analyst.

Another area to be analyzed involves potential social constraints related to an investment. While a project may be legally permissible, it might not be feasible from society's point of view. Social controls in real estate investment analysis have received increased attention in recent years and might require the investor to compensate damaged parties for the negative effects of the project. Potential external effects and their possible costs may effect expected return on the project. Thus, investment projects that create *external effects* must be carefully analyzed.

Other factors that the analyst must consider in this step are physical and structural characteristics, which include the size, shape, and topography of the site; the condition of improvements; transportation access, and personal response factors, such as security. All of these attributes of an investment project are part of the services that the project supplies to the potential demand and must be analyzed carefully.

Step 3: The analyst must forecast the future benefits and costs of the investment. The concept of cash flows from an investment is discussed in detail in Chapter 2. The investor's decision is based on the anticipated amount of cash flow relative to the equity investment. In order to forecast the amount of income from an investment, the analyst goes through each of the following substeps.

Step 3A. From the market analysis the analyst makes forecasts of the rents and vacancies over the holding period of a project and the expected selling price at the end of the holding period.

Step 3B. Estimates of the operating expenses are made. Operating expenses include both fixed and variable expenses such as property taxes, insurance, utilities, and management fees.

Step 3C. The financial markets in which funds are to be borrowed for mortgage financing are analyzed. The supply and demand for mortgage funds set the costs of the borrowing. These costs include the loan-to-value ratio, the interest rate, the term (length) of the mortgage, and the frequency with which payments are to be made. Mortgage techniques must be carefully analyzed for both short-term and long-term financing and their impact on the expected benefits from the investment.

Step 3D. The influence of income taxation must be analyzed. Taxes are important in several ways. The two key areas are the annual income tax liability (or loss) from cash flow of the operation of a project and the tax liability (or loss) resulting from selling a project. Other tax influences that are important in the decision-making process include property exchanges, sale-leaseback techniques, installment sales, and preference taxes. All of these tax impacts must be analyzed in order to estimate the feasibility of an investment.

Many considerations are necessary in this step. For example, in the operations phase the analyst examines the expected rent levels and vacancy rates. Operating expenses must be carefully analyzed. In the financing phase of investment analysis such factors as short-term and long-term financing costs are examined. Financial leverage must be carefully analyzed since the investor would desire to increase the rate of return as result of positive leverage. This also increases the financial risks of a project. The influence of income taxation can have a large impact on a real estate investment decision. The analyst must carefully consider the tax impacts along with possible tax shelter and tax planning concepts. After carefully considering these factors, the analyst can make a forecast of the expected cash flow from the investment.

Step 4. The analyst must take the forecasts of benefits (cash flow) from a project and apply the criteria that are the most appropriate to decide whether the project should be accepted or rejected as compared to the costs of investing. One of the keys to successful investing is correctly identifying the potential cash flows in order to compare them to the cost of the investment. A number of techniques are available for comparing benefits to costs. In each of them the underlying questions are: If the investor pays this cost, what will be his or her rate of return given these expected cash flows? Will this rate of return be high enough to compensate the investor for the risk that he or she must take?

Step 5. The decision to accept or reject the investment is made. Once the benefits and costs have been compared, the investor can then determine if an investment meets his or her objectives. By this comparison, the investor decides to accept or reject an investment.

This brief introduction to the total investment process should give the reader a basic understanding of the many contingencies on which the success of a real estate investment depends. The role of taxation is extremely important since it influences the expected cash flows from a potential investment.

PARTICIPANTS IN REAL ESTATE INVESTMENT PROCESS

We have pointed out that there are four basic participants in the real estate investment process: the equity investor, the mortgage lender, the tenant, and the government (federal, state, and local). Figure 1-2 outlines the basic interrelationships between these participants. The investor must understand how the participants interact and the constraints placed on a real estate investment by each.

We are viewing the investment from the perspective of the equity investor, who usually holds the title to the property. He or she has certain rights—such as the right of use, the right to exclude other people, and the right to sell the property—which come with ownership. These property rights can be viewed as a "bundle" or can be divided and "sold" individually. The equity investor can use any of several different forms of ownership, such as an individual ownership, a partnership, a corporation, or a real estate investment trust (REIT).

Since most real estate investments require large sums of capital, funds must usually be borrowed from a mortgage lender. The mortgage funds can take the form of short-term (such as construction financing) or long-term (permanent) financing. The traditional sources of mortgage funds are savings and loan associa-

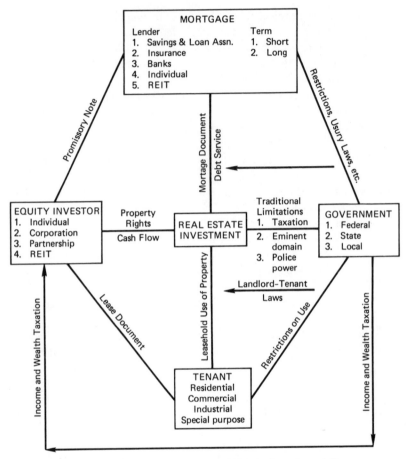

Figure 1-2. Participants in the Real Estate Investment Process.

tions, insurance companies, mutual savings banks, commercial banks, and real estate investment trusts. The mortgage lender is willing to loan on a real estate investment in return for a promise to repay the amount loaned plus interest over the term of the mortgage. This payment of principal and interest is usually called debt service. The mortgage document specifies the conditions of the loan and pledges the real estate as security for the debt. The promissory note is the evidence of the indebtedness and the promise to repay the loan. The mortgage financing aspects of real estate investment are complex from financial, legal, and taxation viewpoints.

The third major participant in the investment process is the user of the real estate. By definition, income-producing real estate has a user other than the owner. This user is referred to as the tenant. The tenant "buys" the right to use the property and in return pays the owner a price. This price is generally referred

12

to as rent. There are many subgroups of tenants. Broad categories include residential, commercial, and industrial tenants. The tenant's right to use the property is generally referred to as a leasehold estate. An important aspect of owning income-producing real estate is the lease document. The lease document serves to protect both the owner (landlord) and the user (tenant). Lease analysis for income-producing property is extremely important for the success of an investment.

The fourth major participant in the real estate investment process is the government. All levels of government—federal, state, and local—have an impact on real estate investments. The traditional influences have been the power of taxation, the power of eminent domain (the right to take private property for public use with compensation), and police power (the right of government to limit the use of property with regard to public safety without compensation). Recent years have seen an even greater government involvement in real estate investment. Intervention such as land-use planning and zoning and environmental controls has made the decision-making process even more complex.

The government has influence on all the interrelationships between the participants. Examples include restrictions on mortgage lenders through usury laws and influences on the landlord-tenant relationship. The areas to be discussed in this book are the income and wealth taxation influences of the government on the equity investor.

TAX INCENTIVES FOR REAL ESTATE INVESTMENTS

The basic motivation for investing is the desire for a return on equity. As was discussed in the overview of the investment process, the rate of return on a real estate investment is influenced by all of the factors that affect the expected cash flows from the investment.

Investors have different investment objectives. All investors are committing certain cash outflows to uncertain cash inflows. Some investors want to hedge themselves against inflation. A hedge against inflation involves investing in an asset whose price increases at a rate at least equal to the rate of inflation. Even better is an investment whose price increases faster than the average inflation rate. This can result when the demand for the asset increases at a greater rate than the demand for other assets. The investor is hoping for "real" appreciation in the value of the property. Tax laws related to taxation on appreciation of property value are favorable to real estate investments.

Another reason for investing is to generate cash flow from a real estate investment. The tax laws concerning the operation of real estate investments make this reason for investing in real estate a significant consideration.

While recent tax law changes, particularly the Tax Reform Act of 1976, have been aimed at eliminating tax benefits, real estate investments continue to be attractive to investors. Well-planned real estate investments, with a correct use of tax benefits and advantages, allow an attractive rate of return on equity capital. The tax advantages that are available to the investor generally fall into two categories: (1) those related to the purchase and holding of a real estate investment, and (2) numerous tax options available when the investor decides to dispose of the investment.

Some tax advantages available to the real estate investor are listed below. Each of these will be discussed in detail in subsequent chapters.

1. The investor in real estate may deduct an allowance for depreciation which allows a recovery of a substantial portion of the investment.

2. The depreciation allowance is unaffected by mortgages. The right to depreciate is based on the total cost rather than the cost of the equity investment. Few investments offer greater opportunity to use leverage concepts.

3. When real estate is held for investment purposes, whether improved or unimproved, the major out-of-pocket costs are deductible. These costs include interest, taxes, insurance, management fees, and other expenses of operating an investment.

4. Some carrying costs, such as taxes or interest, must be capitalized over specified periods up to ten years. Points paid on borrowed funds must be amortized over the term of the loan.

5. The costs of repairs, operation, and maintenance (noncapital expenditures) can be deducted for tax purposes.

6. By pooling resources through the use of a partnership or syndicate, opportunities in real estate investment are made more attractive. This flexibility of ownership and title enables the investor to purchase attractive investments.

7. Real estate held for investment purposes is eligible for a deduction for casualty losses.

8. Incentives for investing in low-income housing have been strengthened. Many advantages, including accelerated depreciation, favorable recapture rules, and other incentives are available for this type of investment.

9. On the sale of an investment, the investor may be taxed at lower capital gains rates.

10. The real estate investor has the option to exchange real property for other like-kind property. Such exchanges may allow the investor to increase his or her equity without tax costs.

11. The investor may elect to defer tax due on sale by using the installment method.

These are only some of the areas of taxation that make real estate an attractive investment. These and others will be discussed in the following chapters.

2

Tax-Shelter Analysis: Basic Principles

INTRODUCTION

Tax considerations enter into every stage of real estate investment decision making. Potential tax liability or saving influences the cash flow from an investment, thus influencing the value or price that an investor could pay and still earn his or her desired rate of return. Real estate has, as a tax shelter, been attractive to high-bracket taxpayers. Tax laws are extremely complex and confusing and thus the potential for error in under- or overvaluing a particular real estate investment is great. To properly structure, operate, and dispose of a real estate investment, a thorough understanding of the rules and alternatives is essential.

Real estate investments are taxed by all levels of government—federal, state, and local. At the federal level, the three basic forms of taxation are the income tax, the estate tax, and the gift tax. Although all of these have an impact on investment decisions, the federal income tax is the primary form discussed in this book. The income tax takes one of two forms: the ordinary income tax and the capital gains tax. While most states have some forms of income taxation, their rates are typically low. State taxes do, however, influence investment decisions in the same manner as the federal taxes. At the local level, the primary form of taxation is the property tax. The property tax is an operating expense item for purposes of federal income taxation.

INCOME TAXATION—
A BRIEF HISTORY

Approximately 80 percent of the tax revenue collected by the federal government comes from taxes imposed on individual and corporation incomes. The income tax is clearly the backbone of the federal tax structure and by far the most important tax influencing real estate investment decisions. The income tax permits the federal government to exercise substantial control over the direction of the nation's economic and social institutions. Table 2-1 outlines some of the more important dates in the history of the income tax in the United States.

The first income tax law by the federal government was enacted in 1862 with the tax rates from 1.5 percent to 5 percent. This tax was designed to aid in financing the Civil War. The tax contained a number of provisions similar to the present structure, such as tax withholding, progressive rates, and returns filed under oath.

This first tax was abolished a decade later, in 1872. From 1872 to 1913, the taxing measures used by the federal government were, to a great extent, excise duties (on liquor and tobacco) and customs receipts (the traditional tax). The controversy over the 1862 income tax was widespread and reached a climax in 1894 when a new income tax law was enacted.

TABLE 2-1. A Brief History of Income Taxes in the United States

Year	Event
1862	First income tax enacted to finance Civil War. A mildly progressive tax with rates of 1.5% to 5%.
1872	1862 tax eliminated.
1894	Second income tax enacted with a flat tax rate of 2% on individual and corporate incomes.
1895	1894 tax ruled unconstitutional by Supreme Court. Court held that the tax required apportionment among the states on the basis of population.
1909	1% excise tax on corporate income enacted.
1909	Sixteenth Amendment to Constitution initiated. This amendment gives the Congress power to lay and collect taxes on income.
1913	Sixteenth Amendment ratified as part of federal Constitution.
1913	Income tax enacted.
1916	Supreme Court upheld validity of tax.
1939	1913 tax law with its subsequent amendments were brought together under a permanent code.
1954	Internal Revenue Code, which is the present governing tax law with subsequent amendments, was established.
1958, 1962, 1964, 1969, 1971, 1976, 1978	Major revisions in Code were made.

The 1894 tax law imposed a flat rate of 2 percent on individual and corporate income. This tax was immediately ruled unconstitutional by the Supreme Court. The next step in tax history was taken in 1909, when proponents of the income tax obtained the enactment of a 1-percent excise tax on corporations. Another important step was taken in 1909 in that the Sixteenth Amendment to the U.S. Constitution was initiated. The amendment reads:

The Congress shall have the power to lay and collect taxes on income, from whatever source derived, without apportionment among the several States, and without regard to any census or enumeration.

The tax of 1894 had been struck down because the Supreme Court held that the income tax was a direct tax and required apportionment among the states on the basis of population. The Sixteenth Amendment was aimed directly at overriding this objection by providing Congress with the power to tax income.

In 1913, the final step in initiating the income tax was taken. By that year a sufficient number of states had ratified the proposed amendment to make it part of the Constitutional law. The Congress enacted the income tax, under the amendment, in the same year. The 1913 Act was a mere sixteen pages in length. In 1939 Congress established a permanent code. In 1954, the Internal Revenue Code was revised. The current income tax law is basically the 1954 Code with subsequent amendments.

While the 1954 Code has been amended in every year since 1954, substantial revisions took place in 1958, 1962, 1964, 1966, 1969, 1971, 1976, and 1978. The current tax laws are largely a product of all the Congresses since the 1913 enactment of the income tax. The Internal Revenue Service (IRS) was created by Congress in 1953 to collect the tax and interpret tax laws. And, as we shall see in the sections to come, the provisions of these laws vitally affect every real estate investment decision.

ESTIMATING CASH FLOWS

How much should an investor pay for a real estate investment? This crucial question should be of greatest concern to the investor.

The *value* of a real estate investment is defined as the present worth of the future cash flows from the investment. Using this definition, the investor must perform two basic steps in order to estimate the price he or she should pay. First, the investor must estimate the income which an investment is expected to generate and secondly, the investor must find the "present value" of the expected income.

How should the income from a real estate investment be measured? In general, a real estate investment has two potential sources of income: (1) the annual

TABLE 2-2. Annual Cash Flow from Operation

	Calculation of After-Tax Cash Flow
	Rent
Multiplied by	Number of units
Equals	Potential gross income (PGI)
Less	Vacancy and bad debt allowance
Plus	Miscellaneous income
Equals	Effective gross income (EGI)
Less	Operating expenses
Equals	Net operating income (NOI)
Less	Debt service
Equals	Before-tax cash flow (BTCF)
Less	Taxes
Equals	After-tax cash flow (ATCF)
	Calculation of Taxes from Operation
	Before-tax cash flow
Plus	Principal payment portion of debt service
Plus	Replacement reserves
Less	Depreciation allowance
Less	Amortized financing costs
Equals	Taxable income (TI)
Multiplied by	Marginal tax rate for investor
Equals	Taxes

income from the operation of the investment, and (2) the income from the reversion (disposition), usually the sale, of the investment. To make correct investment decisions, the investor must formulate expectations about these two potential sources of income. Decisions based on the income from operations without regard to the reversion may not be optimal.

Table 2-2 illustrates how to measure the cash flow from the operation of a real estate investment. Table 2-3 illustrates how to measure the cash flow from the sale of an investment. There are four *levels* of income from an investment:

Annual	*Reversion*
1. Gross income	1. Selling price
2. Net operating income	2. Net sales proceeds
3. Before-tax cash flow	3. Before-tax equity reversion
4. After-tax cash flow	4. After-tax equity reversion

Gross Income. The initial point in setting up the expected cash flow from an investment is to determine the expected gross income from operation and the expected future selling price. The gross income from operation is the rent per unit multiplied by the number of units available for rent. For example, an apartment building has 100 units with an expected rental of $200 per month each. The PGI is thus $200 × 100 × 12 or $240,000 per year. The investor must carefully

TABLE 2-3. Cash Flow from Reversion (Sale)

	Calculation of After-Tax Equity Reversion
	Selling price
Less	Selling expenses
Less	Prepayment penalties on mortgage
Equals	Amount realized (net sales proceeds)
Less	Unpaid mortgage balance
Equals	Before-tax equity reversion (BTER)
Less	Taxes due on reversion
Equals	After-tax equity reversion (ATER)
	Calculation of Taxes Due on Sale
	Amount realized
Less	Adjusted basis
Equals	Total gain
Less	Excess depreciation recapture
Equals	Capital gain
Total taxes =	(Capital gain times capital gain tax rate) plus (Depreciation recapture times ordinary tax rate) plus (Preference income times preference tax rate).

analyze the market in which an investment is competing to formulate expectations regarding rent charges and vacancy allowances.

From the potential gross income, the allowance for vacancy and bad debt is deducted to arrive at effective gross income (EGI) from each year of operation.

Net Operating Income. The second level of income is the net income from operation and the net sales proceeds from the reversion.

The net operating income (NOI) from operation is calculated by deducting the operating expenses from the effective gross income. Operating expenses include such items as property taxes, repairs and maintenance, property insurance, and management fees.

The net sales proceeds (amount realized) from the sale of an investment is calculated by deducting from the expected selling price the selling expenses and any prepayment expenditures associated with early repayment of the mortgage loan.

Before-Tax Cash Flow. From the net operating income each year is deducted the payment on mortgage debt, referred to as debt service, to arrive at the BTCF. The debt service is influenced by the interest rate, the maturity of the loan, the frequency of payments, and the amount borrowed.

The before-tax equity reversion (BTER) is calculated by deducting the unpaid mortgage from the net sales proceeds. Obviously if the expected holding period is less than the mortgage maturity, there will be an unpaid mortgage debt.

After-Tax Cash Flow. The ATCF from operation is calculated by deducting any taxes due from operation from the BTCF. There are two potential sources of taxes from operation: ordinary income tax and minimum tax on preference income from operation. To calculate taxes, the investor must estimate the taxable income and his or her marginal tax rate for each year of operation.

The after-tax equity reversion (ATER) is found by deducting the taxes due on sale from the BTER. Taxes due on sale rise from three potential sources: ordinary income taxes, capital gains taxes, and minimum taxes.

Again, it must be stressed that the cash flows are the *expected* cash flows. Investments are made based on expectations regarding cash flow and the best measures to base one's expectations on are the after-tax cash flow from operation and the after-tax equity reversion from the disposition of the project.

BASIC CHARACTERISTICS OF TAX SHELTERS

Tax shelters take many different forms but usually have one or more of the following elements: tax deferral, leverage, and conversion of ordinary income to capital gain at the time of disposition. Real estate investments allow the investor to take advantage of all three of these elements of tax shelters.

The goal of tax planning is to pay as little tax as possible as late as possible. There is a big difference between tax avoidance and tax evasion. The former is completely legal while the latter is subject to penalties. With corporate tax rates nearly 50 percent and individual marginal tax rates as high as 70 percent on taxable income, tax planning is necessary to maximize investment value. Tax planning for real estate investment is possible because the future tax pattern can be forecast for a number of years in advance.

Tax Deferral

Tax deferral is usually accomplished in real estate investments by the use of accelerated depreciation techniques. The depreciation is a noncash outlay and defers taxes until the time of disposition. The deferral of taxes is simply a straightforward recognition of the time value of money—that is, a dollar today is worth more than a dollar tomorrow. With tax deferral, the taxpayer earns a return on the postponed tax. The numerous laws and regulations concerning taxation of income from real estate investments seek to encourage the taxpayer to engage in some activity that has been judged socially beneficial and, in the process, afford the investor the opportunity to engage in tax planning.

Leverage and Tax Shelters

Leverage is obtained by using borrowed money to finance a real estate investment. Most real estate investments are financed with a large portion of borrowed funds. This simply means a high ratio of debt funds to equity funds. For example, suppose an investment has 25 percent equity and 75 percent borrowed funds. The *leverage factor* is equal to 75 divided by 25, or 3. If the project were financed with 20 percent equity and 80 percent borrowed funds, the leverage factor would be 4 ($80 \div 20$).

The use of leverage maximizes the tax benefits of the accelerated depreciation and creates higher rates of return on the investor's equity. A simple illustration of leverage effects on tax shelters is as follows: An investor buys a property for $200,000 of which $180,000 is depreciable. He borrows $175,000 and provides $25,000 of equity. For tax purposes, he is treated as if he has invested $200,000. If the first-year depreciation deduction is $20,000, an investor in a 70-percent tax bracket would save $14,000 ($20,000 $\times$ .70) in taxes the first year. Obviously since his investment is only $25,000, this represents a substantial return for the first year. An investor in a 50-percent tax bracket would save $10,000 ($20,000 $\times$ .50) in taxes. It's not difficult to see that tax shelters are of more benefit to investors in higher tax brackets.

Several reasons account for the high leverage in real estate investment. The basic reason is that the investor can increase the rate of return on his or her equity position if the cost of borrowing is less than the overall return on the investment.

To illustrate, suppose an investment which had a total value of $300,000 was generating a net operating income of $33,000. This represents an overall rate of return of 11 percent ($33,000 $\div$ $300,000). If the investor uses 100-percent equity funds, her rate of return would be 11 percent. However, suppose she could finance the project by borrowing $240,000 with the remaining $60,000 in equity and suppose further that the debt requires a payment of $24,000. The resulting before-tax cash flow to the investor is $33,000 – $24,000 or $9,000. The investor's rate of return on the equity is now 15 percent ($9,000 $\div$ $60,000)—an increase of 4 percent.

However, this increase in rate of return is also accompanied with an increase in risk, a type of risk generally referred to as *financial risk*—the risk that a project will not generate sufficient income to meet the financial obligations. This risk-return relationship is explained in greater detail in Chapter 6.

A Simple Example

To illustrate the basic concepts of a real estate tax shelter consider the following simple example.

An investor, who is in a 50-percent tax bracket, purchases an apartment building for $100,000. The purchase is financed with $20,000 in equity and a mortgage of $80,000. The debt service on the mortgage is $8,387 per year, of which $7,564 is interest and $823 is principal repayment in the first year. The project is expected to generate a net operating income of $10,000. The depreciation deduction is $3,400.

The before-tax cash flow (BTCF) from the investment is the NOI ($10,000) less debt service ($8,387), or $1,613. To calculate the after-tax cash flow (ATCF), the investor deducts taxes from the BTCF. Taxes are equal to taxable income (TI) multiplied by the tax rate of 50 percent. What is taxable income?

$$TI = BTCF + Principal - Depreciation$$
$$= \$1,613 + \$823 - \$3,400$$
$$= -\$964$$

Notice that taxable income is negative. Does this mean that the investment is losing money? *No:* It means that *for tax purposes*, the project is generating a tax loss. The project *is* generating a positive cash flow.

Taxes are determined thus:

$$Taxes = TI \times Tax\ Rate$$
$$= -\$964 \times .50$$
$$= -\$482$$

Taxes are negative. This means that the investor is able to save $482 in taxes that he otherwise would have paid by using the tax loss from the investment to "shelter" his other taxable income.

The after-tax cash flow (ATCF) from the project for the first year is:

$$ATCF = BTCF - Taxes$$
$$= \$1,613 - (-\$482)$$
$$= \$2,095$$

Notice that the ATCF is larger than BTCF. This is the result of the tax shelter.

This simple illustration demonstrates the calculation of the ATCF for the first year of the investment. The investor must analyze the tax impact on the expected cash flow from operation as well as from the disposition of the investment before making the decision as to whether to invest or not. The following chapters take the investor step-by-step through this analysis.

SOME WORDS OF CAUTION

The investor who invests in real estate simply for tax shelter benefits is usually taking high risks. A real estate investment must make business and economic sense. If the project does not make sound real estate sense from a market viewpoint, it might turn into a nightmare for the investor. The investor must answer the question: Does the investment make business sense? Is there enough demand for such a project? Is there too much competition for such a project? Basic supply and demand analysis is just as applicable to real estate investing as to any other type of investing.

The structure upon which most tax shelters are built is very fragile. The tax laws are very subject to change. Such changes can often have important impacts on a tax shelter. While the investor is encouraged to exert due care and skill to recover all the benefits available in an investment, he or she must be careful to avoid pitfalls in real estate investment.

Several other statements regarding tax-sheltered real estate investments should be made:

1. Tax shelters generally have high risk. Does the expected rate of return compensate the investor for the increased risk?

2. Tax shelters may be the last outpost of *caveat emptor* (let the buyer beware). Investors should know with whom they are dealing and should read all relevant documents carefully. They should not be mislead by the short-run benefits but should determine the total impact of taxation on the investment decision.

3. The decision of whether to invest in a real estate tax shelter is an economic decision. The only distinction between the tax shelter and any other investment is that the tax shelter provides income as a result of sheltering an investor's other taxable income. The expected tax consequence is only one of the factors in determining the economic potential of the investment.

4. Most tax shelters have a sponsor-manager of the project. The ability, reputation, and past experience of the sponsor is a critical factor. Full and complete disclosure of the investment should be demanded by the investor. What is the true role and function of the sponsor in the investment? What is the "track record" of the sponsor in prior deals?

Real estate is sound as an investment opportunity. It has several advantages, particularly tax advantages, that other investments do not afford. Knowing how to use the advantages will help the investor identify desirable real estate investment opportunities.

II

Business Organizations and Tax Considerations

The selection of the legal form of organization for real estate is influenced greatly by tax considerations. However, other factors in addition to tax considerations should be considered in selecting the appropriate business organization of real estate assets. This section outlines the basic structure of each business organization and discusses the factors the investor should consider in selecting the appropriate form for real estate. Particular attention is paid to the influence of tax considerations on choosing the optimum type of organization. Specifically, Chapter 3 discusses the general partnership, the limited partnership, the corporation, the syndicate, the real estate investment trust, and the sole proprietorship forms of business. Chapter 4 discusses the actual formation of various types of business entities for real estate investments.

Choosing the appropriate form of business organization from among the alternatives is a necessary and important step in the analysis of a real estate investment. Several alternatives normally may be suitable. The investor should select the business entity, if any, that enables him or her to reach the investment objectives set forth at the outset. The choice should be made only after careful analysis of the needs and objectives of the owner or owners, often with the advice of legal counsel.

3

Tax Shelters
and the Form
of Organization

INTRODUCTION

Business enterprises exist in a number of different forms. In real estate, the most common are sole proprietorship, corporations, general partnerships, limited partnerships, and real estate investment trusts (REIT's). Tax benefits and hedging against inflation are the primary reasons for investing in real estate. The amount of protection from inflation an investor will realize and the amount of income that is sheltered and deferred will depend to a large extent on the form of organization. Each form of organization differs in the benefits and costs involved. At the same time, each investor may differ as to preferences for investment and corresponding forms of organization. For an investor to realize the maximum benefit from a tax shelter, a thorough understanding of the options available in terms of organization and the tax consequences of each type organization is essential.

This chapter discusses the alternative methods of organizing properties, the characteristics of each type of organization that are especially significant for tax shelters, and the suitability of each type of organization for a particular investment strategy.

TAX SHELTERS AND
REAL ESTATE

The essence of real estate tax shelters is the ability to produce a taxable loss with a positive cash flow. All investments and businesses can produce a tax loss. It is easy to make a poor investment and lose money. But in real estate the tax loss doesn't necessarily indicate a negative cash flow. The income produced by the property may cover all expenses and yet a sizeable tax loss can occur. There are two main reasons for this phenomenon: (1) depreciation allowances and (2) the high leverage potential in real estate financing.

Tax laws allow an investor to depreciate an income-producing improvements. Depreciation is a technique that enables the investor to deduct the supposed reduction in property value that results from age and use. This deduction has little to do with the actual depreciation of the improvement. Depreciation is based on the total value of the improvement, not on the cash invested (equity) or on the income earned. The second factor affecting cash flow is that, in most real estate financing, the proportion of borrowed funds to cash invested (leverage) is very high. The combination of these two factors, depreciation and leverage, on the total value—regardless of the mortgage—can lead to a tax loss with a positive cash flow. In fact, the tax loss is quite often larger than the actual cash investment. While Chapters 6 and 7 will cover these concepts in more detail, the following example will help to give some immediate insight into the impact that depreciation and leverage have on producing a loss with a positive cash flow.

EXAMPLE 3-1:
TAXES AND DEPRECIATION

An individual purchases a $2,000,000 apartment building by paying $200,000 down as equity and borrowing $1,800,000. If the depreciation results in a $400,000 deduction in the first year, and if the investor is in the 70-percent bracket, then the tax liability will be reduced by $400,000 × .70, or $280,000. In this case, the deduction is $200,000 more than the equity and the tax savings are $80,000 more than the amount invested. In essence, the investor finances the investment with an interest-free loan from the government.

Example 3-1 demonstrates that a tax deduction can be accomplished through depreciation without a cash loss. This is not the case with principal payments on a mortgage, or with capital improvements; both represent cash outlays that are not deductible for tax purposes. It is therefore desirable for the investor to maintain a situation where depreciation deductions exceed mortgage principal payments. This allows a positive cash flow with a tax loss. Example 3-2 demonstrates how, in the initial stage, depreciation and mortgage interest offset cash flow and principal payments. Each year the principal payment becomes a greater share of the debt service. At some point in time, when depreciation and mortgage interest will no longer offset cash flow and principal payment, this investment will cease to be a tax shelter.

EXAMPLE 3-2:
TAX LOSS AND CASH FLOW

An investor acquires a warehouse for $750,000 of which $50,000 is allocated to land. The remaining $700,000 is the basis for depreciating the warehouse. The investor pays $50,000 down and takes a $700,000 mortgage at 12 percent for twenty-five years. He will depreciate the building over twenty-five years on a straight-line method. The net operating income is anticipated at $100,000. The debt service on the $700,000 mortgage is $89,290. The before-tax cash flow (BTCF) is equal to the net operating income minus the debt service. This amounts to a BTCF of $10,750. The debt service, $89,250, is for tax purposes divided into principal payment and mortgage interest. The straight-line depreciation of $28,000 is computed by dividing the value of the building, $700,000, by 25. The tax loss is the net operating income (NOI) less interest payments and depreciation— or BTCF plus principal payment less depreciation.

Year	Net Operating Income (NOI)	Debt Service	Before-Tax Cash Flows (BTCF)	Principal Payments	Mortgage Interest	Depreciation	Tax Gain or (Loss)
1	100,000	89,250	10,750	5,250	84,000	28,000	(12,000)
2	100,000	89,250	10,750	5,880	83,370	28,000	(11,370)
3	100,000	89,250	10,750	6,585	82,665	28,000	(10,665)
4	100,000	89,250	10,750	7,376	81,874	28,000	(9,875)
5	100,000	89,250	10,750	8,261	80,989	28,000	(8,989)
10	100,000	89,250	10,750	14,559	74,691	28,000	(2,691)
15	100,000	89,250	10,750	25,687	63,563	28,000	8,437
20	100,000	89,250	10,750	45,223	44,027	28,000	27,973
25	100,000	89,250	10,750	52,747	36,503	28,000	35,497

As Example 3-2 indicates, there is a tax loss for at least the first ten years with a positive before-tax cash flow of $10,750. In later years there is a tax gain, a result of the increased amount of debt service applied to the principal payment and not to interest payment. Principal payments are not deductible; therefore, as the interest payments decrease, the advantage of this project as a tax shelter decreases. At some point, it may be advantageous for the investor to sell or refinance the project. While the crossover point is not necessarily the optimal time for selling an investment, it is a significant point in the holding period of an investment.

This example points out one of the important considerations for deciding on the types of organization. The investor must be able to take the tax loss on his individual tax return to obtain the maximum benefit from the tax shelter. In the first year the tax loss is $12,000. If the investor is in the 50-percent tax bracket this results in a $6,000 reduction in taxes paid on his ordinary income. Adding this $6,000 to the before-tax cash flow of $10,750 gives a $16,750 after-tax cash flow (ATCF) from the warehouse. This will increase the rate of return from the warehouse. If the investor were in the 30-percent tax bracket this would produce a $3,600 reduction in taxes with an after-tax cash flow of $14,350. The rate of return for the investor in the 30-percent bracket would be lower. The higher your taxable income, the greater the benefit from investing in a tax shelter. There are some forms of organization that do not allow the investor to take the tax loss. The next section concentrates on the advantages and disadvantages of alternative forms of business organization.

CHARACTERISTICS OF BUSINESS ORGANIZATIONS

Each type of business organization has associated with it a set of characteristics. The characteristics important for real estate investment tax shelters are:

1. Taxation status
2. Investor liability
3. Transferability
4. Management
5. Restrictions
6. Duration
7. Method of creation

Each of these characteristics will vary with the type of organization.

Taxation Status

Taxation status reflects whether there is an opportunity for a tax shelter on the investor's ordinary income or the possibility of a tax deferral. A tax shelter reduces taxes on income from sources other than real estate. A tax deferral provides a way to postpone taxes. It provides in effect, an interest-free loan from the government. As was seen from Example 3-2, tax losses can be generated from a real estate investment with a positive cash flow. These tax losses must be able to offset ordinary income. If the individual is allowed to offset his or her ordinary income with such tax losses this is referred to as a "flow-through" single tax eligibility. The types of business organizations that allow flow-through tax benefit are individual and general and limited partnerships. Corporate organization results in most cases in double taxation—the corporation pays corporate tax on its income and the investor pays ordinary income tax on the dividends distributed out of the corporation's after-tax earnings. This double taxation may be one of the reasons the stock market has been in such disfavor in recent years. Many states impose a higher tax on corporate income than on individual income.

There are many other taxes that are imposed on corporations but not on sole proprietorships or partnerships. The double taxation can be avoided to some extent in a number of different ways. First, since reasonable salaries paid to employees may be deducted, a group of investors can form a corporation to pay themselves salaries that exactly cover the profits of the real estate investment. Second, the stockholder can make loans to the corporation. The interest on the loan is deductible and the stockholder pays only a single tax on the interest income. Again the Internal Revenue Service limits this technique by restricting the extent of these loans. The third technique is to have the corporation not pay any dividends and to accumulate the earnings. The stock will then sell at a higher price and only a single capital gains tax has to be paid. Here again the IRS imposes a special tax when this technique is used excessively. A combination of the three techniques could, for a group of real estate investors, reduce the double taxation problem to an insignificant level, assuming the investment does not yield extremely high returns.

Liability and Risk

Investors' liability is measured by the amount of risk involved in the investment. Is the possible loss limited to the amount invested or is the possible loss equivalent to the value of the property involved? If the risk is unlimited, the investor could lose his or her entire net worth. The advantage of flow-through tax benefits for certain types of organizations is accomplished in some cases by higher risk. Sole proprietorship and general partnerships have unlimited liability, whereas corporations and limited partners in limited partnerships have limited liability.

The relationship of risk to the extent of liability is on important issue. If an individual investor faces unlimited liability the risks are clearly greater. The compensation for accepting this risk is a higher rate of return on the investment. This is why the observed rates of return on real estate investments are higher. Real estate has more risk associated with it than many other alternative investments so that, even though the return is higher, the chance of serious loss is also higher. Each investor must decide the level of risk to take in choosing different investments.

Transferability and Liquidity

Transferability of interests is vital for flexibility. One of the costs of owning real estate is its lack of liquidity. The possible inability to transfer ownership in real estate increases the problem of liquidity—another factor making real estate a risky investment. When real estate is not readily exchangeable, the cost of exchange in terms of advertising and commissions may be significant. These costs generally require a sufficient holding period to recover expenses. Any situation requiring immediate selling of the property could endanger the rate of return and result in losses. This lack of liquidity should be taken into account by the investor when considering real estate investment and the alternative forms of ownership. Forming an organization such as a corporation that allows investors to freely trade their interest adds a significant amount of flexibility. Holding shares in corporations that specialize in real estate investment is another way to increase flexibility while investing in real estate.

Management

The type of management affects how decisions are made and the extent to which investors participate. Management that is very centralized may reduce administrative involvement and cost. Management cost varies not only with the type of ownership but with the type of investment. Land investment requires less management time whereas apartment building investment requires significantly more time.

Management techniques also vary with the type of organization. Corporations have shareholders who elect directors to set the policy. If a majority of the voting stock is held by stockholders who disagree with the director, he or she can be voted out of office. General partners, in the absence of any agreement to the contrary, have equal voices. This lack of central control in a general partnership may lead to conflict in management when there is a disagreement among the general partners. In limited parnterships the general partners have equal voice but the limited partners have no say as to how the partnership is managed.

Permissible Activities

There are very few restrictions on investment activities based solely on type of organization. Corporations and partnerships, for example, have a lot of flexibility as to their choice of investments. However, real estate investment trusts (REITs) have a number of major restrictions. In REITs a minimum number of shareholders is required. The business activities of REITs are to a large extent restricted to real estate. Their assets must in the most part be in real estate and there are limitations on the gains and the way in which the gains are distributed. Later in this chapter REITs will be covered in more detail. Corporations and partnerships also have regulations that restrict their behavior but these restrictions are far less severe than those governing REITs.

Method of Creation and Duration

Method of creation and duration varies with the type of organization. Corporations are created by the state and may be perpetual. General partnerships are created by agreement of the parties and are terminated by death, agreement, bankruptcy, or withdrawal of a partner. Limited partnerships are created by agreement and are terminated by the rules stated in the same agreement.

Each type of organization is a mixture of these characteristics. New forms of organization have evolved in attempts to merge various advantages and eliminate the disadvantages of these characteristics.

METHODS OF OWNING PROPERTIES

This section will examine the various forms of organization and the factors in real estate that influence their selection. The most significant factors are the characteristics previously discussed, which are listed in Table 3.1. The actual size of the business influences the relative importance of the characteristics. Very large organizations must incorporate to bring a large number of investors together. The corporate structure allows easy transferability with an efficient central management. The negative effect of double taxation is outweighed by the positive impact of limited liability, transferability, central management, and perpetual life.

Real estate investors, however, are generally seeking a method to defer or to shelter income. In such situations the benefits of flow-through tax losses outweigh any of the corporate benefits such as limited liability. It is not surprising, therefore, to find most real estate investors using sole proprietorship or partnership forms of organization. The difficulty of deciding which is the best form of ownership in real estate investment rests mostly on tax considerations.

Individual Ownership, Joint Tenancy, and Tenancy-in-Common

A common form of holding property in real estate is through sole proprietorship. The profits and losses from the property are reported on the individuals income tax returns. Owners are subject to unlimited liability on all debts. They are also liable, in most cases, for personal injury sustained on the property, a fact that makes the investor's entire wealth subject to loss. Also, the property is subject to liens for any other debts.

On the other hand, individual ownership has the advantages of simple management with no possible conflicts, since all the decisions are made by one person with absolute control over the investment. There are no trustees, managers, and boards of directors. Furthermore, in many cases, it is easier to liquidate an entire estate than a fractional share.

Joint tenancy and tenancy-in-common have the same taxation and liability characteristics as sole proprietorship. They are not forms of organization but types of ownership. For example, a partnership may be held as tenancy-in-common. Both joint tenancy and tenancy-in-common have two or more persons involved in the ownership which affects the share of ownership and the rights of survivorship. In a joint tenancy the share of ownership is equal and the survivor

TABLE 3-1. Characteristics of Business Organizations

	Taxation Status	Investor's Liability	Transferability	Management	Restrictions	Method of Creation	Duration
Sole proprietorship	Flow-through (single)	Unlimited	Transferable	Personal	No	Individual	Terminated by death or agreement; deceased interest becomes part of the estate
General partnership	Flow-through (single)	Unlimited	Not transferable	All partners in absence of agreement have equal voice	No	Created by agreement of the parties	Terminated by death, bankruptcy, or withdrawal of a partner
Limited partnership	Flow-through (single)	Limited	Transferable	General partners have equal voice; limited partners have no voice	No	Created by agreement of the parties	Termination provided in the agreement
Corporation	Non-flow-through (double)	Limited	Transferable	Shareholders elect directors who set policy	No	Charter issued by state	Perpetual
REIT	Modified flow-through (tax losses cannot exceed cash distribution)	Limited	Modified	Trustees	Yes	Created by agreement of the parties and charter issued by state	Perpetual

owns the property. In a tenancy-in-common the shares may be unequal and the deceased interest becomes part of the estate. Tenancy-in-common is an especially prevalent form of real estate ownership among nonmarried partners mostly because of the ease of creation. The problem with tenancy-in-common is that all parties must agree to all management and sale decisions.

The popularity of these three forms of ownership is due to flow-through taxation. The tax losses may shelter not only income from the investment but also the other income of the investor. It must be remembered that the risk is greater since all the investor's assets are exposed to possible loss.

Corporations

Corporations are entities of the state and must be chartered by it. The rules and regulations of a corporation are outlined in the charter and vary by state. Corporations are most widely used with large enterprises because of the economies of management and the advantage of limited liability.

The corporation is a legal entity completely separated from the stockholders and management. This means the stockholders can lose only their investment in the corporation and are not liable for the debts of the corporation. If the property is damaged or a lawsuit results in heavy losses, the stockholder risks only the amount of the investment.

The corporation has continual life. The current management can retire and new management enter with no effect on the life of the corporation. The stockholders have the right to sell or buy shares and, if unhappy, can sell out.

The main disadvantages of the corporation are the taxation of income and inability of stockholders to take the tax losses of the corporation on their personal income tax returns. Furthermore, there are fees involved in setting up the corporate charter. Legal advice is usually required. Records and taxes must be kept and paid whether or not there are profits. All policy decisions must be approved by the directors. The corporation pays a corporate tax on earnings and when the earnings are distributed the stockholders pay regular income tax rates on the dividends. This double taxation discourages many real estate ventures from the corporate status.

Another important disadvantage is the inability of the corporation to pass on losses or depreciation allowances to the investors. This is a serious flaw for real estate tax shelters since the non-flow-through character of the corporation eliminates any possibility of sheltering any ordinary income of the investor.

If the real estate investors plan on sheltering only the income produced from the investment then the problem of not being able to pass through the tax losses is insignificant. The corporation is allowed to shelter its own income. The stockholders and management can also decide to reinvest all earning in other corporate investments, thus eliminating the problem of double taxation. If the reinvestments earn profits this will be reflected in the price of the shares and, when they are sold, any profits will be taxed at the capital gain rate. Thus, it is quite possible that a corporate structure can be very useful in certain real estate investment situations. This is especially true for large corporations, earning substantial income from other investments that could be sheltered. In the right situation the advantages of real estate investment and corporate ownership can be combined to form an optimal investment strategy.

Subchapter S Corporations

A corporation that meets certain prescribed requirements can have its income taxed directly to the shareholders, thereby avoiding the double taxation problem that exists in most corporations. These organizations are referred to as Subchapter S corporations.

The Subchapter S corporations are useful during the period of construction before any profits are realized. Operating losses are significant in the early periods and Subchapter S permits the shareholder to claim the operating losses. Unfortunately Subchapter S status terminates if the corporation's rental income exceeds 20 percent of its gross receipts. Most office buildings, shopping centers, and apartment buildings exceed this 20-percent figure. Also the losses claimed cannot exceed the aggregate basis of the property and loans. This is in contrast to the tax treatment given partnerships who can deduct tax losses in excess of their actual investment. Given the restricted conditions of Subchapter S corporations it is not surprising that most real estate investors use partnerships as the means of ownership.

General Partnerships

A general partnership is an association of two or more persons to carry on a business for profit. It has many advantages for the real estate investor. Since it is an agreement among individuals it is a low cost, easy way to form a business. Partnerships are not taxable entities. This means the income or losses of a partnership business are allocated to the partners' individual income taxes. This allows the business to be used as a tax shelter—the main reason partnerships are so popular in real estate.

However, partnerships have some disadvantages, the most serious being unlimited liability. This means that all of the investor's wealth is at risk. Furthermore, a partnership is dissolved any time a member withdraws or dies. This can lead to many complications and interfere with the investment strategy. Finally, all profits and losses are allocated to the partners. Even if profits are reinvested, the partners must still pay income or capital gains tax on the profits. A partner must have other means to pay such taxes.

Limited Partnerships

A limited partnership has one or more general partners and one or more limited partners. The limited partners are not obligated to pay the debts of the partnership. The general partners have unlimited liability whereas the limited partners have limited liability. This type of ownership provides the best of both worlds. The limited partners are allowed to flow-through the tax losses of the partnership, and therefore have the benefit of a tax shelter without the risk of liability. The general partner(s) must be willing to assume the risk of liability for debt of the partnership.

In many real estate projects the general partner is the developer. He or she has the greatest familiarity with the details of the project and is the one who will manage the project. The passive investors can be the limited partners with their liability restricted to their actual investment. The limited partnership is especially useful as a tax shelter in real estate. The limited liability allows the maximum use of the tax advantages of depreciation which generates in the early years a tax loss with a positive income flow.

The Internal Revenue Service has become concerned about the status of limited partnerships. The IRS examines each enterprise that is increasing its corporate characteristics. If the IRS decides that the enterprise is essentially a corporation, not a limited partnership, the enterprise is taxed as a separate entity and investors are taxed again on their income with no chance of deducting any tax losses. Of course, this double taxation eliminates the advantage investors were trying to obtain by forming a limited partnership.

The IRS uses the following set of characteristics to define a corporation: (1) presence of associates, (2) operating for profit, (3) central management, (4) perpetual life, (5) ease of transferability, and (6) limited liability. If a limited or general partnership has most of these characteristics it will be termed as association and subject to double taxation. Since partnership and corporations share the first two characteristics it is necessary to examine the last four characteristics for possible differences.

Many large limited partnerships have central management and therefore are similar to the third corporate feature.

Corporations have perpetual life, whereas partnerships can provide for termination of the enterprise on the death of the general partner. In this case it is important not to allow the term of the partnership to be extended by a vote. The IRS interprets this as perpetual life which could result in the business being classified as a corporation.

Free transferability of interest can apply to corporation or partnership investors. It is possible to set up a partnership with restricted transferability of interests in order to maintain a differential from a corporation.

The last characteristic, liability, is the most used for differentiating a corporation from partnership. The general partner is exposed to unlimited liability. Even though the limited partners have limited liability, in the opinion of the Internal Revenue Service the exposure of the general partner qualifies the entire enterprise as having unlimited liability. The general partner cannot be a "shell" with no assets. The use of a dummy corporation as a general partner to reduce the risk due to liability has been deemed unacceptable by the IRS. The general partner must be risking significant wealth or the IRS will deny the limited partnership status.

The strategy used by most real enterprises to ensure partnership status is to restrict transferability, or provide for termination of the partnership and to expose the general partner to unlimited liability. It is advisable to use of all three characteristics to guard against the possibility of being classified as a corporation and becoming subject to double taxation.

In summary, limited partnerships that are well defined for protection from reclassification by the IRS provide an excellent means for a tax shelter with limited liability.

Real Estate Investment Trusts

Real estate investment trusts (REITs) are large organizations that satisfy a special set of statutory requirements. If the organization meets all the following requirements it is exempted from corporate tax:

1. The REIT must have 100 or more shareholders with no more than 50 percent of shares owned by 5 persons.
2. The REIT must earn 90 percent of the income from passive investments; it must derive 75 percent of its income from real estate investment.
3. The management of the REIT must be committed to trustees.
4. The assets of the REIT must be at least 75 percent in real estate, government securities, and cash; investment in any one corporation cannot exceed 5 percent.
5. Gains from the sale of real estate held for less than four years must amount to no more than 30 percent of the trust's income.
6. At least 90 percent of the REIT taxable income must be distributed to its shareholders every year.

These regulations along with others make the REIT a rather inflexible enterprise for real estate investment. The 90-percent payout requirement of taxable income can put a squeeze on the REIT during times of rapid rising interest rates. This type of pressure has lead to many bankruptcies during high interest years. More importantly, capital and operating losses are not passed through to the investors nor does the REIT have rights to carry such losses forward or backward. Thus the tax shelter benefits are very limited.

Prior to 1960, only a small number of REITs existed. Then in 1960 laws were changed to eliminate double taxation. From 1960 to 1968 trusts grew at a steady rate. In 1968 banks, mortgage lenders, real estate firms, and insurance firms became involved, resulting in rapid growth.

This rapid growth ended abruptly in the 70s with interest rate increases and with significant reduction in real estate development. Many of the investments in real estate were not sound, resulting in a corresponding number of losses and bankrupicies. Since that time, REITs have not been a favorite form of investment for real estate investors. In essence, REITs have the higher risk of real estate investment without the benefit of a tax shelter. They do have the benefit of allowing a small investor to reduce risk by taking advantage of the possible diversification of the REIT's investments. The past performances of REITs would indicate that this possible reduction in risk is not worth the price paid.

REITs vary in their investment strategies. Some emphasize construction and development; others concentrate on permanent mortgages. Many use leverage to a high degree and attempt to borrow short and lend long. Both of these techniques can raise profits. However, when rates on borrowing shifted adversely and when builders failed to complete projects, foreclosures became common. This resulted in many REITs not meeting their commitment to the banks. Their price per share dropped dramatically.

An investor ought to understand completely the management philosophy of the REIT. Some are very conservative; others seek high leverage positions with corresponding high risk. Higher risk means a greater return on average but the chance of experiencing a significant loss is greater. Real estate investment trusts have been available for a relatively short time. Maybe future experience will provide a clearer picture of how representative the past record has been for REITs.

SYNDICATION

A real estate syndicate is a group of people who get together to pool funds for the purpose of investing in real estate. Many real estate investments require a significant amount of equity capital and a syndicate is one way to raise these funds. Syndicates are not a separate form of ownership since any form of ownership allowing more than one member can be used to form the organization. The investment is commonly limited to one property even though several properties could be involved. Private syndicates have a small number of people, maybe two to twenty, that invest in one apartment or office building. Public offering brings in a much larger set of people for the purpose of investing. Syndication is essentially a method to organize people for the purpose of pooling funds for real estate investment.

TAX SHELTERS AND BUSINESS ORGANIZATION: A REVIEW

In Example 3-2 an individual acquired a warehouse for $750,000, of which $50,000 was allocated to land with the remaining $700,000 used as the basis for depreciating the warehouse. The resulting tax shelter from the investment was substantial. Under alternative forms of ownership the tax benefits change. For example, corporate tax rate is

Portion of Taxable Income	Rate (%)
0 to $25,000	17
$25,001 to $50,000	20
$50,001 to $75,000	30
$75,001 to $100,000	40
Over $100,000	46

This corporate tax is paid on earnings before the distribution of dividends which are again taxed at the ordinary income tax rate. For the individual in Example 3-2 this would result in a significant increase in taxes paid with no deferral of taxes or tax shelter of ordinary income. This clearly indicates the benefits of a partnership or sole proprietorship form of business organization.

SUMMARY

The more popular types of business organization in real estate are those that allow a flow-through of tax losses. This provides for the possibility of sheltering ordinary income or, at the very least, provides a way to defer the taxes until a later data. Sole proprietorship, general and limited partnerships all have the flow-through characteristic. In all but the limited partnership the investor is subject to unlimited liability—a significant factor when determining risk. A large portion of the high rate of return earned in real estate is due to the risk. Real estate fluctuates widely with economic conditions of the area; even in times of general economic growth some real estate decreases in value due to poor location. The difficulty involved in acquiring information concerning the best possible investment makes real estate a risky investment.

To avoid the risk of unlimited liability, individuals and groups form limited partnerships or corporations. The limited partners and the shareholders have liability limited to the amount invested. These forms of business especially the limited partnership, have grown in popularity in recent years because of the important reduction of risk. The limited partnership has the added advantage of the single-tax flow-through characteristic, which allows the limited partner to benefit from potential tax shelters.

4

Formation of Business Organizations

INTRODUCTION

The simplest and most common ways to own real estate are individual ownership, joint tenancy, and tenancy-in-common. There are few legal formalities required for individual owners of real estate to create these forms of ownership. The owners must file a deed stating the names of the owners and their shares of the property. Each owner reports his or her share and the corresponding profits or losses attributed to that share on the appropriate Internal Revenue Service form. Joint tenancies and tenancies-in-common are similar to individual ownership except more than one person is involved.

Joint tenancy (joint ownership) has two equal shares of ownership and provides, if one owner should die, that the survivor will then own the property. This form is often used by married couples to avoid the probate court. It does not, however, avoid the possibility of gift taxes for the survivor. Tenants-in-common may have unequal shares of ownership and the deceased's interest becomes part of the deceased's estate. Tenancy-in-common is used in the two states without a partnership statute (Louisiana and Georgia) and among individuals desiring to maintain control. The owners must agree at all times to the terms of a sale or management decision. For tax purposes the tenancy-in-common is treated as a partnership. Tenancy-in-common is often used in joint land ownership where management decisions are few but where control is important. The formation, operation, and dissolution of these three forms of ownership are quite simple. The formation, operation, and dissolution of partnerships and corporations are more complex and require detailed consideration.

THE FORMATION OF A PARTNERSHIP

For hundreds of years the law governing partnerships was determined by the courts. In 1914, the Uniform Partnership Act (UPA) and the Uniform Limited Partnership Act (ULPA) were created by the American Law Institute and the National Conference of Commissioners on Uniform State Laws. The UPA has been adopted by forty-eight states, the exceptions being Georgia and Louisiana, whereas the ULPA has been adopted in every state except Louisiana.

A partnership is an association of two or more persons to carry on as joint owners of business. Even though an oral agreement is acceptable under law, it is far better that the agreement be written and carefully prepared. Oral agreements result in problems in proving the exact contexts of the implied contract. Problems of taxation are more easily solved with a written agreement. The written agreement will clearly state the articles of partnership. The articles of partnership discussed in this section are controlled to a degree by the Uniform Partnership Act, which appears in its entirety in Appendix 4A at the end of this chapter. Limited partnerships are controlled by the Uniform Limited Partnership Act, given in Appendix 4B.

The Sharing of Profits and Losses

With no agreement the partners share equally in all profits and losses. This is true regardless of differences in the individual capital contributions of the investors. Assume three partners contribute $30,000, $20,000, and $10,000 respectively. After the partnership is dissolved and the original contribution returned to each of the partners there remains a $6,000 profit, or $2,000 for each individual. If a loss of $6,000 occurrs before the repayment to contributors, then a $2,000 loss plus the loss of the contributions of $30,000, $20,000, and $10,000 for a total of $66,000 must be shared equally. This amounts to a $22,000 loss for each of the three investors. The investor who contributed $30,000 to this partnership would be entitled to $8,000 ($30,000 – $22,000). The $20,000 contributor would owe $2,000 and the $10,000 contributor would owe $12,000. The last two contributors would have to come up with the money from some other source and pay the $6,000 loss to creditors and $8,000 to the $30,000 contributor. If, however, profits or losses are to be shared relative to the capital contributions, this must be stated in writing. When the written agreement does not specifically state the share of losses, they will be shared on the same basis as profits.

The agreement may state any other compensation entitled to the partners for services or payments rendered. For example, a partnership obtains a loan for $300,000 to invest in a real estate project. One of the partners pays $20,000 for a nonrefundable loan fee. The loan fee is not only deductible in the year paid, but the entire deduction may be allocated to the partner who paid it since he or she bears the economic burden.

When one partner provides services to the partnership he or she is entitled to compensation if stated in the agreement. If not stated the partner is not entitled to compensation for services and is rewarded by the agreed share of the profits. A partner in charge of dissolving the partnership is entitled to compensation for his or her services.

Unless it is written in the partnership agreement a partner is not entitled to interest on capital contributions. However, if a repayment date was set and payment from the partnership is not received, interest can be paid on the late payment of the debt.

There are some exceptions to the general rule that a partner's share is determined by the partnership agreement and with no agreement the partners share equally. The first exception is referred to as the substantial economic effect rule. Each partner must account separately for the income and various deductions representing his or her share. If the partnership agreement allocates a particular item to a partner such as a large expense deduction which is strictly for tax avoidance, the IRS will ignore it. The IRS will, however, consider other possible reasons, such as business purposes, overall tax effects, and, more importantly, the overall economic effect. In general it seems that if the allocation does not have an economic effect it will not be recognized for tax purposes. In other words, the special allocation must have some effect other than tax avoidance.

The second exception deals with the transfer of property or assets from the partners to the partnership. The basis of the assets remains the same. Therefore, the amount of depreciation is limited to the basis established by the contributing partner and in no case can the total depreciation exceed the basis. However, there is a way to allocate the depreciation to reflect the difference between the original basis and current market value when transferred. For example, A and B contribute assets equal to $200,000 each, but A's contribution has a basis of only $50,000. The depreciation at 10 percent would be for A $5,000 on the basis and $20,000 on the current values. B's assets would have a depreciation of $20,000. Assume that the partnership had earnings of $100,000 before deducting depreciation. The income after depreciation is $75,000. In the absence of an agreement each partner will have $37,500 of income. Since partner B contributed $20,000 depreciation and A only $5,000, the agreement could be structured so that A received a $5,000 deduction and B a $20,000 deduction. In that case A and B have a taxable income from the partnership of $35,000 and $17,500 respectively.

The third exception provides techniques to expand the basis for each partner. This is important because, regardless of the losses, the deductions are limited to the amount of basis. Therefore understanding the rules governing the basis is essential. The initial basis for each partner is equal to the amount of cash and property he or she contributed. However this basis can be adjusted by the share of liabilities to each partner. A mortgage for some property owned by the partnership is considered a liability. All the partners share this liability in the same proportion as they share partnership profits. This rule depends on none of the partners having any personal liability for the mortgage loan. For example, C and D form a partnership and contribute assets equal to $200,000 each, with C having a basis of $50,000 and D a basis of $200,000. Using this contributed property C and D purchase real estate for $2,000,000 paying $400,000 equity subject to a $1,600,000 mortgage. The additional basis for the partnership is $1,600,000 with $850,000 for C and $1,000,000 for D.

Partnership Capital

Partnership capital is the money advance made for permanent investment in the business. These capital advances must be repaid upon dissolution of the partnership, before any distribution of profits. An individual may become a partner without a capital contribution. This person would contribute services equal to the capital investment of the other partners. Such partners receive no capital at the time of liquidation.

Partnership Property

A partnership is an entity and as such may use its own property, the property of other partners, or the property of a third person. All property brought into or acquired by the partnership is partnership property. Being a legal entity entitles the partnership to hold property and to do business in its name.

The Firm's Name

If the investors choose a name other than their own, then a public notice as to the actual identity of the partners is required. Failure to post notice results in loss of partnership status in the courts. In most states the partnership has some of the rights of a legal entity. It may sue or be sued. It may declare bankruptcy as a firm. The firm's name and good will may be sold as an asset. Good will is the patronage of old customers, the good reputation, the established location, and potential new customers. The name and good will is often sold on the condition that the previous owners will not compete with the new owners. This should be written in the buy and sell provisions.

The Buy-and-Sell Provisions

A partner may wish to withdraw, or may die unexpectedly. In such cases, the remaining partners must buy his or her interest. Without a written buy and sell agreement many problems could result. A buy-and-sell agreement will avoid these problems by providing a method of determining price with the time and method of payment stipulated.

There are cases of dispute concerning the existence of a partnership. A creditor may be suing the partners and claiming that several other persons are liable because they are also partners. There is no one criterion the courts will use to determine the existence of a partnership. Three important factors are: (1) sharing the profits, (2) joint control of the business, and (3) joint ownership of the property. If the court finds sufficient evidence of these conditions, then a partnership is considered to exist.

OPERATING THE PARTNERSHIP

The operation of the partnership is controlled by the agreement, the statutory law of the state, and, when applicable, the Uniform Partnership Act and the Uniform Limited Partnership Act. Each partner is essentially an agent for the other partners. Therefore the general principles of the law of agency apply. The following is a discussion of the rights, duties, and powers of a partner.

All partners have equal rights to management and conduct of the firm. This right is not altered by the share of profits or the share invested. A majority can overrule the minority in ordinary matters. An agreement or decision that seriously changes the partnership must be agreed to by all partners.

As previously mentioned, partners do not have the right to be paid for their services unless it is explicitly stated in the agreement. No interest is expected on the capital investment. The earning on investment is based on the share of profits.

Each partner has the right to inspect the books and to make copies. A suit for accounting is not usually accepted for settling incidental matters but is within a partner's right upon dissolution of the firm. A partner may demand an accounting of the records when some of the other rights have been violated, such as profits withheld or access to the books denied. A partner has equal rights to possess the partnership property for the purpose of serving the partnership and no right to use the property for other purposes.

There are various duties and powers possessed by each partner. Each partner must at all times consider the material welfare of the other partners. Each partner has the right to be an agent for the partnership. This means each partner has the right to bind the partnership to a contract when it is carried on for the partnership's business. The partner has a right in the real estate business to sell property if the title was in the firm's name and therefore a tenancy in partnership.

In determining the financial powers there are two classes of partner: (1) a trading partner who has the right to buy and sell, to borrow money, and to extend credit, and (2) a nontrading partner who sells his or her services and does not have these rights.

Each partner has the right to receive all information obtained by any other partner affecting the partnership business.

DISSOLUTION OF THE PARTNERSHIP

The ending of a partnership can be broken into three distinct phases: (1) dissolution, (2) winding up, and (3) termination. Dissolution is the beginning of the process which starts when the partners cease to conduct business together. Winding up is the process of converting all assets to cash, paying off creditors, and distributing the profits or losses. Termination occurs when the winding up is finished.

Dissolution can be caused by five basic events: (1) by consent of the partners, (2) by operation of law, (3) when a partner ceases as a member of the partnership, or a new partner enters the firm, (4) by a violation of the agreement, and (5) by court decree.

Partnership agreements are often written to be terminated at the end of a particular project. If no agreement has been made for termination, the partners can at will withdraw. Any withdrawal of a partner results in dissolution. Other types of agreements can be made with regard to the withdrawal of a partner or dissolution of the partnership. For example, specific dates can be set for dissolution, the withdrawing partner may be required to give a one-year notice, or terms for exclusion of a partner can be listed. Regardless of the terms, dissolution can occur with the agreement of all parties.

A partnership dissolves if the business becomes illegal. This most often happens with the loss of a license to practice a particular skill by one of the partners or the loss of the right to do business such as the loss of a liquor license. The operation of law ends a partnership on death of a partner or bankruptcy. The entry of a new partner dissolves the old partnership. (Any single partner can withdraw in violation of the agreement and cause dissolution of the partnership. In such cases the other partners can seek damages from the withdrawing partner.)

A court decree can dissolve a partnership and is used most often in cases of total incapacity of a partner, both physically or mentally, or gross misconduct of a partner including fraud.

The winding-up process involves the liquidating of property, paying debts, and distributing profits. Assuming that the firm has paid all creditors, then assets are distributed as follows:

1. Individual loans plus interest are repaid.
2. Each partner is entitled to his or her contribution of capital.
3. The remaining profits are distributed.

If the partnership experiences a loss, the creditors are paid first. The loss is divided equally among the partners.

Assume that three partners—Irvin, Smith, and Harvey—invested in an apartment building. Serious losses occurred and the partnership was dissolved. The first step was to reduce all assets to cash and then to pay the creditors. Let us look at the financial position of each partner.

The cash after all assets were sold was $400,000. The amount owed to outside creditors was $500,000. Irvin and Harvey made loans to the partnership of $50,000 each. Smith's contribution to capital was $100,000. The overall loss was $300,000. The loss is $100,000 for each partner. The losses actually borne by each partner are summarized as follows:

	Irvin	Smith	Harvey
Loans (unpaid)	$ 50,000	–	$ 50,000
Capital contribution (unpaid)	–	$100,000	–
Personal assets used to pay creditors	$ 50,000	–	$ 50,000
	$100,000	$100,000	$100,000

If Harvey does not have the personal wealth to pay the debt of $50,000, then Smith and Irvin pay an additional $25,000 out of their personal assets. If neither Irvin nor Harvey have the personal wealth then Smith pays an additional $100,000 or the partners declare bankruptcy. This example demonstrates the importance of having full knowledge of the financial position of the other partners.

REAL ESTATE AND THE PARTNERSHIP

The partnership is a useful business organization for investments in real estate. The flow-through characteristic of tax losses and the potential for limited liability have made the partnership a popular form of business. Tenancy-in-common has many of the same characteristics but it is a cumbersome form of ownership for management of income properties. The partnership is not a taxable entity. Taxes are paid by the owners. The partnership is a reporting entity. This means that various policies and tax determinations are made at the partnership level and applied to all members.

Real estate can be transferred to the partnership free of tax. This tax-free transfer results in a carryover of the basis for the property. Assume that Smith and Jones form a partnership. Smith contributes $30,000 worth of real estate and Jones $50,000. The basis is $20,000 and $10,000 respectively. The basis for the partnership is the same, $20,000 and $10,000. No taxable gain is recognized. Where the partnership assumes or pays a mortgage, the original owner is deemed to have received a taxable cash distribution equal to the liability.

Payment to the Developer

Partnerships are often formed with some members providing the capital and some the knowledge of the real estate market. For example, the developer is often the one providing the knowledge. The problem is how to pay the person with the knowledge. A fee for his or her services represents ordinary income and the payment of this fee is usually due before the project is proven successful.

One possible technique is to allow the developer a share of the partnership capital. Unfortunately, the courts have ruled in some cases that this share of capital is payment for services and is taxable as ordinary income. For example, two investors contribute $200,000 each to the partnership and receive two-thirds interest in the investment. A developer acquires the site and arranges for the financing in return for a one-third interest in the partnership for his services. The one-third interest has a value of $66,666. It is taxable as ordinary income.

A second possibility is to give the developer a share of the profit. The IRS rules seem to say that this is a different situation. But the courts have ruled that the profit is taxable as ordinary income, not as a capital gain, because the developer can sell his or her interest in the share of the profits for an immediate cash gain.

The point here is to be able to defer the tax. The best strategy is to have the developer buy into the partnership at the earliest possible stage. The value of the partnership is very low and any contribution of capital after the formation is treated in the normal fashion. In this way the developer is treated as a regular partner with no immediate taxable income. At the same time he or she can share in any taxable losses that might occur through depreciation or debt services.

A business expense paid to a partner by the partnership is fully deductible. The fact that it is paid to a partner does not effect its deductibility. A developer who has received payment for services as ordinary income can avoid paying taxes on that income. This is accomplished by, first, bringing the developer in as a partner and, second, allocating all the cost to the partnership of these services to the developer. The net effect is that the developer will realize taxable income to the extent of the value of the interest in the partnership received for services and, at the same time, be allocated a partnership deduction equal to the taxable income. Remember the payment for the services, whether taken as direct income or as an interest in the partnership, must be an ordinary and necessary business expense. Organization and syndication cost are not deductible the year paid but they may be amortized over sixty months.

THE FORMATION OF A CORPORATION

The corporation is a legal entity separate from its owners. The corporation in many ways is treated as a person. The authority of the state creates the corporation by an approved charter. Since the rules and regulations vary with each state, the following discussion is based on the representative model of a corporation. As a legal entity it can sue or be sued, it does not have liability for the debt of shareholders, and the shareholders do not have personal liability on the contracts of the corporation.

The procedure for incorporation usually requires a minimum of three persons to file an application. The purpose, duration, location, name of agent, and a listing of capital stock is required. After the filing of the application, the initial stockholders meet and elect a board of directors. The board of directors will adopt bylaws, elect officers, and conduct business.

The bylaws state the rules and regulations for doing business and are binding upon all shareholders. The bylaws are subservient to the articles of incorporation. One of the great advantages of corporations is the limitations of shareholder liability. This corporate veil against liability may be pierced if it is used for illegal acts or as a dummy corporation solely for the purpose of shielding investors from liability. The corporation has the right to perpetual existence, a name, to deal in real and personal property, to sue and be sued, to purchase securities, to enter contracts, to make charitable contributions, and to pay pensions.

Just as a partnership finds it important to have a buy and sell agreement, the same is true for a closely held corporation. This type of corporation, with only a few shareholders, must have a means of getting the shareholder out. The withdrawing shareholder is often forced to sell his or her stock at a lower-than-market price and is required in many situations to offer it to the corporation first.

OPERATING THE CORPORATION

The operation of a corporation is provided by three distinct groups: (1) the shareholders, (2) the board of directors, and (3) the elected officers. The shareholders elect the board of directors; the board of directors adopt bylaws and make corporate policy; and the officers carry out the policy.

Shareholders normally exert their power during a regular annual meeting. In most cases the management has collected enough proxies to control any vote taken at the meeting. Shareholders are entitled to vote on elections of directors, major policy issues, mergers, and on dissolution. A shareholder has as many votes as shares of stock. Shareholders have the right to: (1) inspect the books, (2) vote, (3) share in the profits with dividends, (4) exercise the preemptive right, and (5) bring a derivative suit.

The last two items require some clarification. The preemptive right of a shareholder is the right to protect and maintain his or her control and interest in the corporation. This right is exercised when the corporation increases the capital stock. The shareholder has a preemptive right to buy the increased capital stock before it is offered to any potential new shareholders.

The right of derivative suit is the right for a shareholder to bring a suit of equity to enjoin the officers from acting beyond their authority or from doing anything that might injure the assets of the corporation.

The directors are to hire key employees, plan for the future, and supervise the general business activities. Directors hold meetings, are paid according to prior agreement, and are liable for their decisions. Lawsuits brought against directors by shareholders often are the result of directors deriving personal benefit from the corporation based on decisions not beneficial to the shareholders. Directors are expected to maintain good faith by avoiding all conflicts of interest and recommending policy with due care: that is, not to be negligent.

DISSOLUTION OF THE CORPORATION

Corporations are usually chartered for a perpetual life, but may terminate on a date set in the charter. A corporation can voluntarily dissolve before any business begins. If it is in business, however, a written consent of all shareholders or action by the board of directors approved by a majority of shareholders is required for dissolution.

Involuntary dissolutions may be commenced by three groups: the state, the shareholders, or the creditors. The state may cancel a charter for failure to (1) file an annual report, (2) appoint an agent for notices, (3) pay the franchise tax and license fees, (4) use authority appropriately, (5) attain charity legally, and (6) perform the corporate function for a long period of time. The shareholders through the court of equity, can force dissolution. This occurs when a shareholder can prove the corporation is acting illegally, fraudulently, or oppressively. Oppressive conduct is defined as deviation from fair play. Creditors can sue to obtain payment of debts. If judgment is obtained, an execution may be levied against the corporation forcing dissolution for payment of debts.

REAL ESTATE AND THE CORPORATION

As noted in Chapter 3, the corporate form of ownership is not normally suited for real estate ventures for two main reasons. First, double taxation: the before-tax cash flow is subject to a corporate tax and, if the profits are distributed as dividends, they are taxed again as personal income of the shareholders. Second, the tax loss can not be passed to the shareholder and must be absorbed by the corporation's income. Despite these problems there are some cases where a corporate form of ownership is desirable. Corporate ownership avoids liability on the loan or any other obligation. Corporations often have many different businesses under the same corporate structure. If these other businesses generate a surplus of income, then the real estate investment may provide a tax shelter.

One special situation involves the rules governing the incorporation of a new business that was formerly a partnership. The tax losses and interest charges are often greatest during the development of the real estate project. Thus, during the earlier stages a partnership may be the best form of ownership. In later years, when the tax loss has decreased, the advantages of limited liability may be of use. The IRS treats the exchange of property resulting from a change in ownership as an event of no tax significance. This means that the original basis of the property stands. The transfer of property is tax free. This does not eliminate the tax; it just defers the eventual payment. Whether it pays to postpone the tax depends on the different tax brackets of the corporation versus the individuals in the partnership. The way to avoid a tax-free exchange is to violate one of the requirements. The transfer is accomplished by giving to the previous owners securities and stock in the corporation in exchange for the real estate. If some other form of payment (such as cash) is used, the exchange is taxable. The owners of the real estate must control 80 percent of the stock in the new corporation; if they do not, the exchange is taxable.

Many states have usury laws that hinder the sale of real estate. Usury laws put a ceiling on the interest that can be charged on loans; this becomes a problem when the ceiling is below the market-level interest rate. Corporations are exempt from usury laws in most states. Therefore, it may become necessary to set up "straw" corporations for financing the real estate investments. (A straw or dummy corporation serves no corporate purpose except to provide financing.) While this will allow financing, the IRS has held that dummy or straw corporations are taxable entities. This means that the advantages of tax flow-through with the partnership form of business is not available. The investors lose the tax shelter.

Another technique that takes advantage of the limited liability of corporations is the formation of multiple corporations. If the investors own several parcels of speculative real estate it will pay to have a separate corporation for each of them. Thus, each is protected from the others.

Once the business organization is decided upon a complete cash-flow statement must be constructed for each potential investment. This requires knowledge of the operating expenses and a thorough understanding of financing and depreciation techniques. The next three chapters will cover these topics and explain how to construct a cash-flow table that will aid in determining the after-tax rate of return.

The appendices to this chapter contain copies of the Uniform Partnership Act and the Uniform Limited Partnership Act. Any investor planning to form a partnership should read the partnership acts carefully and construct an agreement similar in structure. An example of such an agreement is presented in the last part of this book.

APPENDIX 4A:
THE UNIFORM PARTNERSHIP ACT*

The American law regarding partnerships was developed from the English Common Law. For hundreds of years the law on partnerships was developed almost solely by the courts. In 1914, the American Law Institute and the National Conference of Commissioners on Uniform State Laws created the Uniform Partnership Act (UPA). This act was proposed to each of the various legislatures in the United States and as of 1978, it had been adopted by forty-eight states. The UPA sets out rules to govern the operation of a partnership in the absence of a formal agreement or if certain areas are not covered in the formal agreement.

The partnership form of business entity is widely used in real estate investing. The UPA is included in its entirety to acquaint the reader with the areas that should be covered in the formal partnership agreement. Although the parties can vary many of the rules set forth in this statute, reading it will serve to aid in developing the partnership agreement.

An Act to make uniform the Law of Partnerships
Be it enacted, etc.:

PART I:
PRELIMINARY PROVISIONS

Sec. 1. (Name of Act.) This act may be cited as Uniform Partnership Act.

Sec. 2. (Definition of Terms.) In this act, "Court" includes every court and judge having jurisdiction in the case.

"Business" includes every trade, occupation, or profession.

"Person" includes individuals, partnerships, corporations, and other associations.

"Bankrupt" includes bankrupt under the Federal Bankruptcy Act or insolvent under any state insolvent act.

"Conveyance" includes every assignment, lease, mortgage, or encumbrance.

"Real property" includes land and any interest or estate in land.

Sec. 3. (Interpretation of Knowledge and Notice.) (1) A person has "knowledge" of a fact within the meaning of this act not only when he has actual knowledge thereof, but also when he has knowledge of such other facts as in the circumstances shows bad faith.

(2) A person has "notice" of a fact within the meaning of this act when the person who claims the benefit of the notice

(a) States the fact to such person, or

(b) Delivers through the mail, or by other means of communication, a written statement of the fact to such person or to a proper person at his place of business or residence.

Sec. 4. (Rules of Construction.) (1) The rule that statutes in derogation of the common law are to be strictly construed shall have no application to this act.

(2) The law of estoppel shall apply under this act.

(3) The law of agency shall apply under this act.

(4) This act shall be so interpreted and construed as to effect its general purpose to make uniform the law of those states which enact it.

(5) This act shall not be construed so as to impair the obligations of any contract existing when the act goes into effect, nor to affect any action or proceedings begun or right accrued before this act takes effect.

---

*National Conference of Commissioners on Uniform State Laws (1914).

Sec. 5. (Rules for Cases Not Provided for in this Act.) In any case not provided for in this act the rules of law and equity, including the law merchant, shall govern.

PART II:
NATURE OF PARTNERSHIP

Sec. 6. (Partnership Defined.) (1) A partnership is an association of two or more persons to carry on as co-owners a business for profit.

(2) But any association formed under any other statute of this state, or any statute adopted by authority, other than the authority of this state, is not a partnership under this act, unless such association would have been a partnership in this state prior to the adoption of this act; but this act shall apply to limited partnerships except in so far as the statutes relating to such partnerships are inconsistent herewith.

Sec. 7. (Rules for Determining the Existence of a Partnership.) In determining whether a partnership exists, these rules shall apply:

(1) Except as provided by Section 16 persons who are not partners as to each other are not partners as to third persons.

(2) Joint tenancy, tenancy in common, tenancy by the entireties, joint property, common property, or part ownership does not of itself establish a partnership, whether such co-owners do or do not share any profits made by the use of the property.

(3) The sharing of gross returns does not of itself establish a partnership, whether or not the persons sharing them have a joint or common right or interest in any property from which the returns are derived.

(4) The receipt by a person of a share of the profits of a business is prima facie evidence that he is a partner in the business, but no such inference shall be drawn if such profits were received in payment:

(a) As a debt by installments or otherwise,

(b) As wages of an employee or rent to a landlord,

(c) As an annuity to a widow or representative of a deceased partner,

(d) As interest on a loan, though the amount of payment vary with the profits of the business.

(e) As the consideration for the sale of a goodwill of a business or other property by installments or otherwise.

Sec. 8. (Partnership Property.) (1) All property originally brought into the partnership stock or subsequently acquired by purchase or otherwise, on account of the partnership, is partnership property.

(2) Unless the contrary intention appears, property acquired with partnership funds is partnership property.

(3) Any estate in real property may be acquired in the partnership name. Title so acquired can be conveyed only in the partnership name.

(4) A conveyance to a partnership in the partnership name, though without words of inheritance, passes the entire estate of the grantor unless a contrary intent appears.

PART III:
RELATIONS OF PARTNERS TO PERSONS DEALING WITH THE PARTNERSHIP

Sec. 9. (Partner Agent of Partnership as to Partnership Business.) (1) Every partner is an agent of the partnership for the purpose of its business, and the act of every partner, including the execution in the partnership name of any instrument, for apparently carrying on in the usual way the business of the partnership of which he is a member binds the partnership, unless the partner so acting has in fact no authority to act for the partnership in the particular matter, and the person with whom he is dealing has knowledge of the fact that he has no such authority.

(2) An act of a partner which is not apparently for the carrying on of the business of the partnership in the usual way does not bind the partnership unless authorized by the other partners.

(3) Unless authorized by the other partners or unless they have abandoned the business, one or more but less than all the partners have no authority to:

(a) Assign the partnership property in trust for creditors or on the assignee's promise to pay the debts of the partnership,

(b) Dispose of the goodwill of the business,

(c) Do any other act which would make it impossible to carry on the ordinary business of a partnership,

(d) Confess a judgment,

(e) Submit a partnership claim or liability to arbitration or reference.

(4) No act of a partner in contravention of a restriction on authority shall bind the partnership to persons having knowledge of the restriction.

Sec. 10. (Conveyance of Real Property of the Partnership.) (1) Where title to real property is in the partnership name, any partner may convey title to such property by a conveyance executed in the partnership name; but the partnership may recover such property unless the partner's act binds the partnership under the provisions of paragraph (1) of section 9 or unless such property has been conveyed by the grantee or a person claiming through such grantee to a holder for value without knowledge that the partner, in making the conveyance, has exceeded his authority.

(2) Where title to real property is in the name of the partnership, a conveyance executed by a partner, in his own name, passes the equitable interest of the partnership, provided the act is one within the authority of the partner under the provisions of paragraph (1) of section 9.

(3) Where title to real property is in the name of one or more but not all the partners, and the record does not disclose the right of the partnership, the partners in whose name the title stands may convey title to such property, but the partnership may recover such property if the partners' act does not bind the partnership under the provisions of paragraph (1) of section 9, unless the purchaser or his assignee, is a holder for value, without knowledge.

(4) Where the title to real property is in the name of one or more or all the partners, or in a third person in trust for the partnership, a conveyance executed by a partner in the partnership name, or in his own name, passes the equitable interest of the partnership, provided the act is one within the authority of the partner under the provisions of paragraph (1) of section 9.

(5) Where the title to real property is in the names of all the partners a conveyance executed by all the partners passes all their rights in such property.

Sec. 11. (Partnership Bound by Admission of Partner.) An admission or representation made by any partner concerning partnership affairs within the scope of his authority as conferred by this act is evidence against the partnership.

Sec. 12. (Partnership Charged with Knowledge of or Notice to Partner.) Notice to any partner of any matter relating to partnership affairs, and the knowledge of the partner acting in the particular matter, acquired while a partner or then present to his mind, and the knowledge of any other partner who reasonably could and should have communicated it to the acting partner, operate as notice to or knowledge of the partnership, except in the case of a fraud on the partnership committed by or with the consent of that partner.

Sec. 13. (Partnership Bound by Partner's Wrongful Act.) Where, by any wrongful act or omission of any partner acting in the ordinary course of the business of the partnership or with the authority of his co-partners, loss or injury is caused to any person, not being a partner in the partnership, or any penalty is incurred, the partnership is liable therefor

to the same extent as the partner so acting or omitting to act.

Sec. 14. (Partnership Bound by Partner's Breach of Trust.) The partnership is bound to make good the loss:

(a) Where one partner acting within the scope of his apparent authority receives money or property of a third person and misapplies it; and

(b) Where the partnership in the course of its business receives money or property of a third person and the money or property so received is misapplied by any partner while it is in the custody of the partnership.

Sec. 15. (Nature of Partner's Liability.) All partners are liable

(a) Jointly and severally for everything chargeable to the partnership under sections 13 and 14.

(b) Jointly for all other debts and obligations of the partnership; but any partner may enter into a separate obligation to perform a partnership contract.

Sec. 16. (Partner by Estoppel.) (1) When a person, by words spoken or written or by conduct, represents himself, or consents to another representing him to any one, as a partner in an existing partnership or with one or more persons not actual partners, he is liable to any such person to whom such representation has been made, who has, on the faith of such representation, given credit to the actual or apparent partnership, and if he has made such representation or consented to its being made in a public manner he is liable to such person, whether the representation has or has not been made or communicated to such person so giving credit by or with the knowledge of the apparent partner making the representation or consenting to its being made.

(a) When a partnership liability results, he is liable as though he were an actual member of the partnership.

(b) When no partnership liability results, he is liable jointly with the other persons, if any, so consenting to the contract or representation as to incur liability, otherwise separately.

(2) When a person has been thus represented to be a partner in an existing partnership, or with one or more persons not actual partners, he is an agent of the persons consenting to such representation to bind them to the same extent and in the same manner as though he were a partner in fact, with respect to persons who rely upon the representation. Where all the members of the existing partnership consent to the representation, a partnership act or obligation results; but in all other cases it is the joint act or obligation of the person acting and the persons consenting to the representation.

Sec. 17. (Liability of Incoming Partner.) A person admitted as a partner into an existing partnership is liable for all the obligations of the partnership arising before his admission as though he had been a partner when such obligations were incurred, except that this liability shall be satisfied only out of partnership property.

PART IV: RELATIONS OF PARTNERS TO ONE ANOTHER

Sec. 18. (Rules Determining Rights and Duties of Partners.) The rights and duties of the partners in relation to the partnership shall be determined, subject to any agreement between them, by the following rules;

(a) Each partner shall be repaid his contributions, whether by way of capital or advances to the partnership property and share equally in the profits and surplus remaining after all liabilities, including those to partners, are satisfied; and must contribute toward the losses, whether of capital or otherwise, sustained by the partnership according to his share in the profits.

(b) The partnership must indemnify every partner in respect of payments made and personal liabilities reasonably incurred by him in the ordinary and proper conduct of its business, or for the preservation of its business or property.

(c) A partner, who in aid of the partnership makes any payment or advance beyond the amount of capital which he agreed to contribute, shall be paid interest from the date of the payment or advance.

(d) A partner shall receive interest on the capital contributed by him only from the date when repayment should be made.

(e) All partners have equal rights in the management and conduct of the partnership business.

(f) No partner is entitled to remuneration for acting in the partnership business, except that a surviving partner is entitled to reasonable compensation for his services in winding up the partnership affairs.

(g) No person can become a member of a partnership without the consent of all the partners.

(h) Any difference arising as to ordinary matters connected with the partnership business may be decided by a majority of the partners; but no act in contravention of any agreement between the partners may be done rightfully without the consent of all the partners.

Sec. 19. (Partnership Books.) The partnership books shall be kept, subject to any agreement between the partners, at the principal place of business of the partnership, and every partner shall at all times have access to and may inspect and copy any of them.

Sec. 20. (Duty of Partners to Render Information.) Partners shall render on demand true and full information of all things affecting the partnership to any partner or the legal representative of any deceased partner or partner under legal disability.

Sec. 21. (Partner Accountable as a Fiduciary.) (1) Every partner must account to the partnership for any benefit, and hold as trustee for it any profits derived by him without the consent of the other partners from any transaction connected with the formation, conduct, or liquidation of the partnership or from any use by him of its property.

(2) This section applies also to the representatives of a deceased partner engaged in the liquidation of the affairs of the partnership as the personal representatives of the last surviving partner.

Sec. 22. (Right to an Account.) Any partner shall have the right to a formal account as to partnership affairs:

(a) If he is wrongfully excluded from the partnership business or possession of its property by his co-partners,

(b) If the right exists under the terms of any agreement,

(c) As provided by Section 21,

(d) Whenever other circumstances render it just and reasonable.

Sec. 23. (Continuation of Partnership Beyond Fixed Term.) (1) When a partnership for a fixed term or particular undertaking is continued after the termination of such term or particular undertaking without any express agreement, the rights and duties of the partners remain the same as they were at such termination, so far as is consistent with a partnership at will.

(2) A continuation of the business by the partners or such of them as habitually acted therein during the term, without any settlement or liquidation of the partnership affairs, is prima facie evidence of a continuation of the partnership.

PART V: PROPERTY RIGHTS OF A PARTNER

Sec. 24. (Extent of Property Rights of a Partner.) The property rights of a partner are (1) his rights in specific partnership property, (2) his interest in the partnership, and (3) his right to participate in the management.

Sec. 25. (Nature of a Partner's Right in Specific Partnership Property.) (1) A partner is co-owner with his partners of specific partnership property holding as a tenant in partnership.

(2) The incidents of this tenancy are such that:

(a) A partner, subject to the provisions of this act and to any agreement between the partners, has an equal right with his partners to possess specific partnership property for partnership purposes; but he has no right to possess such property for any other purpose without the consent of his partners.

(b) A partner's right in specific partnership property is not assignable except in connection with the assignment of rights of all the partners in the same property.

(c) A partner's right in specific partnership property is not subject to attachment or execution, except on a claim against the partnership. When partnership property is attached for a partnership debt the partners, or any of them, or the representatives of a deceased partner, cannot claim any right under the homestead or exemption laws.

(d) On the death of a partner his right in specific partnership property vests in the surviving partner or partners, except where the deceased was the last surviving partner, when his right in such property vests in his legal representative. Such surviving partner or partners, or the legal representative of the last surviving partner, has no right to possess the partnership property for any but a partnership purpose.

(e) A partner's right in specific partnership property is not subject to dower, courtesy, or allowances to widows, heirs, or next of kin.

Sec. 26. (Nature of Partner's Interest in the Partnership.) A partner's interest in the partnership is his share of the profits and surplus, and the same is personal property.

Sec. 27. (Assignment of Partner's Interest.) (1) A conveyance by a partner of his interest in the partnership does not of itself dissolve the partnership, nor, as against the other partners in the absence of agreement, entitle the assignee, during the continuance of the partnership to interfere in the management or administration of the partnership business or affairs, or to require any information or account of partnership transactions, or to inspect the partnership books; but it merely entitles the assignee to receive in accordance with his contract the profits to which the assigning partner would otherwise be entitled.

(2) In case of a dissolution of the partnership, the assignee is entitled to receive his assignor's interest and may require an account from the date only of the last account agreed to by all the partners.

Sec. 28. (Partner's Interest Subject to Charging Order.) (1) On due application to a competent court by any judgment creditor of a partner, the court which entered the judgment, order, or decree, or any other court, may charge the interest of the debtor partner with payment of the unsatisfied amount of such judgment debt with interest thereon; and may then or later appoint a receiver of his share of the profits, and of any other money due or to fall due to him in respect of the partnership, and make all other orders, directions, accounts and inquiries which the debtor partner might have made, or which the circumstances of the case may require.

(2) The interest charged may be redeemed at any time before foreclosure, or in case of a sale being directed by the court may be purchased without thereby causing a dissolution:

(a) With separate property, by any one or more of the partners, or

(b) With partnership property, by any one or more of the partners with the consent of all the partners whose interests are not so charged or sold.

(3) Nothing in this act shall be held to deprive a partner of his right, if any, under the exemption laws, as regards his interest in the partnership.

**PART VI:
DISSOLUTION AND WINDING UP**

Sec. 29. (Dissolution Defined.) The dissolution of a partnership is the change in the relation of the partners caused by any partner ceasing to be associated in the carrying on as distinguished from the winding up of the business.

Sec. 30. (Partnership Not Terminated by Dissolution.) On dissolution the partnership is not terminated, but continues until the winding up of partnership affairs is completed.

Sec. 31. (Causes of Dissolution.) Dissolution is caused: (1) Without violation of the agreement between the partners,

(a) By the termination of the definite term or particular undertaking specified in the agreement,

(b) By the express will of any partner when no definite term or particular undertaking is specified,

(c) By the express will of all the partners who have not assigned their interests or suffered them to be charged for their separate debts, either before or after the termination of any specified term or particular undertaking,

(d) By the expulsion of any partner from the business bona fide in accordance with such a power conferred by the agreement between the partners;

(2) In contravention of the agreement between the partners, where the circumstances do not permit a dissolution under any other provision of this section, by the express will of any partner at any time;

(3) By any event which makes it unlawful for the business of the partnership to be carried on or for the members to carry it on in partnership;

(4) By the death of any partner;

(5) By the bankruptcy of any partner or the partnership;

(6) By decree of court under Section 32.

Sec. 32. (Dissolution by Decree of Court.)
(1) On application by or for a partner the court shall decree a dissolution whenever:

(a) A partner has been declared a lunatic in any judicial proceeding or is shown to be of unsound mind,

(b) A partner becomes in any other way incapable of performing his part of the partnership contract,

(c) A partner has been guilty of such conduct as tends to affect prejudicially the carrying on of the business,

(d) A partner wilfully or persistently commits a breach of the partnership agreement, or otherwise so conducts himself in matters relating to the partnership business that it is not reasonably practicable to carry on the business in partnership with him,

(e) The business of the partnership can only be carried on at a loss,

(f) Other circumstances render a dissolution equitable.

(2) On the application of the purchaser of a partner's interest under Sections 27 or 28:

(a) After the termination of the specified term or particular undertaking,

(b) At any time if the partnership was a partnership at will when the interest was assigned or when the charging order was issued.

Sec. 33. (General Effect of Dissolution on Authority of Partner.) Except so far as may be necessary to wind up partnership affairs or to complete transactions begun but not then finished, dissolution terminates all authority of any partner to act for the partnership,

(1) With respect to the partners,

(a) When the dissolution is not by the act, bankruptcy or death of a partner; or

(b) When the dissolution is by such act, bankruptcy or death of a partner, in cases where Section 34 so requires.

(2) With respect to persons not partners, as declared in Section 35.

Sec. 34. (Right of Partner to Contribution from Copartners After Dissolution.) Where

the dissolution is caused by the act, death or bankruptcy of a partner, each partner is liable to his copartners for his share of any liability created by any partner acting for the partnership as if the partnership had not been dissolved unless

(a) The dissolution being by act of any partner, the partner acting for the partnership had knowledge of the dissolution, or

(b) The dissolution being by the death or bankruptcy of a partner, the partner acting for the partnership had knowledge or notice of the death or bankruptcy.

Sec. 35. (Power of Partner to Bind Partnership to Third Persons After Dissolution.)
(1) After dissolution a partner can bind the partnership except as provided in Paragraph (3)

(a) By any act appropriate for winding up partnership affairs or completing transactions unfinished at dissolution;

(b) By any transaction which would bind the partnership if dissolution had not taken place, provided the other party to the transaction

(I) Had extended credit to the partnership prior to dissolution and had no knowledge or notice of the dissolution; or

(II) Though he had not so extended credit, had nevertheless known of the partnership prior to dissolution, and, having no knowledge or notice of dissolution, the fact of dissolution had not been advertised in a newspaper of general circulation in the place (or in each place if more than one) at which the partnership business was regularly carried on.

(2) The liability of a partner under paragraph (1b) shall be satisfied out of partnership assets alone when such partner had been prior to dissolution.

(a) Unknown as a partner to the person with whom the contract is made; and

(b) So far unknown and inactive in partnership affairs that the business reputation of the partnership could not be said to have been in any degree due to his connection with it.

(3) The partnership is in no case bound by any act of a partner after dissolution

(a) Where the partnership is dissolved because it is unlawful to carry on the business, unless the act is appropriate for winding up partnership affairs; or

(b) Where the partner has become bankrupt; or

(c) Where the partner has no authority to wind up partnership affairs; except by a transaction with one who

(I) Had extended credit to the partnership prior to dissolution and had no knowledge or notice of his want of authority; or

(II) Had not extended credit to the partnership prior to dissolution, and, having no knowledge or notice of his want of authority, the fact of his want of authority has not been advertised in the manner provided for advertising the fact of dissolution in paragraph (1bII).

(4) Nothing in this section shall affect the liability under section 16 of any person who after dissolution represents himself or consents to another representing him as a partner in a partnership engaged in carrying on business.

Sec. 36. (Effect of Dissolution on Partner's Existing Liability.) (1) The dissolution of the partnership does not of itself discharge the existing liability of any partner.

(2) A partner is discharged from any existing liability upon dissolution of the partnership by an agreement to that effect between himself, the partnership creditor and the person or partnership continuing the business; and such agreement may be inferred from the course of dealing between the creditor having knowledge of the dissolution and the person or partnership continuing the business.

(3) Where a person agrees to assume the existing obligations of a dissolved partnership, the partners whose obligations have been assumed shall be discharged from any liability to any creditor of the partnership who, knowing of the agreement, consents to a material alteration in the nature or time of payment of such obligations.

(4) The individual property of a deceased partner shall be liable for all obligations of the partnership incurred while he was a partner but subject to the prior payment of his separate debts.

Sec. 37. (Right to Wind Up.) Unless otherwise agreed the partners who have not wrongfully dissolved the partnership or the legal representative of the last surviving partner, not bankrupt, has the right to wind up the partnership affairs; provided, however, that any partner, his legal representative or his assignee, upon cause shown, may obtain winding up by the court.

Sec. 38. (Rights of Partners to Application of Partnership Property.) (1) When dissolution is caused in any way, except in contravention of the partnership agreement, each partner as against his co-partners and all persons claiming through them in respect of their interests in the partnership, unless otherwise agreed, may have the partnership property applied to discharge its liabilities, and the surplus applied to pay in cash the net amount owing to the respective partners. But if dissolution is caused by expulsion of a partner, bona fide under the partnership agreement; and if the expelled partner is discharged from all partnership liabilities, either by payment or agreement under Section 36(2), he shall receive in cash only the net amount due him from the partnership.

(2) When dissolution is caused in contravention of the partnership agreement the rights of the partners shall be as follows:

(a) Each partner who has not caused dissolution wrongfully shall have,

(I) All the rights specified in paragraph (1) of this section, and

(II) The right, as against each partner who has caused the dissolution wrongfully, to damages for breach of the agreement.

(b) The partners who have not caused the dissolution wrongfully, if they all desire to continue the business in the same name, either by themselves or jointly with others, may do so, during the agreed term for the partnership and for that purpose may possess the partnership property, provided they secure the payment by bond approved by the court, or pay to any partner who has caused the dissolution wrongfully, the value of his interest in the partnership at the dissolution, less any damages recoverable under clause (2aII) of the section, and in like manner indemnify him against all present or future partnership liabilities.

(c) A partner who has caused the dissolution wrongfully shall have:

(I) If the business is not continued under the provisions of paragraph (2b) all the rights of a partner under paragraph (1), subject to clause (2aII), of this section,

(II) If the business is continued under paragraph (2b) of this section the right as against his co-partners and all claiming through them in respect of their interests in the partnership, to have the value of his interests in the partnership, less any damages caused to his co-partners by the dissolution, ascertained and paid to him in cash, or the payment secured by bond approved by the court, and to be released from all existing liabilities of the partnership; but in ascertaining the value of the partner's interest the value of the goodwill of the business shall not be considered.

Sec. 39. (Rights Where Partnership Is Dissolved for Fraud or Misrepresentation.) Where a partnership contract is rescinded on the ground of the fraud or misrepresentation of one of the parties thereto, the party entitled to rescind is, without prejudice to any other right, entitled,

(a) To a lien on, or right of retention of, the surplus of the partnership property after satisfying the partnership liabilities to third persons for any sum of money paid by him for the purchase of an interest in the partnership and for any capital or advances contributed by him; and

(b) To stand, after all liabilities to third persons have been satisfied, in the place of the creditors of the partnership for any payments made by him in respect of the partnership liabilities; and

(c) To be indemnified by the person guilty of the fraud or making the representation against all debts and liabilities of the partnership.

Sec. 40. (Rules for Distribution.) In settling accounts between the partners after dissolution, the following rules shall be observed, subject to any agreement to the contrary:

(a) The assets of the partnership are;

(I) The partnership property,

(II) The contributions of the partners necessary for the payment of all the liabilities specified in clause (b) of this paragraph.

(b) The liabilities of the partnership shall rank in order of payment, as follows:

(I) Those owing to creditors other than partners,

(II) Those owing to partners other than for capital and profits,

(III) Those owing to partners in respect of capital,

(IV) Those owing to partners in respect of profits.

(c) The assets shall be applied in the order of their declaration in clause (a) of this paragraph to the satisfaction of the liabilities.

(d) The partners shall contribute, as provided by Section 18(a) the amount necessary to satisfy the liabilities; but if any, but not all, of the partners are insolvent, or, not being subject to process, refuse to contribute, the other parties shall contribute their share of the liabilities, and, in the relative proportions in which they share the profits, the additional amount necessary to pay the liabilities.

(e) An assignee for the benefit of creditors or any person appointed by the court shall have the right to enforce the contributions specified in clause (d) of this paragraph.

(f) Any partner or his legal representative shall have the right to enforce the contributions specified in clause (d) of this paragraph, to the extent of the amount which he has paid in excess of his share of the liability.

(g) The individual property of a deceased partner shall be liable for the contributions specified in clause (d) of this paragraph.

(h) When partnership property and the individual properties of the partners are in possession of a court for distribution, partnership creditors shall have priority on partnership property and separate creditors on individual property, saving the rights of lien or secured creditors as heretofore.

(i) Where a partner has become bankrupt or his estate is insolvent the claims against his separate property shall rank in the following order:

(I) Those owing to separate creditors,

(II) Those owing to partnership creditors,

(III) Those owing to partners by way of contribution.

Sec. 41. (Liability of Persons Continuing the Business in Certain Cases.) (1) When any new partner is admitted into an existing partnership, or when any partner retires and assigns (or the representative of the deceased partner assigns) his rights in partnership property to two or more of the partners, or to one or more of the partners and one or more third persons, if the business is continued without liquidation of the partnership affairs, creditors of the first or dissolved partnership are also creditors of the partnership so continuing the business.

(2) When all but one partner retire and assign (or the representative of a deceased partner assigns) their rights in partnership property to the remaining partner, who continues the business without liquidation of partnership affairs, either alone or with others, creditors of the dissolved partnership are also creditors of the person or partnership so continuing the business.

(3) When any partner retires or dies and the business of the dissolved partnership is continued as set forth in paragraphs (1) and (2) of this section, with the consent of the retired partners or the representative of the deceased partner, but without any assignment of his right in partnership property, rights of creditors of the dissolved partnership and of the creditors of the person or partnership continuing the business shall be as if such assignment had been made.

(4) When all the partners or their representatives assign their rights in partnership property to one or more third persons who promise to pay the debts and who continue the business of the dissolved partnership, creditors of the dissolved partnership are also creditors of the person or partnership continuing the business.

(5) When any partner wrongfully causes a dissolution and the remaining partners continue the business under the provisions of section 38(2b), either alone or with others, and without liquidation of the partnership affairs, creditors of the dissolved partnership are also creditors of the person or partnership continuing the business.

(6) When a partner is expelled and the remaining partners continue the business either alone or with others, without liquidation of the partnership affairs, creditors of the dissolved partnership are also creditors of the person or partnership continuing the business.

(7) The liability of a third person becoming a partner in the partnership continuing the business, under this section, to the creditors of the dissolved partnership shall be satisfied out of partnership property only.

(8) When the business of a partnership after

dissolution is continued under any conditions set forth in this section the creditors of the dissolved partnership, as against the separate creditors of the retiring or deceased partner or the representative of the deceased partner, have a prior right to any claim of the retired partner or the representative of the deceased partner against the person or partnership continuing the business, on account of the retired or deceased partner's interest in the dissolved partnership or on account of any consideration promised for such interest or for his right in partnership property.

(9) Nothing in this section shall be held to modify any right of creditors to set aside any assignment on the ground of fraud.

(10) The use by the person or partnership continuing the business of the partnership name, or the name of a deceased partner as part thereof, shall not of itself make the individual property of the deceased partner liable for any debts contracted by such person or partnership.

Sec. 42. (Rights of Retiring or Estate of Deceased Partner When the Business Is Continued.) When any partner retires or dies, and the business is continued under any of the conditions set forth in Section 41(1, 2, 3, 5, 6), or Section 38(2b), without any settlement of accounts as between him or his estate and the person or partnership continuing the business, unless otherwise agreed, he or his legal representative as against such persons or partnership may have the value of his interest at the date of dissolution ascertained, and shall receive as an ordinary creditor an amount equal to the value of his interest in the dissolved partnership with interest, or, at his option or at the option of his legal representative, in lieu of interest, the profits attributable to the use of his right in the property of the dissolved partnership; provided that the creditors of the dissolved partnership as against the separate creditors, or the representative of the retired or deceased partner, shall have priority on any claim arising under this section, as provided by Section 41(8) of this act.

Sec. 43. (Accrual of Actions.) The right to an account of his interest shall accrue to any partner, or his legal representative, as against the winding up partners or the surviving partners or the person or partnership continuing the business, at the date of dissolution, in the absence of any agreement to the contrary.

PART VII: MISCELLANEOUS PROVISIONS

Sec. 44. (When Act Takes Effect.) This act shall take effect on the ———— day of ———— one thousand nine hundred and ————.

Sec. 45. (Legislation Repealed.) All acts or parts of acts inconsistent with this act are hereby repealed.

APPENDIX 4B:
THE UNIFORM LIMITED
PARTNERSHIP ACT*

Be it enacted, etc., as follows:

Sec. 1. (Limited Partnership Defined.) A limited partnership is a partnership formed by two or more persons under the provisions of Section 2, having as members one or more general partners and one or more limited partners. The limited partners as such shall not be bound by the obligations of the partnership.

Sec. 2. (Formation.) (1) Two or more persons desiring to form a limited partnership shall

(a) Sign and swear to a certificate, which shall state

    I.   The name of the partnership,

    II.   The character of the business,

    III.   The location of the principal place of business,

    IV.   The name and place of residence of each member; general and limited partners being respectively designated,

    V.   The term for which the partnership is to exist,

---

*National Conference of Commissioners on Uniform State Laws (1976).

VI. The amount of cash and a description of and the agreed value of the other property contributed by each limited partner,

VII. The additional contributions, if any, agreed to be made by each limited partner and the times at which or events on the happening of which they shall be made,

VIII. The time, if agreed upon, when the contribution of each limited partner is to be returned,

IX. The share of the profits or the other compensation by way of income which each limited partner shall receive by reason of his contribution,

X. The right, if given, of a limited partner to substitute an assignee as contributor in his place, and the terms and conditions of the substitution,

XI. The right, if given, of the partners to admit additional limited partners,

XII. The right, if given, of one or more of the limited partners to priority over other limited partners, as to contributions or as to compensation by way of income, and the nature of such priority,

XIII. The right, if given, of the remaining general partner or partners to continue the business on the death, retirement or insanity of a general partner, and

XIV. The right, if given, of a limited partner to demand and receive property other than cash in return for his contribution.

(b) File for record the certificate in the office of [here designate the proper office].

(2) A limited partnership is formed if there has been substantial compliance in good faith with the requirements of paragraph (1).

Sec. 3. (Business Which may Be Carried On.) A limited partnership may carry on any business which a partnership without limited partners may carry on, except [here designate the business to be prohibited].

Sec. 4. (Character of Limited Partner's Contribution.) The contributions of a limited partner may be cash or other property, but not services.

Sec. 5. (A Name Not to Contain Surname of Limited Partner; Exceptions.) (1) The surname of a limited partner shall not appear in the partnership name, unless

(a) It is also the surname of a general partner, or

(b) Prior to the time when the limited partner became such the business had been carried on under a name in which his surname appeared.

(2) A limited partner whose name appears in a partnership name contrary to the provisions of paragraph (1) is liable as a general partner to partnership creditors who extend credit to the partnership without actual knowledge that he is not a general partner.

Sec. 6. (Liability for False Statements in Certificate.) If the certificate contains a false statement, one who suffers loss by reliance on such statement may hold liable any party to the certificate who knew the statement to be false.

(a) At the time he signed the certificate, or

(b) Subsequently, but within a sufficient time before the statement was relied upon to enable him to cancel or amend the certificate, or to file a petition for its cancellation or amendment as provided in Section 25(3).

Sec. 7. (Limited Partner Not Liable to Creditors.) A limited partner shall not become liable as a general partner unless, in addition to the exercise of his rights and powers as a limited partner, he takes part in the control of the business.

Sec. 8. (Admission of Additional Limited Partners.) After the formation of a limited partnership, additional limited partners may be admitted upon filing an amendment to the original certificate in accordance with the requirements of Section 25.

Sec. 9. (Rights, Powers and Liabilities of a General Partner.) (1) A general partner shall have all the rights and powers and be subject to all the restrictions and liabilities of a partner in a partnership without limited partners, except that without the written consent or ratification of the specific act by all the limited partners, a general partner or all of the general partners have no authority to

(a) Do any act in contravention of the certificate,

(b) Do any act which would make it impossible to carry on the ordinary business of the partnership,

(c) Confess a judgment against the partnership,

(d) Possess partnership property, or assign their rights in specific partnership property, for other than a partnership purpose,

(e) Admit a person as a general partner,

(f) Admit a person as a limited partner, unless the right to do so is given in the certificate,

(g) Continue the business with partnership property on the death, retirement or insanity of a general partner, unless the right so to do is given in the certificate.

Sec. 10. (Rights of a Limited Partner.) (1) A limited partner shall have the same rights as a general partner to

(a) Have the partnership books kept at the principal place of business of the partnership, and at all times to inspect and copy any of them,

(b) Have on demand true and full information of all things affecting the partnership, and a formal account of partnership affairs, whenever circumstances render it just and reasonable, and

(c) Have dissolution and winding up by decree of court.

(2) A limited partner shall have the right to receive a share of the profits or other compensation by way of income, and to the return of his contribution as provided in Sections 15 and 16.

Sec. 11. (Status of Person Erroneously Believing Himself a Limited Partner.) A person who has contributed to the capital of a business conducted by a person or partnership erroneously believing that he has become a limited partner in a limited partnership, is not, by reason of his exercise of the rights of a limited partner, a general partner with the person or in the partnership carrying on the business, or bound by the obligations of such person or partnership; provided that on ascertaining the mistake he promptly renounces his interest in the profits of the business, or other compensation by way of income.

Sec. 12. (One Person Both General and Limited Partner.) (1) A person may be a general partner and a limited partner in the same partnership at the same time.

(2) A person who is a general, and also at the same time a limited partner, shall have all the rights and powers and be subject to all the restrictions of a general partner; except that, in respect to his contribution, he shall have the rights against the other members which he would have had if he were not also a general partner.

Sec. 13. (Loans and Other Business Transactions with Limited Partner.) (1) A limited partner also may loan money to and transact other business with the partnership, and, unless he is also a general partner, receive on account of resulting claims against the partnership, with general creditors, a pro rata share of the assets. No limited partner shall in respect to any such claim

(a) Receive or hold as collateral security any partnership property, or

(b) Receive from a general partner or the partnership any payment, conveyance, or release from liability, if at the time the assets of the partnership are not sufficient to discharge partnership liabilities to persons not claiming as general or limited partners.

(2) The receiving of collateral security, or a payment, conveyance, or release in violation of the provisions of paragraph (1) is a fraud on the creditors of the partnership.

Sec. 14. (Relation of Limited Partners Inter Se.) Where there are several limited partners the members may agree that one or more of the limited partners shall have a priority over other limited partners as to the return of their contributions, as to their compensation by way of income, or as to any other matter. If such an agreement is made it shall be stated in the certificate, and in the absence of such a statement all the limited partners shall stand upon equal footing.

Sec. 15. (Compensation of Limited Partner.) A limited partner may receive from the partnership the share of the profits or the compensation by way of income stipulated for in the certificate; provided, that after such payment is made, whether from the property of the partnership or that of a general partner, the partnership assets are in excess of all liabilities of the partnership except liabilities to limited partners on account of their contributions and to general partners.

Sec. 16. (Withdrawal or Reduction of Limited Partner's Contribution.) (1) A limited partner shall not receive from a general partner or out of partnership property any part of his contribution until

(a) All liabilities of the partnership, except liabilities to general partners and to limited partners on account of their contributions, have been paid or there remains property of the partnership sufficient to pay them,

(b) The consent of all members is had, unless the return of the contribution may be rightfully demanded under the provisions of paragraph (2), and

(c) The certificate is cancelled or so amended as to set forth the withdrawal or reduction.

(2) Subject to the provisions of paragraph (1) a limited partner may rightfully demand the return of his contribution

(a) On the dissolution of a partnership, or

(b) When the date specified in the certificate for its return has arrived, or

(c) After he has given six months' notice in writing to all other members, if no time is specified in the certificate either for the return of the contribution or for the dissolution of the partnership,

(3) In the absence of any statement in the certificate to the contrary or the consent of all members, a limited partner, irrespective of the nature of his contribution, has only the right to demand and receive cash in return for his contribution.

(4) A limited partner may have the partnership dissolved and its affairs wound up when

(a) He rightfully but unsuccessfully demands the return of his contribution, or

(b) The other liabilities of the partnership have not been paid, or the partnership property is insufficient for their payment as required by paragraph (1a) and the limited partner would otherwise be entitled to the return of his contribution.

Sec. 17. (Liability of Limited Partner to Partnership.) (1) A limited partner is liable to the partnership

(a) For the difference between his contribution as actually made and that stated in the certificate as having been made, and

(b) For any unpaid contribution which he agreed in the certificate to make in the future at the time and on the conditions stated in the certificate.

(2) A limited partner holds as trustee for the partnership

(a) Specific property stated in the certificate as contributed by him, but which was not contributed or which has been wrongfully returned, and

(b) Money or other property wrongfully paid or conveyed to him on account of his contribution.

(3) The liabilities of a limited partner as set forth in this section can be waived or compromised only by the consent of all members; but a waiver or compromise shall not affect the right of a creditor of a partnership, who extended credit or whose claim arose after the filing and before a cancellation or amendment of the certificate, to enforce such liabilities.

(4) When a contributor has rightfully received the return in whole or in part of the capital of his contribution, he is nevertheless liable to the partnership for any sum, not in excess of such return with interest, necessary to discharge its liabilities to all creditors who extended credit or whose claims arose before such return.

Sec. 18. (Nature of Limited Partner's Interest in Partnership.) A limited partner's interest in the partnership is personal property.

Sec. 19. (Assignment of Limited Partner's Interest.) (1) A limited partner's interest is assignable.

(2) A substituted limited partner is a person admitted to all the rights of a limited partner who has died or has assigned his interest in a partnership.

(3) An assignee, who does not become a substituted limited partner, has no right to require any information or account of the partnership transactions or to inspect the partnership books; he is only entitled to receive the share of the profits or other compensation by way of income, or the return of his contribution, to which his assignor would otherwise be entitled.

(4) An assignee shall have the right to become a substituted limited partner if all the members (except the assignor) consent thereto or if the assignor, being thereunto empowered by the certificate, gives the assignee that right.

(5) An assignee becomes a substituted limited partner when the certificate is appropriately amended in accordance with Section 25.

(6) The substituted limited partner has all the rights and powers, and is subject to all the restrictions and liabilities of his assignor, except those liabilities of which he was ignorant at the time he became a limited partner and which could not be ascertained from the certificate.

(7) The substitution of the assignee as a limited partner does not release the assignor from liability to the partnership under Sections 6 and 17.

Sec. 20. (Effect of Retirement, Death or Insanity of a General Partner.) The retirement, death or insanity of a general partner dissolves the partnership, unless the business is continued by the remaining general partners

(a) Under a right so to do stated in the certificate, or

(b) With the consent of all members.

Sec. 21. (Death of Limited Partner.) (1) On the death of a limited partner his executor or administrator shall have all the rights of a limited partner for the purpose of settling his estate, and such power as the deceased had to constitute his assignee a substituted limited partner.

(2) The estate of a deceased limited partner shall be liable for all his liabilities as a limited partner.

Sec. 22. (Rights of Creditors of Limited Partner.) (1) On due application to a court of competent jurisdiction by any judgment creditor of a limited partner, the court may charge the interest of the indebted limited partner with payment of the unsatisfied amount of the judgment debt; and may appoint a receiver, and make all other orders, directions, and inquiries which the circumstances of the case may require.

In those states where a creditor on beginning an action can attach debts due the defendant before he has obtained a judgment against the defendant it is recommended that paragraph (1) of this section read as follows:

On due application to a court of competent jurisdiction by any creditor of a limited partner, the court may charge the interest of the indebted limited partner with payment of the unsatisfied amount of such claim; and may appoint a receiver, and make all other orders, directions, and inquiries which the circumstances of the case may require.

(2) The interest may be redeemed with the separate property of any general partner, but may not be redeemed with partnership property.

(3) The remedies conferred by paragraph (1) shall not be deemed exclusive of others which may exist.

(4) Nothing in this act shall be held to deprive a limited partner of his statutory exemption.

Sec. 23. (Distribution of Assets.) (1) In settling accounts after dissolution the liabilities of the partnership shall be entitled to payment in the following order:

(a) Those to creditors, in the order of priority as provided by law, except those to limited partners on account of their contributions, and to general partners,

(b) Those to limited partners in respect to their share of the profits and other compensation by way of income on their contributions,

(c) Those to limited partners in respect to the capital of their contributions,

(d) Those to general partners other than for capital and profits,

(e) Those to general partners in respect to profits,

(f) Those to general partners in respect to capital.

(2) Subject to any statement in the certificate or to subsequent agreement, limited partners share in the partnership assets in respect to their claims for capital, and in respect to their claims for profits or for compensation by way of income on their contributions respectively, in proportion to the respective amounts of such claims.

Sec. 24. (When Certificate Shall Be Cancelled or Amended.) (1) The certificate shall be cancelled when the partnership is dissolved or all limited partners cease to be such.

(2) A certificate shall be amended when

(a) There is a change in the name of the partnership or in the amount or character of the contribution of any limited partner,

(b) A person is substituted as a limited partner,

(c) An additional limited partner is admitted,

(d) A person is admitted as a general partner,

(e) A general partner retires, dies or becomes insane, and the business is continued under Section 20,

(f) There is a change in the character of the business of the partnership,

(g) There is a false or erroneous statement in the certificate,

(h) There is a change in the time as stated in the certificate for the dissolution of the partnership or for the return of a contribution,

(i) A time is fixed for the dissolution of the partnership, or the return of a contribution, no time having been specified in the certificate, or

(j) The members desire to make a change in any other statement in the certificate in order that it shall accurately represent the agreement between them.

Sec. 25. (Requirements for Amendment and for Cancellation of Certificate.) (1) The writing to amend a certificate shall

(a) Conform to the requirements of Section 2(1a) as far as necessary to set forth clearly the change in the certificate which it is desired to make, and

(b) Be signed and sworn to by all members, and an amendment substituting a limited partner or adding a limited or general partner shall be signed also by the member to be substituted or added, and when a limited partner is to be substituted, the amendment shall also be signed by the assigning limited partner.

(2) The writing to cancel a certificate shall be signed by all members.

(3) A person desiring the cancellation or amendment of a certificate, if any person designated in paragraphs (1) and (2) as a person who must execute the writing refuses to do so, may petition the [here designate the proper court] to direct a cancellation or amendment thereof.

(4) If the court finds that the petitioner has a right to have the writing executed by a person who refuses to do so, it shall order the [here designate the responsible official in the office designated in Section 2] in the office where the certificate is recorded to record the cancellation or amendment of the certificate; and where the certificate is to be amended, the court shall cause to be filed for record in said office a certified copy of its decree setting forth the amendment.

(5) A certificate is amended or cancelled when there is filed for record in the office [here designate the office designated in Section 2] where the certificate is recorded

(a) A writing in accordance with the provisions of paragraph (1), or (2) or

(b) A certified copy of the order of court in accordance with the provisions of paragraph (4).

(6) After the certificate is duly amended in accordance with this section, the amended certificate shall thereafter be for all purposes the certificate provided for by this act.

Sec. 26. (Parties to Actions.) A contributor, unless he is a general partner, is not a proper party to proceedings by or against a partnership, except where the object is to enforce a limited partner's right against or liability to the partnership.

Sec. 27. (Name of Act.) This act may be cited as The Uniform Limited Partnership Act.

Sec. 28. (Rules of Construction.) (1) The rule that statutes in derogation of the common law are to be strictly construed shall have no application to this act.

(2) This act shall be so interpreted and construed as to effect its general purpose to make uniform the law of those states which enact it.

(3) This act shall not be so construed as to impair the obligations of any contract existing when the act goes into effect, nor to affect any action on proceedings begun or right accrued before this act takes effect.

Sec. 29. (Rules for Cases Not Provided for in this Act.) In any case not provided for in this act the rules of law and equity, including the law merchant, shall govern.

Sec. 30.[1] (Provisions for Existing Limited Partnerships.) (1) A limited partnership formed under any statute of this state prior to the adoption of this act, may become a limited partnership under this act by complying with

---

[1] Sections 30, 31, will be omitted in any state which has not a limited partnership act.

the provisions of Section 2; provided the certificate sets forth

(a) The amount of the original contribution of each limited partner, and the time when the contribution was made, and

(b) That the property of the partnership exceeds the amount sufficient to discharge its liabilities to persons not claiming as general or limited partners by an amount greater than the sum of the contributions of its limited partners.

(2) A limited partnership formed under any statute of this state prior to the adoption of this act, until or unless it becomes a limited partnership under this act, shall continue to be governed by the provisions of [here insert proper reference to the existing limited partnership act or acts], except that such partnership shall not be renewed unless so provided in the original agreement.

Sec. 31.[1] (Act [Acts] Repealed.) Except as affecting existing limited partnerships to the extent set forth in Section 30, the act (acts) of [here designate the existing limited partnership act or acts] is (are) hereby repealed.

III

Taxation
and Operations

A real estate investment has two potential sources of cash-flow income: the annual cash flow from the operation after all expenses have been paid and the cash flow after expenses from the sale of the investment. The investor is interested in the amount of cash flow he or she has left from these two sources after *all* expenses have been met. Expenses fall into three major categories: operating expenses (or, in the case of sale, selling expenses), financing expenses, and income taxes. Part 3 is concerned with techniques for estimating the cash flow from annual operations of a real estate investment. The cash flow from the disposition of the investment will be discussed in Part 4.

   Chapter 5 outlines the interrelationship between operating expenses and taxes. Chapter 6 discusses the impact of financing decisions on the annual cash flow. Chapter 7 examines the impact of the taxation on the annual cash flow. Particular attention is paid to the influence of the depreciation deduction. Chapter 7 also provides a detailed example showing how to set up the annual cash flow statement for a real estate investment.

5

Operating Expenses and Tax Analysis

INTRODUCTION

The initial starting point in all income investments is potential gross income (PGI). A duplex renting for $200 per unit per month will generate an annual potential gross income of $4,800. A fourteen-unit apartment complex renting for $300 per unit per month will generate an annual potential gross income of $50,400. Since the earning capacity of an apartment complex is expressed on a unit basis, it is always critical to obtain an accurate count of the number of units in the property. The number of units multiplied by the unit rental is the potential gross income. The units must be defined consistently. If half the units have one bedroom and half have two bedrooms, the units are different even if they are the same size. The mechanics of estimating potential gross income are simple and are based on 100-percent occupancy. Assume a 100-unit apartment property containing 60 two-bedroom units with a rental of $300 per month and 40 one-bedroom units with a rental of $200 per month. The PGI would be calculated as follows:

$$40 \text{ units} \times \$200 = \$8,000 \ \times 12 = \$96,000$$

$$60 \text{ units} \times \$300 = \$18,000 \times 12 = \underline{\$216,000}$$

$$\text{Annual PGI} = \$312,000$$

The monthly PGI is equal to $8,000 for the one-bedroom units and $18,000 for the two-bedroom units for a total monthly PGI of $26,000.

The gross income can be divided by the sales price to give a gross multiplier. These gross multipliers are used by many buyers to compare investment projects. If on the average the gross multiplier for duplexes or apartments is 7, this would suggest a sales price for the above duplex and apartments of $33,600 ($4,800 × 7), $352,800 ($50,400 × 7), and $2,184,000 ($312,000 × 7), respectively. The gross multiplier is determined for an area from previous sales and income data. The problem with this approach is that it does not adjust for the benefits of the project as a tax shelter or take account of differences in the goals of individual investors.

All real estate investments will generate some form of tax shelter. The extent of this tax benefit will depend to a great extent on an individual's tax bracket. The acceptable rate of return and the corresponding sales price a buyer is willing to pay may be greater for a buyer in the 70-percent tax bracket than for one in the 30-percent bracket. Thus, potential gross income and gross income multipliers may be misleading in determining what a specific individual should pay for a particular real estate investment. Instead of relying on these measures alone, an investor should be concerned with the taxable income from the project. The computed taxable income will allow the buyer to determine the after-tax rate of return. It is quite possible and beneficial for the investor to have a negative taxable income. Thus, not only is income from the project sheltered but other ordinary income, as well.

The first step in determining taxable income is the derivation of net operating income (NOI). NOI is computed by subtracting operating expenses from effective gross income (EGI). The remainder of this chapter is concerned with deriving NOI and with providing the best possible strategy for minimizing taxable income through proper handling of deductible operating expenses.

EFFECTIVE GROSS INCOME

Potential gross income is a somewhat naive concept. Few real estate investors expect to maintain no vacancies for all of their rental units throughout the year. There will usually be some vacancies and some renters who have not paid their rents. A common error is to underestimate the reduction in gross income resulting from vacancies and bad debts. This reduced rental income after deductions from PGI for vacancies and bad debts is called effective gross income (EGI). The goal is to estimate effective (actual) gross income accurately. If the project is a used rental property, then it is best to examine the past occupancy rates. If the property is new, then it would be necessary to conduct a real estate market analysis of the area to determine future demand and expected vacancies. Taking account of potential vacancies and bad debts provides a much more reliable assessment of effective gross income and expected rate of return.

For example, the fourteen-unit apartment complex discussed in the introduction with an annual potential gross income of $50,400 is expected to have ten units vacant for one month during the year. This reduces gross income by $3,000. Also, it is expected that two tenants will fail to pay their rent for one month each during the year, further reducing gross income by $600. It is required that all miscellaneous income be added to gross income. If two laundry machines in the apartment complex produce an income of $50 per month each, this would increase annual gross income by $1,200. In this case the final figure for effective gross income is $48,000, an almost 5-percent reduction. The annual allowance for income loss from vacancy and turnover or from nonpayment of rent must be made before any forecast of expected rate of return. In many cases some judgment is made as to what is a typical number of vacancies. Market comparables are often used to determine the average income loss for a similar type of investment. If the market comparables indicate a 5-percent loss for one-bedroom units and a 6-percent loss for two-bedroom units, then the effective gross income for the 100-unit property is:

One-bedroom units		
Potential gross income (PGI)	$ 96,000	
Minus 5-percent vacancy and income loss	(4,800)	
Plus miscellaneous income (laundry machines, etc.)	1,000	
Total Rent		$ 92,200
Two-bedroom units		
Potential gross income (PGI)	$216,000	
Minus 6-percent vacancy and income loss	(12,960)	
Plus miscellaneous income (laundry machines, etc.)	1,000	
Total Rent		204,040
Effective gross income (EGI)		$296,240

Notice that different units are not given the same vacancy allowance since one- and two-bedroom apartments appeal to different markets with different vacancy rates.

In summary, effective gross income (EGI) is the potential gross income (PGI) less allowances for vacancies and bad debts, plus miscellaneous income. In the next section the more difficult problem of how to compute operating expenses is examined. We can then estimate net operating income, which is effective gross income minus operating expenses.

OPERATING EXPENSES

Operating expenses represent the cost of providing services and maintaining the physical property of the real estate investment. The investor will always want to minimize the actual operating cost subject to the constraint of maintaining the building at some acceptable level to achieve the most rental income. Operating

expenses vary with the age of the building and with the past level of maintenance. Each investor must know the operating expenses for the specific building
under consideration to correctly estimate the expected rate of return.

Once the operating expenses are determined, useful techniques are available for using these expenses for reducing taxable income. Operating expenses
are subtracted from effective gross income to compute net operating income
(NOI). Net operating income is the basis for figuring the taxable income. The
lower the NOI, the lower the taxable income or, in the case of a taxable loss, the
greater the tax shelter.

What is the best strategy concerning operating expenses? Normally, taxpayers claim deductions for expenses in the year that they are paid. In some
cases, however, these expenses can be deferred to another year. This may be advantageous in years in which the real estate property does not produce significant income and when the investor has no ordinary income to shelter. In some
situations the investor's ordinary income may fluctuate to such an extent that it
would pay to defer the operating expenses to the year of his or her highest taxable income. This would reduce the taxes paid and increase the rate of return. It
is important to know not only the amount of operating expenses but to what extent they can be shifted to another year. The main criterion for tax reduction is
whether the operating expense is deductible in the year paid or whether it can be
capitalized over the life of the project. To capitalize an expense, it must be divided by the life of the project with a certain portion deductible for a given year.
This reduces the investor's deductions for the year the expense actually occurred
but increases them for later years. In most cases the deductions for any given
year do not completely shelter all income. Therefore, it pays to have the maximum tax write-off as early as possible, thus providing more income at an earlier
date. This assumes the investor's tax bracket remains relatively stable. The rules
and the best strategy to follow depend on the type of operating expense being
considered. The various types of expenses will now be examined.

Repairs and Maintenance

Repairs and maintenance are intended to continue the operating efficiency
of the property over its life. Capital improvements are intended to add value to,
lengthen the life of, or change the use of the property. Repairs and maintenance
are deductible in the year the expenditure is paid. The cost of capital addition is
depreciated over the improvement's useful life. If the repairs and maintenance
improve the value of the property, the Internal Revenue Service treats them as a
capital improvement. This means that the total cost of the repair cannot be deducted in the year of the expenditure. Although the cost will eventually be recovered through depreciation, this is not as advantageous as a complete deduction
in the year the expense occurred. The following example shows some expenditures and how they are treated for tax purposes:

Expenditure	Qualified as a repair	Qualified as a capital improvement
Heating system	Replacing the motor	New gas furnace replacing coal furnace
Roofing	Replacing shingles	New roof
Plumbing	Fixing the washer	Adding new gas water heater
Painting	Repainting	Repainting the additions of a new room
Walls	Repainting	Partition to create office

There are many other examples and court cases dealing with the distinction between repairs and capital expenditures. The results are not always consistent. The cost of painting and decorating is deductible. Resurfacing a parking lot or adding insulating material is deductible. Any repairs or maintenance that improves the capital value may be denied as current operating expenses. Examples are adding a new room for the storage of tools, replacing the attic fans with air conditioning, and replacing the plywood floor with hardwood. Machinery and equipment with a life of more than one year will be treated as a capital expenditure.

The decision as to whether a particular expenditure is a repair or capital improvement can have rather important tax effects. A $4,000 expenditure on roofing if deducted in the same year could result in a $2,000 tax savings for an investor in the 50-percent bracket. If that same expenditure is treated as a capital improvement, assuming the roofing has a useful life of twenty years and using straight-line depreciation, the investor would have only a $200 deduction the first year. The tax savings would be $100 a year for twenty years.

In general, the greater the size of the expenditure, the more likely it will be treated as a capital expenditure. If the improvement increases the value of the building by making it more useful or if better materials are used to improve the quality, then the expense related to the improvement must be capitalized and recovered through annual depreciation over the life of the improvement.

In most situations, the best strategy regarding repairs and maintenance is to keep the property in excellent condition. The expenses are deductible in the same year. When the investor sells the building, the value of the repairs and maintenance is reflected in a higher sales price for the property. This additional value can be taxed at the capital gain rate which is lower than the ordinary income rate.

Real Estate Taxes

Taxes are deductible as operating expenses when property is held for the production of income. The taxes are deductible the year that they are paid. The real estate tax must be apportioned between the buyer and seller for the year of sale. This is true even when the buyer pays all the taxes for the year. Taxes are deductible only by the owner of the property. If a husband or wife pays the tax on property owned by the spouse, no deduction is allowed. State and local personal property taxes along with mortgage recording and transfer taxes are also deductible.

Taxpayers are required to capitalize construction-period interest and taxes in the year paid and amortize them over a ten-year period. Some portion of the cost may be deducted the first year with the remaining cost phased in over the amortized period as set forth in the schedule in Table 5-1.

This IRS rule on construction interest and taxes has reduced the potential tax shelter during the early years of the investment. For example, assume an investor buys an apartment building in 1980. There is an immediate deduction of $16\frac{2}{3}$ percent of the construction-period interest and taxes paid. The balance of $83\frac{1}{3}$ percent must be delayed until the apartment is ready for rental or sale. At that time the investor may deduct $16\frac{2}{3}$ percent of the interest and taxes each year for the next five years. There are different phase-in schedules for nonresidential and low-income real estate.

It is possible for taxes and interest even under the phase-in schedule to generate tax losses. An investor may find that the tax losses are larger than the income to be sheltered. It may be to the investor's advantage to defer some of these deductions for later years. This is possible by capitalizing the taxes and interest over a period of ten years. When the property is unimproved or unproductive this can be done on a year-to-year basis. If the property is productive the decision to capitalize expenses cannot be reversed.

Taxes for local benefit, sometimes called special assessments, are not deductible to the extent that they increase the value of the property. They are treated as a capital improvement and must be amortized over the useful life. Real property tax for the general welfare is deductible.

Sales taxes on material used in construction or repairs are deductible. If a partnership is formed to construct and operate an apartment building then the sales tax for materials is deductible if the law imposes the tax on the buyer and if the partnership, not the general contractor, is the purchaser of the material. In

TABLE 5-1. Phase-In Schedule for Capitalization of Interest and Taxes Paid or Accrued during Construction for Residential Real Property

The Year Taxes and Interest Paid or Accrued	Percent Deductible Each Year
1978	25
1979	20
1980	$16\frac{2}{3}$
1981	$14\frac{2}{7}$
1982	$12\frac{1}{2}$
1983	$11\frac{1}{9}$
Thereafter	10

construction, it must be made clear that the buyer is responsible for the sales tax. A general contractor has the right to deduct the sales tax under a fixed-dollar-amount contract. In this case the investor should indicate on a separate agreement that the contractor is acting as the agent for the investor.

Insurance and Casualty

Insurance premiums against fire, storm, theft, and accidents are deductible if the investor pays for more than one year.

A casualty is the destruction of property resulting from a sudden, unexpected event. Examples are fires, storms, earthquakes, sonic booms, floods, and other acts of nature. The progressive deterioration of property is not treated as a casualty. It is the sudden, unusual, or unexpected nature of the event that qualifies the loss for deduction.

If the property is totally destroyed by casualty, the amount to be deducted is the adjusted basis of the property less any insurance received and salvage value. If the projects are partially destroyed, the amount deductible is the lesser of the loss in property value or the adjusted basis of the property. Repair cost is valid evidence of loss of value. The taxpayer must show that repairs are necessary to restore property to prior condition and do not result in an increase in value of the property.

Fees and Commissions

Fees and commissions for services that produce current benefits are deductible. The cost of collecting rents and managing property are deductible in the year paid. If the benefit of the service extends beyond the year paid then it must be capitalized amd amortized over the length of benefit. Long-term leases and the cost of securing a mortgage loan must be amortized over the relevant term. Lawyers' and architects' fees, brokerage commissions, and title expenses all must be added to the leases and recovered through the annual depreciation allowance.

In many cases, individual investors in real estate spend a great deal of their own personal time on the project. Such time would include that spent on possible remodeling, decorating, construction, keeping the books, collecting the rent, and filing the tax return. This time has a value. Each person must decide on his or her subjective valuation of the time spent working on the investment. This value is treated as an expense when computing the rate of return of the project. The IRS does not treat this as an expense unless the corporation or partnership pays the investor a salary or the individual declares an income. In this case the investor has to pay taxes on the salary. He or she may be better off to allow the work to be implicitly capitalized into the value of the investment. In this way, the worst that could happen is that a capital gains tax will be imposed on the additional value contributed by the investor's efforts. Management services may not be capitalized into the value. In this case it may be best for tax purposes to pay the investor a salary. In any case, the contributions of time by the investor should be treated as an expense when computing the rate of return. Many investors have overstated their rate of return by not counting the value of their own time.

Material and Supplies

If records are kept on material and supplies, then the deduction is limited to the value actually used during the year. If no record is maintained on consumption, the entire amount expended can be deducted. Records of expenditures must be kept, but careful records of consumption and use of material and supplies is not advised.

NET OPERATING INCOME

Net operating income is effective gross income less operating expenses. In analyzing the potential rate of return from an investment, buyers have a tendency to underestimate operating expenses. The operating expenses can vary with the type of investment. The following examples will show how to estimate expenses and NOI for four types of property: an apartment, a shopping center, a warehouse, and an office building.

In most cases, four broad categories can be used for expenses: repairs and maintenance, utilities, administrative fees, and insurance and taxes.

Apartment-Building Expenses

Example 5-1 provides a breakdown of expenses for a typical apartment building. The example is hypothetical, but the actual amounts are representative of apartment expenses. There are several ways to collect information on expenses. The past three to five years of operating experience of the property is a good guide. It is important to check the quality of management during this period. If the management is different from the norm then adjustments should be made in the expense estimates so that the management costs are typical. A second approach is to study several other similar projects on the market. The experience of comparable properties is an excellent guide for the subject's property. Thirdly, there are a number of published studies that provide information on typical occupancy and income loss of different types of property. Such surveys give regional differences and serve as guides to reasonable standards. Example 5-1 lists the annual income and operating expenses for a fourteen-unit apartment complex.

EXAMPLE 5-1:
ANNUAL INCOME AND OPERATING EXPENSES FOR A
FOURTEEN-UNIT APARTMENT COMPLEX

Income			
Rents—apartments		$50,400	
Rents—parking garage		1,400	
Laundry machines		1,200	
Total Potential Gross Income			$53,000
Vacancies		3,000	
Nonpayment of rent		600	−3,600
Effective Gross Income			49,400
Operating Expenses			
Repairs and Maintenance			
Total payroll expenses	400		
Supplies	80		
Painting and decorating	400		
Maintenance	400		
Services	80		
Miscellaneous expenses	80		
Subtotal Repairs and Maintenances		1,440	
Utilities			
Electricity	3,600		
Gas	900		
Water	50		
Heating fuel	1,000		
Subtotal Utilities		5,550	
Administration			
Management fees	3,000		
Other administrative expenses	500		
Subtotal Administrative		3,500	
Taxes and Insurance			
Insurance	500		
Real estate property taxes	8,000		
Sales taxes	100		
Other taxes	50		
Subtotal Taxes and Insurance		8,650	
Total All Expenses			−19,140
Net Operating Income (NOI)			$30,260

Shopping-Center Expenses

A shopping-center expense statement would be similar in form but would have some differences in the items included for operating expenses. More expense would be involved in maintaining the appearance of the lots and plants.

The management fee is 10 to 15 percent of the common area charge. The lease would reveal many different responsibilities between landlord and tenant as compared to an apartment complex. The leases should not be made for too long a period. Shorter lease terms allow the landlord to renegotiate with the smaller tenants for higher rents or to weed out weak tenants. The major tenant leases should be for at least twenty years. The major tenants provide security of the continued success of the shopping center. Caution should be used when granting options, since these generally favor the tenant.

Most rents are in terms of a percentage of gross sales. Gross sales should be carefully defined and accurately reported. The landlord should have the right to check all records. An article audit should be scheduled every two years.

The use clause is a statement that preserves the tenant mix. Competition should not be avoided. Exclusives are damaging to the total sales. Escalator clauses establish either full-share or cost-of-living indices to compensate for increased costs of operations. A tax-stop clause requires the tenant to pay a pro rata share of any increase in real estate taxes.

EXAMPLE 5-2:
ANNUAL INCOME AND OPERATING EXPENSE
FOR A SHOPPING CENTER

Income		
Total rent	$895,000	
Common area charges	76,500	
Other charges	13,500	
Total Potential Gross Income		$985,000
Vacancies		−40,000
Effective Gross Income		945,000
Operating Expenses		
Building maintenance	36,000	
Maintenance of parking lot, mall, and other public areas	72,000	
Advertising and promotion	72,000	
General and administrative	49,500	
Real estate taxes	139,500	
Insurance	13,500	
Total All Expenses		−382,500
Net Operating Income (NOI)		$562,500

There are a few unique expenses connected with shopping centers. Every shopping center has a common area. Everything outside of the leasable area is referred to as the common area. This generally includes parking, loading areas, service roads, public restrooms, landscaped areas, and access roads.

The lease will stipulate a common area charge that the tenant is required to pay. The pro rata system based on rent or gross rental area is preferable since each tenant pays his or her proportional share and no ceiling is established. The charges connected with common areas can vary from insurance premiums for liability to snow removal charges, all of which are deductible as operating expenses.

The preceding discussion was not meant to be a complete example of how to invest in shopping centers. It does present some insights into how to set up an expense chart and how to arrive at net operating income for a shopping center.

Warehouse Expenses

A warehouse expense statement is similar in structure to other real estate investments. The difference is mostly due to the reduced number of items. One of the attractions of warehouse investments is the low management cost. In many cases warehouses are leased to one firm for an extended period of time. This low turnover of a small number of tenants reduces management cost and the risk of high vacancy rates. However, if the lease expires or the tenant defaults then the cost of obtaining a new tenant may be significant. An investor can expect a possible several-month vacancy for every turnover of a tenant. In evaluating the potential rate of return on the expenses of a warehouse investment, it is very important to know the characteristics of the lease. What is the term of the lease? What are the provisions for increasing the rent? What are the conditions for showing future increases in cost? The answers to these questions determine the appropriate estimate of expenses. The longer and more stable the lease the lower would be the projected expenses.

EXAMPLE 5-3:
ANNUAL INCOME AND OPERATING EXPENSES
FOR A WAREHOUSE

Income		
Total rent	$12,000	
Vending machines	300	
Total Potential Gross Income		$12,300
Vacancies		−400
Effective Gross Income		11,900
Operating Expenses		
Building maintenance	1,000	
Management fees	1,000	
Real estate taxes	1,900	
Insurance	800	
Total Expenses		−4,700
Net Operating Income (NOI)		$7,200

In this case, the difference between effective gross income and operating expenses is $7,200, which is the net operating income. This is the annual income after expenses that this warehouse is expected to generate under typical management and economic conditions.

Office-Building Expenses

The office-building industry is another separate component of real estate. The growth and rate of return of office space fluctuates with the economic conditions. Regional differences in migration have produced significant differences in the rate of return of investing in office buildings. A list of expenses for a typical office building in the United States follows:

EXAMPLE 5-4:
ANNUAL INCOME AND OPERATING EXPENSES FOR AN OFFICE BUILDING WITH 250,000 SQUARE FEET

Income			
Rental income			
Office area	$1,300,000		
Store area	350,000		
Storage area	25,000		
Special area	75,000		
Total rental income		$1,750,000	
Miscellaneous income		20,000	
Total Potential Gross Income			$1,770,000
Vacancies	70,000		
Nonpayment of rent	20,000		-90,000
Effective Gross Income			1,680,000
Operating Expense			
Category A			
Cleaning	$ 190,000		
Electrical systems	25,000		
Heating	20,000		
Air conditioning	30,000		
Elevators	45,000		
General building costs	100,000		
Administrative costs	70,000		
Energy	200,000		
Total Expenses Category A		680,000	
Category B			
Alterations in building	27,000		
Decorating	10,000		
Total Expenses Category B		37,000	

Category C		
Insurance	$ 15,000	
Real estate tax—land	60,000	
Real estate tax—building	250,000	
Personal property tax	30,000	
Total Expenses Category C		355,000
Total Operating Expenses		−1,072,000
Net Operating Income (NOI)		$ 608,000

The operating expenses average about 64 percent of total income. The categories A, B, and C are a standard classification in office building accounting, representing operating, construction, and fixed cost respectively. This system of accounting includes in Category A energy costs, covering electricity, gas and steam, chilled water, etc., purchased to operate the building. The electrical, heating, and air conditioning costs include the maintenance costs only.

A CASH-FLOW STATEMENT FOR REAL ESTATE

Although there were some differences among the four examples just given, they all followed the same basic format. The first step is to estimate potential gross income (PGI), then subtract from PGI any losses due to bad debts or vacancies and add any miscellaneous income to arrive at effective gross income (EGI). Finally, subtract operating expenses from EGI to get net operating income.

Note that in all cases net operating income is less than potential gross income and that vacancies and expenses vary with the type of investment. The net operating income is therefore a more reliable measure of the possible benefits of investing in a real estate project. It is important to account for all possible income and expenses because the net effect is to change the investor's taxable income and the after-tax rate of return.

Table 5-2 presents an annual operating cash-flow statement for a real estate investment. This cash-flow statement will be referred to repeatedly throughout the book. The table lists the relevant categories to tabulate in determining the after-tax cash flow which is used to determine the after-tax rate of return. Table 5-2 is completed up to net operating income for the apartment building given in the first example. The following chapters will continue to progress in such a fashion to complete the cash-flow table.

TABLE 5-2. Annual Operating Cash-Flow Statement for a Real Estate Investment

	Year									
	1	2	3	4	5	6	7	8	9	10
Potential gross income (PGI)	$50,400	$52,920	$55,566	$58,344	$61,262	$64,325	$67,541	$70,918	$74,464	$78,187
Less vacancies and bad debts	(3,600)	(3,780)	(3,969)	(4,167)	(4,376)	(4,595)	(4,824)	(5,066)	(5,319)	(5,638)
Plus miscellaneous income	2,600	2,730	2,867	3,010	3,160	3,318	3,484	3,658	3,841	4,033
Effective gross income (EGI)	49,400	51,870	54,464	57,187	60,046	63,048	66,201	69,510	72,986	76,582
Less operating expenses	19,140	20,100	21,500	22,560	25,260	25,460	27,540	27,580	28,620	30,100
Net operating income (NOI)	30,260	31,770	32,964	34,627	34,786	37,588	38,661	41,930	44,366	46,482
Less debt service										
Before-tax cash flow (BTCF)										
Plus principal										
Less depreciation										
Plus replacement reserves										
Less amortized costs										
Taxable income (TI)										
Multiplied by tax rate										
Taxes										
After-tax cash flow (ATCF) (BTCF minus taxes)										

6

Financing
and Taxes

INTRODUCTION

Historically the American people have a tradition of paying off their debts. The ideal was to own your home or business free and clear. This risk-adverse psychology was generated in the eighteenth and nineteenth centuries from a recurring cycle of depression and recession. Since World War II and especially since 1960, the economy has had continual inflation with mild recessions. The constant growth of inflation has produced the new philosophy of buy now, pay later. This strategy means that investors try to maintain a low equity position, that is, to minimize their cash investment. This is the same as attempting to maximize their leverage. The maximum leverage is obtained with the amount of equity equal to zero. This gives a loan-to-value ratio of 1, or an equity-to-value ratio of 0. During inflationary periods the debtor, especially the investor with low equity, benefits relative to the creditor since the debtor pays his or her debt with cheaper dollars. This assumes that the inflation is unexpected. A creditor who expects inflation will charge a higher interest rate to compensate for being paid back with cheaper dollars.

Even without inflation, leverage increases the possible rate of return for a second reason. For example, developers often try to get a 100-percent loan on a real estate project. If their project sells for a profit, the developer has earned a very high rate of return because of the leverage. If the project sells for a loss the developer will suffer serious losses because of the leverage. This increase in the range of possible outcomes makes the investment a greater risk. Leverage provides the opportunity to make or lose a greater amount of wealth; the expected return in a leveraged real estate investment is greater but the risk of loss is also greater.

Federal taxes are a third important reason for leverage. The value of the improvements (land cannot be depreciated) when sold is used by the new owner to determine the basis for depreciation. The amount of cash (equity) invested in the project does not limit the basis or the extent of depreciation. In fact, the total dollar value of the depreciation may far exceed any cash investment. Thus, the tax benefit of depreciation may completely offset any equity required for the purchase of the improvements. The fundamental benefit of a tax shelter is the ability it provides to depreciate the basis of the improvements regardless of the amount of equity. The lower the equity (or the greater the leverage) for a given amount of depreciation, the greater the tax shelter. A second impact of federal taxes comes from the rule that borrowed funds are not taxable income. An owner can refinance property and cash out his or her equity. For example, if an apartment building appreciates by $100,000 the owner can liquidate part of the investment tax free simply by borrowing $100,000 against the property. Obviously when the investor liquidates in this fashion, the price (cost) is the interest paid on the loan. Fortunately the interest is tax deductible.

The rest of this chapter deals with the techniques of financing and the strategy that should be employed to maximize the amount of income covered by the tax shelter.

FINANCIAL LEVERAGE
AND RISK

Most investors use debt financing to purchase real estate. This is done to supplement the available equity and to increase leverage. Investors usually do not have the cash to purchase property on a 100-percent equity basis. Without mortgage financing, most real estate transactions would not take place. Corporations, partnerships, syndicates, and others use debt financing to buy properties. Business often seeks to maximize debt financing to ensure the efficient use of a limited cash supply. Thus, debt financing increases the possible leverage and extends the available cash.

Leverage is used to acquire an income-producing property in the expectation of a rate of return on the equity higher than the cost of borrowing the money. If the property does produce a higher rate of return, the technique of leveraging will result in a greater return on the equity.

EXAMPLE 6-1

A warehouse valued at $100,000 produces a net operating income of $10,000 per year. If the investor pays cash for the property, the equity is equal to $100,000. This is a 10-percent rate of return ($10,000 ÷ $100,000). If the investor borrows 60 percent of the $100,000 at 7-percent interest, his annual interest per year is $4,200 (60,000 × .07). For simplicity only the interest cost will be considered here. The payment on the principal is assumed to be made at the end of the loan. This is referred to as a balloon payment. Out of the annual returns of $10,000 from the warehouse, $4,200 must be paid for interest. The warehouse must earn 4.2 percent ($4,200 ÷ $100,000) on the total investment to cover the debt service. The remaining $5,800 represents a 14.5-percent ($5,800 ÷ $40,000) return on the equity.

This example can be expressed as follows:

Total investment in the warehouse =	100% × .10 = 10.00%
Mortgage interest	= 60% × .07 = 4.20%
Equity (40%)	= 10.00% − 4.20% = 5.80%
Return on equity	= 5.80% ÷ .40 = 14.50%

The same method can be used to explore the impact of increasing the leverage. If the investor places 20 percent down on the warehouse the equity will be $20,000. Assuming the same rate of return on the investment and the same mortgage rate the results are as follows:

Total investment in the warehouse =	100% × .10 = 10.00%
Mortgage interest	= 80% × .07 = 5.60%
Equity (20%)	= 10.00% − 5.60% = 4.40%
Return on equity	= 4.40% ÷ .20 = 22.00%

If the investor could obtain a 95-percent loan at the same rate of interest the results would be:

Total investment in the warehouse =	100% × .10 = 10.00%
Mortgage interest	= 95% × .07 = 6.65%
Equity (5%)	= 10.00% − 6.65% = 3.35%
Return on equity	= 3.35% ÷ .05 = 67.00%

The examples demonstrate clearly the advantages of leverage. The return on equity went from 14.5 percent to 67 percent by decreasing the equity from 40 percent to 5 percent.

What the examples do not show is the increased risk. As the investor decreases the equity (increases the leverage) the rate of return on equity becomes more sensitive to the rate of return on the entire investment. If the rate of return on the investment falls to 5 percent with the same mortgage rate the following will result:

1. *Equity 40%*

Total investment in the warehouse	=	100% ×	.05	=	5.00%
Mortgage interest	=	60% ×	.07	=	4.20%
Equity (40%)	=	5.00% − 4.20%	=		.80%
Return on equity	=	.80% ÷	.40	=	2.0%

2. *Equity 20%*

Total investment in the warehouse	=	100% ×	.05	=	5.00%
Mortgage interest	=	80% ×	.07	=	5.60%
Equity (20%)	=	5.00% − 5.60%	=		−.60%
Return on equity	=	−.60% ÷	.20	=	−3.00%

3. *Equity 5%*

Total investment in the warehouse	=	100% ×	.05	=	5.00%
Mortgage interest	=	95% ×	.07	=	6.65%
Equity (5%)	=	5.00% − 6.65%	=		−1.65%
Return on equity	=	−1.65% ÷	.05	=	−33.00%

Thus if the rate of return on the warehouse falls from 10 percent to 5 percent the possible rates of return of different levels of equity fall from 2 percent to a negative 33 percent. A downward trend in the economy which reduces the rate of return on the investment can result in heavy losses when the investor is highly leveraged. Each increase in leverage results in a higher risk. The risk is expressed as the potential of greater losses from a decrease in the overall rate of return.

THE MORTGAGE

The mortgage is a contract between the lender (mortgagee) and the borrower (mortgagor). The lender agrees to loan money to the borrower for the purchase of real estate. The real estate in question is used to secure the loan. If the borrower fails to pay the loan in accordance with the contract, the lender can force the sale of the property to pay for the loan.

The interest on the loan and the principal payment are determined in the agreement. The standard mortgage has a fixed interest throughout the loan. The interest and the principal payment (amortization) is split on each payment during the life of the loan. The sum of principal payment and interest is called the debt service. The amount of interest and principal payed each month or year depends on the agreement between the lender and the borrower. (Alternative forms of debt financing will be explored later in the chapter.)

The Terms of the Mortgage

The terms of a mortgage comprise the costs to the borrower: the amount the borrower can borrow, the length of time he or she may have the funds, the timing of paying back the loan, and the interest rate per year. Once the amount to be borrowed, the interest rate, the maturity (length of time), and the frequency of payments are determined, the payment to be made each period can be calculated. This payment is usually referred to as the debt service. The factors that determine the mix of the terms for a particular mortgage vary with the area, the availability of funds, and the characteristics of the borrower.

The most common type of mortgage loan is fully amortized with level payments and a fixed interest. The following discussion of loan terms uses this standard form.

The Interest Rate

The interest rate is the annual cost per dollar of loan. Most mortgages have a fixed interest rate throughout the term of the loan. A change in the interest rate has a direct effect on the cost of the loan and the return to equity in the investment. Holding other things constant the higher the interest rate, the lower the equity return.

Recall Example 6-1 where the investor has a $100,000 warehouse with a 10-percent rate of return. The investor borrowed 60 percent of the cost at a 7-percent rate of interest for an annual interest payment of $4,200. Ignoring amortization and using percentages the rate of return on equity is as follows:

Total investment in the warehouse = 100% X .10 = 10.00%
Mortgage interest   = 60% X .07 = 4.20%
Equity   = 10.00% - 4.20% = 5.80%
Return on equity   = 5.80% ÷ .40 = 14.5%

The return on equity is 14.5 percent. If the interest rate increases to 10 percent the return on equity is as follows:

Total investment in the warehouse = 100% X .10 = 10.00%
Mortgage interest   = 60% X .10 = 6.00%
Equity   = 10.00% - 6.00% = 4.00%
Return on equity   = 4.00% ÷ .40 = 10.00%

Thus an increase in the interest rate on the loan from 7 percent to 10 percent decreases the rate of return on the equity from 14.5 percent to 10 percent. A decrease in the interest rate to 4 percent would have the following effect:

$$
\begin{array}{lll}
\text{Total investment in the warehouse} = & 100\% \times .10 & = 10.00\% \\
\text{Mortgage interest} & = 60\% \times .04 & = 2.40\% \\
\text{Equity} & = \overline{10.00\% - 2.40\%} & = 7.60\% \\
\text{Return on equity} & = 7.60\% \div .40\% & = 19.00\%
\end{array}
$$

These calculations demonstrate the inverse relationship between the interest the investor pays on the loan and the rate of return on equity. This assumes that nothing else that could affect the investment has changed with the change in the interest rate. In reality, higher interest rates lower the demand for real estate which in turn could lower the price of the warehouse. Higher rates also affect the amount of money available for loans which in turn could change the required loan-to-value ratio. Thus the preceding method of calculating the impact of changes in the interest rate on equity return is best used when comparing alternative loans. At any point in time different lenders may charge different rates of interest. It is clear from the examples that the borrower should seek the lowest rate for a given set of other terms.

Points

Points and the interest rate charged on a loan are closely related. With usury laws the lender is often forced to lend money at an interest below the market rate of interest. Under this situation a lender must seek alternatives to the interest rate for making the appropriate charges for the loan. If no alternatives are available the lender will cease to make loans. One technique is to discount the loan. This means that the lender states that the loan is for $100,000 on paper but actually gives the investor only $97,000. The investor must pay back $100,000, not $97,000. In this case the "points" were equal to 3 percent ($3,000 ÷ $100,000) of the total loan. This 3 percent is referred to as 3 points. Assume the investor borrowed the money at 7 percent. The annual interest charges (again, ignoring amortization) are $7,000. The 7 percent is called the normal rate of interest. The effective or actual rate of interest is 7.21 percent ($7,000 ÷ $97,000). Discounting has two effects: First, it increases the interest rate which reduces the equity return; and second, it has the impact of increasing the amount of equity since the borrower is loaned a smaller amount. Both reduce the equity rate of return. Points are to be avoided if possible but remember they generally occur because of artificial restrictions placed on the market by government intervention. Without points there would be fewer loans made. The strategy is to accept them but to seek the lowest cost possible from competitive lenders.

Deductions for Mortgage Costs

The borrower incurs a number of costs when obtaining a loan. These include attorney and appraisal fees, title and survey costs, and commission fees and other possible charges by the loan institution. The investor would prefer to deduct all these expenses in the same year for a greater tax shelter. Unfortunately, if the loan is for investment purposes these costs must be amortized over the term of the loan. For example, an investor pays $10,000 in costs for a $100,000 ten-year loan to finance an apartment building. If these costs represent attorney and commission fees, they must be deducted at the rate of $1,000 per year ($10,000 ÷ 10).

If additional costs are imposed for a new loan these are deductible over the life of the new loan. An investor who prepays the loan can deduct all remaining unamortized mortgage costs and any prepayment penalties in the same year.

Interest costs are deductible the year they are paid. Prepaid interest up to twelve months is deductible if it does not distort income. The deductibility of prepaid interest has in recent years been severely limited by the IRS based on the principle that most prepayment distorts income. Assume a loan of $100,000 at 10-percent interest for twenty years is obtained by an investor. The interest payment (ignoring amortization) in the first year is $10,000. This entire $10,000 interest payment is deductible in the first year.

As discussed in this section, a lender may charge points. A point is equal to one percent of the loan. Points may be paid by the borrower's separate funds or deducted from the loan. Prior to 1976 points were deductible in the year paid. This is still true for personal residences but for all investment properties the additional cost due to points must be amortized over the life of the loan. Assume again that a loan of $100,000 at 10-percent interest for twenty years is obtained by an investor. In this case the lender charges 3 points, or $3,000. The interest cost (again ignoring amortization) is $10,000, which is deductible in the first year. The points which cost the investor another $3,000 must be divided by 20, the number of years of the loan. This provides a deduction of $150 per year for the life of the loan. If the loan is prepaid in the fifth year then the remaining unamortized mortgage cost can be deducted in the fifth year. If any prepayment penalties are incurred, the investor may deduct these also. Prepayment penalties influence both the taxable income and the cash flow in the year of sale.

Loan-to-Value Ratios

The loan-to-value ratio is the percentage of value represented by the loan. If an investor borrows $80,000 to finance a $100,000 warehouse the loan-to-value ratio is 80 percent. The equity is the amount of the down payment required by the lender. In this case it is $20,000, a 20-percent equity. Both the loan-to-value and equity ratios are expressed as a percentage of value.

The lower the equity, the higher the loan-to-value ratio and the higher the leverage. An 80-percent loan-to-value ratio or a 20-percent equity is correspondingly a leverage factor of 5 (100% ÷ 20%). A 60-percent loan-to-value ratio represents a leverage factor of 2.5 (100% ÷ 40%).

If other factors are held constant, a higher loan-to-value ratio will mean a higher equity return. This assumes that the investment return is higher than the mortgage rate. If the investment is unsuccessful—that is, the investment rate of return is lower than the mortgage rate—the higher loan-to-value ratio will lead to lower equity returns. A higher loan-to-value ratio also means the investment is more vulnerable to a decline in property value or a decline in income from the rental. Equity rates of return are subject to wider fluctuations with higher loan-to-value ratios. This was demonstrated in Example 6-1. A higher loan-to-value ratio leads to the investor paying a larger total amount for the property because of greater interest costs. Remember, the important criterion for investments is not the total amount paid for some probable period of time but the return on equity.

Length of the Loan

The length of the loan is referred to as the loan maturity. A twenty-year loan will be fully paid in twenty years. The longer the term, the greater the amount paid by the borrower for the investment. Lenders have a tendency to restrict the loan maturity to somewhat less than the economic life of the real estate asset. For any given amount of money loaned the greater the maturity, the smaller the payments on that loan. These smaller payments reduce the cash outflow each year. This reduces the equity position for the early years thus increasing the equity return. Before any examples are given to demonstrate the effects of a change in maturity, a thorough understanding of amortization is necessary.

Amortization

Amortization refers to the repayment of the principal over a specific time period. The most common loans have payments sufficient over the life of the loan to amortize it fully at maturity (to pay off the loan by the end of the scheduled payment). The typical loan has equal monthly payments which include interest on the outstanding loan and the payment on the principal. The interest due each month or year is based on the agreed rate of interest times the amount of the loan outstanding. The initial payments have a larger amount of interest relative to the principal payment because the loan outstanding is very large. As the payments are made the principal is gradually reduced. This reduces the proportion of interest paid and increases the principal paid each year until the loan maturity is reached.

This combination of interest and principal payment is called debt service. When most investors think of taking a loan the first question that occurs is,

"What will the debt service be?" A simple way to compute the debt service is to use a table that has an annual or monthly listing of mortgage constants. The mortgage constant is the annual debt service divided by the original amount of the loan. This mortgage constant is usually expressed as a monthly or annual percentage. They are not the same; use monthly when the frequency of payment is monthly and annual tables when annual payments are called for.

Tables A-2 and A-3 in the Appendix present monthly and annual mortgage constants respectively. The tables are set up for $1.00 values. To arrive at the debt service for any loan, multiply the amount borrowed times the mortgage constant for a given loan maturity and interest rate. For example, an investor purchases a warehouse for $100,000 with $20,000 as equity with a monthly payment schedule on a loan for $80,000 at 10 percent. The monthly mortgage constant for a twenty-year loan at 10 percent is .009650. The monthly debt service is $772 (.009650 × $80,000). The investor must make a payment of $772 each month for twenty years. At the end of twenty years the loan will be amortized (paid off). Many payment tables are provided by banks and other loan institutions. These tables usually give the amount of monthly debt service for a given interest rate, mortgage maturity (term), and loan amount. The problem with these tables is that the loans are nice, even numbers like $30,000, $40,000, and $50,000. If the investor's loan is for $52,182, the payment book is of little value. By using a mortgage constant concept any loan amount can be converted into a monthly or annual debt service.

The next step is to compute the amount outstanding, the percentage outstanding, and the split of debt service between interest and principal payment. Assume again, that an investor has purchased a warehouse for $100,000. The equity is $20,000 and the $80,000 loan is for twenty years at 10 percent. The installments are made monthly. As demonstrated in the previous example the mortgage constant for such a loan is .00965 which gives a monthly debt service of $772 (.00965 × $80,000). The division of interest and principal for each $772 payment is as shown in Table 6-1.

These numbers were calculated as follows. The original amount outstanding is $80,000. The debt service is a constant amount of $772 per month. The interest rate is 10 percent annually or .10 ÷ 12 per month; therefore, the amount of interest in Month 1 is $666.66 ($80,000 × .10 ÷ 12). The total debt service

TABLE 6-1. Division of Interest and Principal on $80,000 for 20 Years at 10 Percent

Month	Amount Outstanding	Debt Service	Interest Payment	Principal Payment
0	$80,000.00	—	—	—
1	79,894.66	$772.00	$666.66	$105.34
2	79,788.45	772.00	665.79	106.21
3	79,681.35	772.00	664.90	107.10
4	79,573.36	772.00	664.01	107.99
5	79,464.47	772.00	663.11	108.89

(payment) is $772 and the interest payment is $666.66; therefore, the principal payment is $105.74 ($772 - $666.66). The original balance, $80,000, minus the principal payment in Month 1 gives the amount outstanding after one month as $79,894.66. Using this new balance the interest payment in the second month is $665.79 ($79,894.66 × .10 ÷ 12). The principal payment in the second month is $106.21 ($772 - $664.79). The amount outstanding at the end of the second month is 79,788.45. This process can be continued for each month.

Note that at the end of five months, the amount outstanding is $79,464.47. The original amount outstanding was $80,000. Thus at the end of five months the percentage amount outstanding is 99.33% ($79,464.47 ÷ $80,000.00). Why bother to know the amount outstanding or the interest-principal split? The reason is taxes. An investor can deduct the interest payments from the net operating income. This results in a significant reduction in taxes. For any given year the interest payments must be known. This presents a small problem. Usually the investors will not want to compute the entire 240 months or some portion thereof to arrive at the total interest paid for any given year. A shortcut is to solve for the amount outstanding for any given month. Once the investor has the amount outstanding it is easy to solve for the interest paid.

To find the proportion outstanding at the end of any given month, the following equation can be used:

$$\text{Proportion outstanding} = \frac{\text{Mortgage constant for total mortgage term}}{\text{Mortgage constant for remaining term}}$$

For instance, the mortgage constant for the warehouse example was .009650. This was based on a $80,000 loan for twenty years (240 months) at 10 percent with monthly installments. The investor wants to know the proportion outstanding after the thirty-sixth month. This gives a remaining term of 204 months. Using Table A-3, we find the mortgage constant at 10 percent for seventeen years is .01021. The percentage outstanding is

$$\frac{.00965}{.01021} = .9450$$

Multiply this proportion by the original loan amount of $80,000 to get the amount outstanding:

$$.945 \times \$80,000 = \$75,600$$

For the first month of the fourth year the monthly debt service for a $80,000 loan at 10 percent is $772. This debt service remains the same throughout the loan period. The interest payment for the first month would be $630 ($75,600 ×

.10 ÷ 12). The principal payment would be $142 ($772 – $630). Following Table 6-1 the investor could compute the interest-principal split for each month of the fourth year.

Table 6-2 provides a format of a mortgage amortization schedule which should be used by the investor. The schedule is structured assuming a fixed interest rate. Above each table the amount borrowed, interest rate, maturity of the loan (term), frequency of payments (monthly, semiannual, or annual), loan-to-value ratio, mortgage constant, and debt service are listed. The reader should be familiar with all these terms before proceeding onward. In Table 6-2 we consider a $100,000 loan for an apartment building at 11-percent interest with annual payments. The term is twenty-five years with a loan-to-value ratio of .80. The mortgage constant is .118740 and the debt service is $11,874 per year (.11874 X $100,000). The purchase price was $125,000. The investor can use Table 6-2 for observing the interest cost of the mortgage for each of the ten years. These interest costs are important in determining the before-tax cash flow. Table 6-3 presents the same investment but with a higher interest rate (14 percent), a higher loan-to-value ratio (.95), and a shorter term (twenty years). Comparing Tables 6-2 and 6-3 it can be seen that the interest payments are higher in Table 6-3 but are falling at a faster rate. Which one is the preferred loan structure? It depends on the investment goals, the ordinary income of the investors, and other factors. The purpose of this section is to demonstrate the techniques necessary to compute the amount outstanding, the debt service, and the interest-principal split.

TABLE 6-2. Mortgage Amortization Schedule for a $100,000 Loan

Amount borrowed: $100,000.00
Interest rate: 11%
Maturity term: 25 years
Frequency of payments: Annual
Loan-to-value ratio: .80
Mortgage constant: .11874
Debt service: $11,874.00

Year	Percent Outstanding	Amount Outstanding	Debt Service	Interest Payment	Principal Payment
0	100.00	$100,000.00	–	–	–
1	99.13	99,126.00	$11,874.00	$11,000.00	$ 874.00
2	98.16	98,155.86	11,874.00	10,903.86	970.14
3	97.08	97,079.00	11,874.00	10,797.14	1,076.86
4	95.88	95,883.00	11,874.00	10,678.69	1,195.31
5	94.56	94,556.90	11,874.00	10,547.20	1,326.80
6	93.08	93,084.16	11,874.00	10,401.26	1,472.74
7	91.45	91,449.41	11,874.00	10,239.26	1,634.74
8	89.63	89,634.86	11,874.00	10,059.44	1,814.56
9	87.62	87,620.69	11,874.00	9,859.83	2,014.17
10	85.38	85,384.96	11,874.00	9,638.28	2,235.72

TABLE 6-3. Mortgage Amortization Schedule for a $118,750 Loan

Amount borrowed: $118,750.00
Interest rate: 14%
Maturity term: 20 years
Frequency of payments: Annual
Loan-to-value ratio: .95
Mortgage constant: .150986
Debt service: $17,929.59

Year	Percent Outstanding	Amount Outstanding	Debt Service	Interest Payment	Principal Payment
0	100.00	$118,750.00	–	–	–
1	98.90	117,445.41	$17,929.59	$16,625.00	$1,304.59
2	97.65	115,958.18	17,929.59	16,442.36	1,487.23
3	96.22	114,262.73	17,929.59	16,234.14	1,695.45
4	94.59	112,329.92	17,929.59	15,996.78	1,932.81
5	92.74	110,126.52	17,929.59	15,726.19	2,203.40
6	90.62	107,614.65	17,929.59	15,417.71	2,511.88
7	88.21	104,751.11	17,929.59	15,066.05	2,863.54
8	85.46	101,486.67	17,929.59	14,665.16	3,264.43
9	82.33	97,765.22	17,929.59	14,208.13	3,721.46
10	78.76	93,522.76	17,929.59	13,687.13	4,242.46

Alternative Mortgage Loans

The preceding discussion dealt with fully amortized loans with a fixed interest and equal annual or monthly payments. The most common alternative is the partially amortized mortgage loan. These loans are not fully amortized over the term. The portion that is not amortized must be paid in a lump sum at fixed intervals or typically at the end of the loan period (maturity). This lump-sum payment is called a balloon payment.

Partially Amortized Loans

In some cases an investor purchases a property and pays interest only for a certain time period, then makes a balloon payment at the end of the loan period. A more common approach is to set the loan for one maturity but calculate the debt service on the basis of a larger amortization period. This reduces the debt service during the life of the loan but will require a balloon payment at the end.

Estimating the Balloon Payment

The borrower is usually interested in knowing in advance what the outstanding balance of the loan will be at maturity. This outstanding balance is the balloon payment. Table 6-4 presents an example of a $100,000 loan that is due in ten years. The amortization schedule and debt service is based on a thirty-

TABLE 6-4. Mortgage Amortization Schedule for a $100,000 Loan

Amount borrowed: $100,000.00
Interest rate: 10%
Maturity term: 10 years
Frequency of payments: Annual
Loan-to-value ratio: .80
Mortgage constant: .10608, based on a 30-year term
Debt service: $10,607.90

Year	Percent Outstanding	Amount Outstanding	Debt Service	Interest Payment	Principal Payment
0	100.00	$100,000.00	–	–	–
1	99.39	99,392.10	$10,607.90	$10,000.00	$ 607.90
2	98.72	98,723.41	10,607.90	9,939.21	668.69
3	97.99	97,987.85	10,607.90	9,872.34	735.56
4	97.18	97,178.74	10,607.90	9,798.79	809.11
5	96.29	96,288.71	10,607.90	9,717.87	890.03
6	95.31	95,309.68	10,607.90	9,628.87	979.03
7	94.23	94,232.75	10,607.90	9,530.97	1,076.93
8	93.05	93,048.12	10,607.90	9,423.27	1,184.63
9	91.75	91,745.05	10,607.90	9,304.01	1,303.09
10	90.31	90,311.65	10,607.90	9,174.50	1,433.40

year schedule. Table 6-4 indicates the results—the debt service is $10,607.90. If the debt service had been based on a ten-year due date it would have been much higher $16,274.50. The amount outstanding at the end of ten years is $90,311.65. This would be the required balloon payment. A shortcut method as discussed previously would be to compute the proportion outstanding based on the relative mortgage constants.

$$\text{Proportion outstanding} = \frac{\text{Mortgage constant for the total term (30 years)}}{\text{Mortgage constant for the remaining term (20 years)}}$$

$$= \frac{.10608}{.11746} = .9031$$

Thus the balloon payment would be $90,310 (.9031 × $100,000). This is the same (except for the rounding error) as the amount obtained from the longer procedure.

Graduated-Payment and Variable-Rate Mortgages

There are two new approaches that have entered the mortgage market: (1) the graduated-payment mortgage and (2) the variable-rate mortgage. The graduated-payment mortgage (GPM) requires a systematic increase in the investor's monthly payment throughout the life of the mortgage. This allows the investor to make lower payments initially and thus, when compared to a fixed-rate mortgage (FRM), will allow the investor to qualify for a larger mortgage. The process would increase the principal outstanding in the early years and then gradually reduce the principal in the later years as the payments become greater.

The variable-rate mortgage (VRM) is a loan that allows for changes in the interest rate. The interest rate is usually tied to an index rate. The result of an interest rate change is a change in the monthly payment or the length of the maturity. The variable-rate mortgage allows the loan institution to pass on the cost or the benefits of changes in the interest rate, thus making loan institutions more willing to give out loans during periods of expectedly higher interest rates.

FINANCIAL MARKET TRENDS

Many individuals, institutions, and businesses compete for the available money supply. Thus, real estate investors are not only competing with each other but with all other users of money. Interest rates are essentially the price of early availability. If you want to buy something today and must borrow money, someone else must give up their consumption or investment. The interest rate is the price of borrowed money and, like all prices, is a mechanism for allocating resources.

The mortgage market must compete for funds in the marketplace. If alternative investments became more attractive, the funds available for mortgages will be reduced. This has happened in the past during so-called tight money markets. High interest rates have always occurred in recent times because of Federal Reserve Board (Fed) policies. If the Fed increases the money supply at a faster rate, the short-run effect is to decrease the interest rate but the long-run effect is to increase the inflation rate. Thus it is not tight money that makes interest rates higher but loose money.

Two reasons for the reduction in mortgages during loose-money periods are the usury laws and Regulation Q. Usury laws and regulations restrict the interest rates that loan institutions can charge or pay out. Thus, as interest rates become higher because of expected inflation, the money-lending institution is unable to compete for funds. Investors draw out their money and invest it elsewhere. This results in tight money for mortgages during a loose-money period. The only solution is to eliminate Regulation Q and usury laws. Recently, savings and loan institutions have been allowed to pay competitive interest rates. This has increased the amount of mortgage money available during high interest rate periods.

Without a doubt the most relevant information concerning expected interest rates is the change in the money supply by the Fed. An increase in the money supply will increase interest rates in the long run (four to nine months).

SOURCES OF FUNDS

The mortgage market is a rather loose, undefined gathering of borrowers and lenders. There are few organizations that attempt to bring these groups together. Mortgage brokers find qualified borrowers and willing lenders, for a fee. Mortgage bankers use their own funds, sometimes from short-term loans, to make loans and then try to sell the mortgages to other lenders for a profit. Mortgage correspondents act as agents for mortgage lenders such as life insurance companies. Their main function as agents is to secure loans.

The elements of supply for mortgages are the money available, the competition from other borrowers, and the current policies established by the lenders. Some of the sources of mortgage funds are:

1. Commercial banks, which lend on all types of real estate. They are generally more conservative with low loan-to-value ratios and short maturities.
2. Mutual savings banks, which are concentrated in the Northeast and specialize in apartment and commercial loans. Compared to commercial bank loans, their loan-to-value ratios are higher and their loan maturities longer.
3. Savings and loan associations, which are a major source of residential mortgages. They usually concentrate on local markets with rather high loan-to-value ratios and long maturities.
4. Life insurance companies, which loan money for high-credit, low-risk, large-value income-producing property. They are often involved in shopping centers, resorts, and industrial parks.
5. Other sources are trusts, mortgage intermediaries, and public agencies all of which make loans for mortgages.

BEFORE-TAX CASH FLOW

In Chapter 5 the annual operating cash-flow statement for a real estate investment was completed up to net operating income (NOI). The goal is to estimate after-tax cash flow (ATCF) which will be the basis for estimating an after-tax rate of return. This chapter takes the next step in reaching that goal by demonstrating how to arrive at before-tax cash flow. Before-tax cash flow is simply net operating income less debt service. Table 6-5 continues the example of the apartment building cash flow statement in Table 5-2. The purchase price is assumed to be $350,000. The investor places $100,000 down as equity and takes a $250,000 loan for thirty years at 10-percent interest. The mortgage constant is .10608 and the debt service is $26,520 per year (.10608 × $250,000). As can be seen from the table, the before-tax cash flow is low in the early years but increases substantially by Year 10. This is because NOI has been increasing with debt service remaining fixed.

TABLE 6-5. Annual Operating Cash-Flow Statement for a Real Estate Investment

	Year									
	1	2	3	4	5	6	7	8	9	10
Potential gross income (PGI)	$50,400	$52,920	$55,566	$58,344	$61,262	$64,325	$67,541	$70,918	$74,464	$78,187
Less vacancies and bad debts	(3,600)	(3,780)	(3,969)	(4,167)	(4,376)	(4,595)	(4,824)	(5,066)	(5,319)	(5,638)
Plus miscellaneous income	2,600	2,730	2,867	3,010	3,160	3,318	3,484	3,658	3,841	4,033
Effective gross income (EGI)	49,400	51,070	54,464	57,187	60,046	63,048	66,201	69,510	72,986	76,582
Less operating expenses	19,140	20,100	21,500	22,560	25,260	25,460	27,540	27,580	28,620	30,100
Net operating income (NOI)	30,260	31,770	32,964	34,627	34,786	37,588	38,661	41,930	44,366	46,482
Less debt service	26,520	26,520	26,520	26,520	26,520	26,520	26,520	26,520	26,520	26,520
Before-tax cash flow (BTCF)	3,740	5,250	6,444	8,107	8,266	11,068	12,141	15,410	17,846	19,962
Plus principal										
Less depreciation										
Plus replacement reserves										
Less amortized costs										
Taxable income (TI)										
Multiplied by tax rate										
Taxes										
After-tax cash flow (ATCF) (BTCF minus taxes)										

The estimation of debt service in Table 6-5 allows the investor or lender to compute one more additional statistic, the debt coverage ratio. The debt coverage ratio is the net operating income divided by the debt service. This indicates to the lender how much of the debt service is covered by the income from the investment. It is another measure of risk to the lender. The range for the debt coverage ratio is approximately 1.00 to 1.40. In general, lenders like to see net operating income about 20 percent greater than the debt service. This gives the lender some assurance that even in an economic downturn the borrower will have sufficient income to pay debt service.

The next chapter will consider the impact of depreciation on estimating after-tax cash flow.

7

Calculating Annual After-Tax Cash Flow

INTRODUCTION

The preceding two chapters were concerned with estimating operating expenses and debt service on the mortgage indebtedness for a real estate investment. The projected gross income from the project less operating expenses and debt service results in the before-tax cash flow to the investor. The investor, however, is more interested in the cash flow after income taxes. Thus the income taxes for each year of operation must be forecast. The before-tax cash flow less taxes results in after-tax cash flows.

In order to estimate the amount of taxes in each year, the investor must know the taxable income and the tax rate. A key part of calculating taxable income from an investment is the depreciation allowance. The depreciation allowance is an accounting concept that only rarely corresponds with actual losses in the value of an investment. The depreciation allowance is simply a deduction against taxable income for investment assets. It is an incentive device offered to investors to encourage investment in real estate and serves as a method for recovering the cost of an investment.

This chapter first discusses the impact of the depreciation allowance on the cash flow from a real estate investment. Our goal is to illustrate how the annual cash flow from operating real estate investments is forecast. Chapters 8 and 9 will discuss the cash flow from the disposition of a real estate investment.

DEPRECIATION

The main purpose of depreciation is to allow the taxpayer to make deductions from his or her taxable income for the recovery of the cost of the depreciable property. Depreciation produces tax deductions without any cash outlay. Thus the investor has an incentive to maximize the depreciation deduction, thereby reducing taxable income, which in turn reduces the tax liability.

Depreciation deductions are allowed because it is viewed that depreciable assets gradually wear out, thus leading to a gradual loss in their value—a loss which is, in effect, a cost of owning the property.

The cumulative depreciation deductions taken by the taxpayer on a real estate investment usually bears little or no relationship to the real change in the value of the property. Typically, in fact, the situation is such that the taxpayer has a deduction for depreciation while the property value is actually rising. The net result is the creation of a tax-free cash flow.

Two types of property are allowed depreciation deductions:

1. Property used in trade or business
2. Property held for production of income (investment)

Property used by the taxpayer for personal purposes, such as the taxpayer's residence, is not depreciable. Depreciation is only allowed on property that has a limited useful life, such as buildings and machines. Land is not depreciable since, at least for tax purposes, it has an infinite useful life. Certain land improvements such as paving curbs and gutters may be depreciable. The depreciation of land improvements, in general, depends on whether they permanently improve the land or improve it only so long as a particular building or structure remains useful. Property held for sale to customers is also depreciable.

The depreciation deduction in any year is that amount which should be set aside in accordance with a reasonably consistent plan so that the aggregate amount set over the useful life of the asset plus the salvage value will equal the cost or basis of the property. The depreciation deduction depends on three factors:

1. The cost or basis; that is, the total amount to be depreciated
2. The useful life of the asset; that is, the period of time over which the asset is to be depreciated
3. The method of depreciation

Since much of the investment in a real estate asset is depreciable, the depreciation deduction may have three results:

1. All of the cash flow from a project may be sheltered from taxes.
2. Part of the cash flow from an investment may be sheltered.

3. More than the cash flow from the investment may be sheltered from income taxes. This results in a reduction in the taxpayer's other taxable income, thus reducing his or her taxes.

Determining the Depreciable Amount

The first step in estimating the depreciation deduction each year is to determine the amount to be depreciated. Basis is the term used to describe the value of property for tax purposes and is used for determining (1) the amount of annual depreciation deductions and (2) the investor's gain or loss on the property at the time of sale. The total depreciable amount is generally the original cost *plus* the cost of any additions *less* the cost of the land. Only the building is depreciable.

The basis of a real estate investment is generally its cost to the present owner. This cost includes cash, mortgages, and other real estate given in exchange for the property. For example, suppose an investor purchases a property for cash and also assumes a mortgage. The cash and the amount of the mortgage are added together to figure the basis of the investment. When an investor gives cash and property in a taxable exchange (exchanges are discussed later), the cash and the basis of the old property are added together to determine the basis of the new investment.

Certain items may affect the cost of an investment and thus change the depreciable basis. These include expenditures for capital improvements, certain legal fees, and the cost of title insurance. Other items, such as financing costs, do not affect the basis. These financing costs, however, as discussed in the previous chapter, can be deducted over the life of the mortgage.

To determine the depreciable amount, the investor must (1) estimate the salvage value and (2) allocate the total cost between land and building. In most real estate investments, the salvage value is zero since it typically costs more to demolish the building than the value of the components of the building. The expected cost of removal at the end of its useful life may be deducted from the anticipated proceeds to arrive at a net salvage value. For most real estate investment this results in a negative net salvage value. The salvage value for tax purposes then becomes zero.

A real estate investment, from a tax perspective, consists of two parts: a depreciable building and nondepreciable land. This total cost must be allocated between land and building. The investor should try to allocate as much as possible of the total cost to the building in order to maximize the depreciation deduction. The tax regulations offer little information on how to allocate between the land and building.

In making the allocation to building and land, the portion of the cost to be allocated to each is based on the market value of each at the time of acquisition. There are several methods an investor might use to allocate the total acquisition cost between land and building. First, a professional appraisal can be used. An independent appraisal, however, might be expensive. But obviously if there is a chance it could save the investor money, it certainly might be worth the cost. For example, suppose an investor makes an investment for a total cost of $100,000. If the building-to-total value ratio is 80 percent, the depreciable amount is $80,000. If this ratio drops to 75 percent, the depreciable amount is $75,000. On the other hand, if the ratio were to increase to 85 percent the depreciable amount would increase to $85,000. The increase or decrease in depreciable amount would represent a considerable increase or decrease in depreciation deductions for the investor. This in turn translates into a savings or loss in taxes.

A second method to allocate between land and building is to use the relative values placed on each by the local tax assessor. Suppose the tax assessor has set the assessed value of the building at $50,000 and the assessed value of the land at $15,000. This represents a building-to-total assessed value ratio of 77 percent ($50,000 ÷ 65,000). Using this ratio, the investor would allocate $77,000 of the $100,000 cost to the building and the remaining $23,000 to land value.

To further illustrate the importance of increasing the depreciable amount Table 7-1 shows the present value of alternative depreciation deductions for different rates of return. For example a depreciation amount of $90,000 using a life of twenty years and straight-line depreciation, creates a depreciation deduction of $4,500 per year ($90,000 ÷ 20). For an individual in the 50-percent tax bracket, this deduction creates a tax savings of $2,250 per year. The present value of this depreciation deduction at a 10-percent rate of return is $19,155. This is less than the apparent tax savings of $45,000. ($90,000 X .50) since the deduction must be taken over a twenty-year period. Obviously deductions taken in later years are worth less than the same deductions in earlier years. The investor thus has an incentive to take the largest deduction possible in the early years of the asset. Table 7-1 also shows that the higher the rate of return desired, the lower the *present value* of the tax savings created by the depreciation deduction.

TABLE 7-1. Present Value of Alternative Depreciable Amounts

Total Depreciable Amount	Amount[a] per Year	Tax Savings[b]	Present Value of Savings at:		
			10%	12%	15%
$ 70,000	$3,500	$1,750	$14,899	$13,072	$10,954
80,000	4,000	2,000	17,027	14,939	12,519
90,000	4,500	2,250	19,156	16,806	14,983
100,000	5,000	2,500	21,284	18,674	15,648
110,000	5,500	2,750	23,412	20,541	17,213
120,000	6,000	3,000	25,541	22,408	18,778
130,000	6,500	3,250	27,669	24,276	20,340
150,000	7,500	3,750	31,926	28,010	23,472

[a]Useful life equal to 20 years; straight-line amount.
[b]Tax rate equal to 50 percent.

Using Table 7-1 an investor can see the advantage of increasing the depreciable amount. If the investor can increase the depreciable amount by $10,000, an additional tax savings would result of approximately $2,128 at a 10-percent rate of return. It would obviously benefit the investor to pay an appraiser if the investor knew for certain that the depreciable basis would increase by $10,000 and if the appraisal cost less than $2,128.

Whatever method is used, the investor should be careful in dividing the total cost between land and building.

Estimating the Useful Life

The second major factor influencing the depreciation deduction is the length of time over which an investment is to be depreciated. This period of time is referred to as the useful life. The useful life depends on such factors as replacement policy of the investor, repair policy, and obsolescence. The useful life on a real estate investment usually bears little resemblence to the physical life.

As noted, a real estate investment consists of two components when viewed from a tax perspective: the land and the building. The land is nondepreciable, being viewed by the tax courts as a nonwasting asset. The building is depreciable. Obviously, there is an incentive from a tax aspect to overvalue the building since it is depreciable.

The useful life of a real estate investment is the period during which it is expected to be held for the production of income. The investor has an incentive from a tax viewpoint to use the shortest possible useful life, thereby increasing the depreciation deduction and thus reducing taxable income. This can be seen in Table 7-2, showing the percentage depreciation under alternative useful lives and various depreciation methods. The shorter the useful life, the greater the depreciation deduction in each year.

The Internal Revenue Service has issued certain guidelines for useful life of real estate as shown in Table 7-3. These useful lives are simply guidelines. They are not hard and fast rules and do not take into account many key factors necessary to determine useful life such as type of construction and economic obsoles-

TABLE 7-2. Depreciation per Year (percent)

Useful Life (years)	Depreciation Method			
	Straight-Line	125%	150%	200%
10	10.00%	12.50%	15.00%	20.00%
15	6.66	8.33	10.00	13.33
20	5.00	6.25	7.50	10.00
25	4.00	5.00	6.00	8.00
30	3.33	4.17	5.00	6.60
$33\frac{1}{3}$	3.00	3.75	4.50	6.00
40	2.50	3.13	3.75	5.00
50	2.00	2.5	3.00	4.00

TABLE 7-3. Internal Revenue Service Guidelines for Useful Life Determination

Type of Real Estate	Useful Life (years)
Apartment buildings	40
Factories	45
Hotels	40
Office buildings	45
Warehouses	60
Farm buildings	25
Theatre buildings	40
Pavement, sidewalks, sewers	20
Garages	45

cence. These guidelines are merely aids in the determination of useful life. In general, the useful life for real estate investments is shorter than these guidelines.

Expert opinion is particularly useful in defending the useful life in real estate investments. Many of the factors that determine the useful life of a particular building can be appraised by experts. A list of such factors includes among others, location and character of the building and its neighborhoods, quality and nature of construction and materials, past and future maintenance, present condition and use, and the shifting of land values.

Selecting the Depreciation Method

The final step in determining the depreciation deduction is selecting the depreciation method. There are three major categories of depreciation techniques:

1. Straight-line method
2. Accelerated methods
   a. 200-percent declining balance (double-declining balance)
   b. 150-percent declining balance
   c. 125-percent declining balance
   d. Sum-of-the-years' digits (SOYD)
3. Component method

Not all of the techniques are allowed on all types of real estate investments. Table 7-4 indicates which depreciation techniques are allowed with various types of real estate investments.

Real estate investments, for tax purposes are classified as residential and nonresidential. Residential real estate is defined as that for which at least 80 percent of the gross rental collections comes from the rental of housing units. New residential property qualifies for any type of depreciation technique. The property must be new in the sense that its original use commences with the current owner. New nonresidential real estate can be depreciated with every technique

TABLE 7-4. Allowed Depreciation Methods for Real Estate Investments

Type of Investment	Straight-Line	125%	150%	200%	Sum-of-the-years'-Digits	Component
			Depreciation Method			
Used Nonresidential	Yes	No	No	No	No	Yes
New Nonresidential	Yes	Yes	Yes	No	No	Yes
Used residential[a]	Yes	Yes	No	No	No	Yes
New residential	Yes	Yes	Yes	Yes	Yes	Yes

[a]Useful life of at least 20 years; if useful life is fewer than 20 years, then the 125% method is not allowed.

except the double-declining balance (200 percent) and sum-of-the-years' digits methods.

Used residential real estate with a useful life of greater than twenty years can be depreciated using the straight-line and the 125-percent declining balance methods. If the useful life is less than twenty years, only straight-line is allowed. Used nonresidential real estate can only be depreciated using the straight-line method.

The component depreciation technique can be applied to any type of real estate investment. It should be noted that if the "composite" asset can be depreciated with an accelerated method, the components can be depreciated using the accelerated method. For example, the components for a new residential real estate investment can be depreciated using the 200-percent declining balance method.

Calculating the Depreciation Deduction: An Example

To illustrate the depreciation deduction calculation under each of these methods, the following example is used:

> Property type: New residential
> Total costs: $250,000
> Building cost: $200,000
> Land cost: $50,000
> Useful life: 25 years
> Salvage value: None

Table 7-5 shows the depreciation deduction in each year under the various methods. Notice that the sum-of-the-years' digits method produces the largest deduction in the early years. Also it is important to note that using the 125-percent, 150-percent, or 200-percent methods results in accumulated depreciation deduction of less than the $200,000. This remaining balance becomes important in understanding the concept of switching from the accelerated techniques to the straight-line method (to be discussed later).

TABLE 7-5. Depreciation of a $200,000 New Residential Property Under Various Methods

Year	Straight-Line	125%	150%	200%	Sum-of-the-Years' Digits
1	$ 8,000.00	$ 10,000.00	$ 12,000.00	$ 16,000.00	$ 15,384.62
2	8,000.00	9,500.00	11,280.00	14,720.00	14,769.23
3	8,000.00	9,025.00	10,603.20	13,542.40	14,153.85
4	8,000.00	8,573.75	9,967.01	12,459.01	13,538.46
5	8,000.00	8,145.06	9,368.99	11,462.29	12,923.08
6	8,000.00	7,737.81	8,806.85	10,545.30	12,307.69
7	8,000.00	7,350.92	8,278.44	9,701.68	11,692.31
8	8,000.00	6,883.37	7,781.73	8,925.55	11,076.92
9	8,000.00	6,634.20	7,314.83	8,211.50	10,461.54
10	8,000.00	6,302.49	6,875.94	7,554.58	9,846.15
11	8,000.00	5,987.37	6,463.38	6,950.22	9,230.77
12	8,000.00	5,688.00	6,075.58	6,394.20	8,615.38
13	8,000.00	5,403.60	5,711.04	5,882.66	8,000.00
14	8,000.00	5,133.42	5,368.38	5,412.05	7,384.62
15	8,000.00	4,876.75	5,046.28	4,979.08	6,769.23
16	8,000.00	4,632.91	4,743.50	4,580.76	6,153.85
17	8,000.00	4,401.27	4,458.89	4,214.30	5,538.46
18	8,000.00	4,181.20	4,191.36	3,877.15	4,923.08
19	8,000.00	3,912.14	3,939.88	3,566.98	4,307.69
20	8,000.00	3,773.54	3,703.48	3,281.62	3,692.31
21	8,000.00	3,584.86	3,481.27	3,019.09	3,076.92
22	8,000.00	3,405.62	3,272.40	2,777.57	2,461.54
23	8,000.00	3,235.34	3,076.05	2,555.36	1,846.15
24	8,000.00	3,073.57	2,891.49	2,350.93	1,230.77
25	8,000.00	2,919.89	2,718.00	2,162.86	615.39
Accumulated depreciation	$200,000.00	$144,522.08	$157,127.14	$175,127.14	$200,000.00
Switch to straight-line in		Year 7	Year 10	Year 14	

Straight-Line Method. Under the straight-line method, an equal amount of depreciation is deducted each year. In the example, the useful life is twenty-five years. Thus $\frac{1}{25}$ (4 percent) of the building costs is deducted each year. The amount of depreciation to be taken is $8,000 ($200,000 × .04). This is illustrated in Column 1 of Table 7-5.

Accelerated Methods. Table 7-5 also summarizes the amount of depreciation allowance under the four accelerated methods: 125 percent, 150 percent, 200 percent (double-declining), and sum-of-the-years' digits. Tables 7-6 through 7-9 illustrate in more detail these accelerated methods. These tables show the depreciation amount, the cumulative depreciation, and the book value of the building over the entire twenty-five-year useful life.

125-Percent Declining Balance Method. As the name implies, under the 125-percent declining balance method, the percentage depreciation each year is

TABLE 7-6. 125-Percent Declining Balance Method

Year	Depreciation Amount	Cumulative Depreciation	Book Value of Building
0	0.00	0.00	$200,000.00
1	$10,000.00	$ 10,000.00	190,000.00
2	9,500.00	19,500.00	180,500.00
3	9,025.00	28,525.00	171,475.00
4	8,573.75	37,098.75	162,901.25
5	8,145.06	45,243.81	154,756.19
6	7,737.81	52,981.62	147,018.38
7	7,350.92	62,332.54	139,667.46
8	6,983.37	67,315.91	132,684.09
9	6,634.20	73,950.11	126,049.89
10	6,302.49	80,252.60	119,747.40
11	5,987.37	86,239.97	113,760.03
12	5,688.00	91,927.97	108,072.03
13	5,403.60	97,331.57	102,668.43
14	5,133.42	102,464.99	97,535.01
15	4,876.75	107,341.74	92,658.26
16	4,632.91	111,974.65	88,025.35
17	4,401.27	116,375.92	93,624.08
18	4,181.20	120,557.12	79,442.88
19	3,972.14	124,529.26	75,470.74
20	3,773.54	128,302.80	71,697.20
21	3,584.86	131,887.66	68,112.34
22	3,405.62	135,293.28	64,706.72
23	3,235.34	138,528.62	61,471.38
24	3,073.57	141,602.19	58,397.81
25	2,919.89	144,522.08	55,477.92

125 percent of the straight-line percentage, on the declining balance. Table 7-6 illustrates how this method works. The original amount to be depreciated is $200,000. The straight-line percentage is 4 percent. Thus the percentage taken each year is 4 percent times 1.25 or 5 percent. This is 5 percent each year on the declining balance. Thus the first year's amount is $10,000 ($200,000 X .05). The book value at the end of the first year is thus $190,000 ($200,000 - $10,000). The amount of depreciation allowed in the second year is $9,500 ($190,000 X .05). The book value at the end of the second year is $180,500 ($190,000 - $9,500). The depreciation deduction in the third year is 5 percent of $180,500 or $9,025. This process is continued until the end of the useful life.

Notice that after the twenty-five-year life the total cumulative depreciation is $144,522 with a remaining book value of $55,478. Thus the 125-percent technique results in a substantial depreciation amount that is not taken.

150-Percent Declining Balance Method. Table 7-7 illustrates the 150-percent declining balance method. The technique works like the 125-percent method except the depreciation percentage is 150 percent of the straight-line percentage, on the declining balance. Again, the depreciable basis is $200,000 and the straight-line percentage is 4 percent. The 150-percent declining balance percentage is 6 percent (4 percent X 1.5). The depreciation amount in the first year is $12,000 ($200,000 X .06). The book value at the end of the first year is $188,000 ($200,000 − $12,000). The depreciation deduction in the second year is $11,280 ($188,000 X .06). This process is continued for each year.

Notice that in the early years, the depreciation deduction under the 150-percent method exceeds the 125-percent deduction. This continues until the nineteenth year. The total cumulative depreciation deductions under the 150-percent method exceeds that for the 125-percent method, but there is still a large book value at the end of the useful life of twenty-five years.

200-Percent Declining Balance Method. Table 7-8 illustrates the 200-percent (double-declining) balance method. As the name implies, the double-declining balance method calculates the percentage depreciation deduction at double the straight-line percentage on the declining balance. Using the basis of $200,000 and the twenty-five year life, the 200-percent declining balance per-

TABLE 7-7. 150-Percent Declining Balance Method

Year	Depreciation Amount	Cumulative Depreciation	Book Value of Building
0	0.00	0.00	$200,000.00
1	$12,000.00	$ 12,000.00	188,000.00
2	11,280.00	23,280.00	176,720.00
3	10,603.20	33,883.20	166,116.80
4	9,967.01	43,850.21	156,149.79
5	9,368.99	53,219.20	146,780.80
6	8,806.85	62,026.05	137,973.95
7	8,278.44	70,304.49	129,695.51
8	7,781.73	78,086.22	121,913.78
9	7,314.83	85,401.05	114,598.95
10	6,875.94	92,276.99	107,723.01
11	6,463.38	98,740.37	101,259.63
12	6,075.58	104,815.95	95,184.05
13	5,711.04	110,526.99	89,473.01
14	5,368.38	115,895.37	84,104.63
15	5,046.28	120,941.65	79,058.35
16	4,743.50	125,685.15	74,314.85
17	4,458.89	130,144.04	69,855.96
18	4,191.36	134,335.40	65,664.60
19	3,939.88	138,275.28	61,724.72
20	3,703.48	141,978.76	58,021.24
21	3,481.27	145,460.03	54,539.97
22	3,272.40	148,732.43	51,267.57
23	3,076.05	151,808.48	48,191.52
24	2,891.49	154,699.97	45,300.03
25	2,718.00	157,417.97	42,582.03

TABLE 7-8. 200-Percent Declining Balance Method

Year	Depreciation Amount	Cumulative Depreciation	Book Value of Building
0	0.00	0.00	$200,000.00
1	$16,000.00	$ 16,000.00	184,000.00
2	14,720.00	30,720.00	169,280.00
3	13,542.40	44,262.40	155,737.60
4	12,459.01	56,721.41	143,278.59
5	11,462.29	68,183.70	131,816.30
6	10,545.30	78,729.00	121,271.00
7	9,701.68	88,430.68	111,569.32
8	8,925.55	97,356.23	102,643.77
9	8,211.50	105,567.73	94,432.27
10	7,554.58	113,122.31	86,877.69
11	6,950.22	120,072.53	79,927.47
12	6,394.20	126,466.73	73,533.27
13	5,882.66	132,349.39	67,650.61
14	5,412.05	137,761.44	62,238.56
15	4,979.08	142,740.52	57,259.48
16	4,580.76	147,321.28	52,678.72
17	4,214.30	151,535.58	48,464.42
18	3,877.15	155,412.73	44,587.27
19	3,566.98	158,979.71	41,020.29
20	3,281.62	162,261.33	37,738.67
21	3,019.09	165,280.42	34,719.58
22	2,777.57	168,057.99	31,942.01
23	2,555.36	170,613.35	29,386.65
24	2,350.93	172,964.28	27,035.72
25	2,162.86	175,127.14	24,872.86

centage is 8 percent (4 percent X 2). The depreciation deduction in the first year is thus $16,000 ($200,000 X .08). The depreciation deduction for the second year is $14,720 ($184,000 X .08). The deduction in the remaining years is calculated in a similar manner using the same percentage and the declining balance.

The 200-percent declining balance method results in a larger depreciation deduction in the earlier years relative to the 125-percent and 150-percent methods. This can be seen in Table 7-5, which summarizes the amounts under the various methods. The 200-percent declining balance method also results in a larger total accumulated depreciation amount taken over the useful life.

Sum-of-the-Years'-Digits Method. The last accelerated method is the sum-of-the-years' digits (SOYD) method. The percentage depreciation allowance taken under the SOYD method is not related to the straight-line method. Table 7-9 illustrates the depreciation deduction using the SOYD method.

To determine the deduction, the investor first calculates the proportion to be taken each year. This proportion is calculated by dividing the number of years remaining by the sum of all years' digits in the useful life of the property.

Using the example, the useful life is twenty-five years. The sum of the

TABLE 7-9. Sum-of-the-Years'-Digits Method

Year	Depreciation Amount	Cumulative Depreciation	Book Value of Building
0	0.00	0.00	$200,000.00
1	$15,384.62	$ 15,384.62	184,615.38
2	14,769.23	30,153.85	169,846.15
3	14,153.85	44,307.70	155,692.30
4	13,538.46	57,846.16	142,153.84
5	12,923.08	70,769.24	129,230.76
6	12,307.69	83,076.93	116,923.07
7	11,692.31	94,769.24	105,230.76
8	11,076.92	105,846.16	94,153.84
9	10,461.54	116,307.70	83,692.30
10	9,846.15	126,153.85	73,846.15
11	8,615.38	144,000.00	56,000.00
12	9,230.77	135,384.62	64,615.38
13	8,000.00	152,000.00	48,000.00
14	7,384.62	159,384.62	40,615.38
15	6,769.23	166,153.85	33,846.15
16	6,153.85	172,307.70	27,692.30
17	5,538.46	177,846.16	22,153.84
18	4,923.08	182,769.24	17,230.76
19	4,307.69	187,076.93	12,923.07
20	3,692.31	190,769.24	9,230.76
21	3,076.92	193,846.16	6,153.84
22	2,461.54	196,307.70	3,692.30
23	1,846.15	198,153.85	1,846.15
24	1,230.77	199,384.61	615.39
25	615.39	200,000.00	—

years' digits $(1 + 2 + 3 + 4 \cdots + 25)$ is 325. Thus the first's depreciation percentage is 7.6923 percent $(25 \div 325)$. This results in a depreciation deduction in the first year of $15,385 ($200,000 $\times$ .076923). The percentage deduction in the second year is 7.38 percent $(24 \div 325)$. This results in a deduction of $14,769 ($200,000 $\times$ .0738). Notice that the percentage is taken on the entire depreciable basis, not on the declining balance. This process is continued for each year of the useful life.

To simplify the summing of the years' digits, the following equation can be used:

$$\text{Sum of digits} = \frac{\text{Life} \times (\text{Life} + 1)}{2}$$

In the example, the denominator for the proportion calculations is

$$\frac{25 \times (25 + 1)}{2} = 325.$$

Notice that the SOYD method results in a cumulative deduction equal to the original total depreciable amount ($200,000). Thus, there is not any remaining book value for the improvements.

Switching Depreciation Methods. A real estate investor is not restricted to the use of only one depreciation method for all of his or her properties but is allowed to use different methods for different properties. However, for a particular property the investor can switch from one depreciation method to another only with the permission of the IRS. The exception is the switch from the accelerated techniques to the straight-line method.

This switching is attractive to the investor who would like to depreciate the total amount as soon as possible, thus obtaining the greatest tax benefits from the depreciation deduction. The 125-percent, 150-percent, and 200-percent declining balance methods have an undepreciated balance at the end of the useful life. At some point during the useful life, the straight-line amount on the remaining balance will exceed the accelerated method. Thus, the investor, in order to maximize the depreciation deduction, should then switch to the straight-line method. An investor who has switched to straight-line, can only switch back again with permission.

To determine the year in which it becomes advantageous to switch, the investor takes the outstanding book value at the end of any year and divides it by the remaining useful life. If this straight-line amount exceeds what would have taken using the accelerated method, the investor should switch to the straight-line method. For example, Table 7-8 illustrates the 200-percent declining balance method. After the tenth year, book value is $86,878 and the remaining useful life is fifteen years. The straight-line amount is $5,792 ($86,878 ÷ 15). The accelerated amount in the eleventh year is $6,950, which exceeds the straight-line amount of $5,792. The investor would thus *not* switch after ten years. Doing the same calculations for various years results in the fourteenth year being determined as the year in which to switch.

After thirteen years, the book value of the improvement is $67,651. The remaining useful life is twelve years. Thus, the straight-line amount is $5,638 ($67,651 ÷ 12). The accelerated amount in the fourteenth year is $5,412 which is less than the straight-line amount ($5,638). Thus the investor should switch to the straight-line method *in* the fourteenth year (after thirteen years).

This same procedure can be used to determine the year in which to switch using the 125-percent and 150-percent declining balance methods. For the 125-percent method, the investor would switch in the seventh year and under the 150-percent method, in the tenth year.

Another method for determining the last year in which to use the accelerated method is to use the following equation:

$$\text{Life} - \frac{\text{Life}}{\text{Method}} + 1 = \text{Last year to use accelerated method}$$

This equation gives the last year in which to use the accelerated method. For example, using the 200-percent declining balance method, the last year in which to use the accelerated method is

$$25 - \frac{25}{2} + 1 = 13.5$$

The investor should switch *after* the thirteenth, that is, *in* the fourteenth year. If a fraction of a year results with the equation, it is always rounded *up* to determine the year in which to switch.

Table 7-10 shows the last year in which to use the accelerated depreciation methods under various useful lives. These years are correct regardless of the amount to be depreciated. It should be noted that it is never advantageous to switch from the SOYD method to straight-line. The SOYD depreciation amount will always exceed the straight-line amount.

Component Depreciation Method. The third major depreciation technique is the component method in which the total depreciable basis is divided into its various components and each component is depreciable according to its useful life, unlike the "composite" method, which assumes one rate of depreciation for the entire structure.

The component method could allow the investor to maximize the tax shel-

TABLE 7-10. Last Year to Use Accelerated Methods for Various Useful Life and Methods

Useful Life (years)	Last Year to Use Accelerated		
	125-Percent Method	150-Percent Method	200-Percent Method
15	4th	6th	8th
20	5th	7th	11th
21	5th	8th	11th
22	5th	8th	12th
23	5th	8th	12th
24	5th	9th	13th
25	6th	9th	13th
26	6th	9th	14th
27	6th	10th	14th
28	6th	10th	15th
29	6th	10th	15th
30	7th	11th	16th
31	7th	11th	16th
32	7th	11th	17th
33	7th	12th	17th
34	7th	12th	18th
35	8th	12th	18th
40	9th	14th	21st
45	10th	16th	23rd
50	11th	17th	26th

ter from an investment. The component method is somewhat more expensive to implement since it requires that the total depreciable amount be split into a basis for each of the components and an estimate made of the useful life for each. As a result, the component method has been relatively underutilized by real estate investors.

To illustrate the component method, suppose the building in the preceeding example can be divided into the various components:

Component	Basis	Useful Life (years)
Heating and air conditioning	$25,000	10
Interior walls and floors	$30,000	20
Plumbing	$8,000	15
Roofing	$12,000	10
Electrical	$25,000	15
Building shell	$100,000	40
Total	$200,000	

Tables 7-11 through 7-13 illustrate the component method using straight-line, 150-percent declining balance, and 200-percent declining balance methods on the components. It should be noted that if the type of investment qualifies for an accelerated method, the components can be depreciated using that method.

Comparing the total amount of depreciation deduction in Tables 7-11, 7-12, and 7-13 with the depreciation deductions in Table 7-5 and using the composite method in the early years of the investment, notice that a larger depreciation deduction results from using the component method in this example. This reflects the relative amount of each component and the useful life of each being taken into account.

The IRS took the position for many years that the component depreciation could be used only on new rather than used property. Lately, however, it has been recognized that the component method can be employed on existing buildings. The total cost must be carefully allocated among the various components based on their value as of the date of purchase. The useful life of each component is assigned based on the condition of the components at the time of acquisition. It is probably advisable that the investor use qualified independent appraisers to justify cost allocations and useful life estimates when the component method is employed with existing property. In the case of a new property, it is relatively easy to allocate based on the actual cost of the separate components.

Obviously, the investor should also carefully analyze switching from the accelerated method to straight-line when the component method is used. The same rules outlined in the preceding section apply in this case.

TABLE 7-11. Depreciation Amount Under Component Method Using Straight-Line

				Component			
Year	Building	Roofing	Electricity	Plumbing	Heating & Air Conditioning	Interior Walls & Floors	Total
1	$ 2,500.00	$ 1,200.00	$ 1,666.66	$ 533.33	$ 2,500.00	$ 1,500.00	$ 9,900.00
2	2,500.00	1,200.00	1,666.66	533.33	2,500.00	1,500.00	9,900.00
3	2,500.00	1,200.00	1,666.66	533.33	2,500.00	1,500.00	9,900.00
4	2,500.00	1,200.00	1,666.66	533.33	2,500.00	1,500.00	9,900.00
5	2,500.00	1,200.00	1,666.66	533.33	2,500.00	1,500.00	9,900.00
6	2,500.00	1,200.00	1,666.66	533.33	2,500.00	1,500.00	9,900.00
7	2,500.00	1,200.00	1,666.66	533.33	2,500.00	1,500.00	9,900.00
8	2,500.00	1,200.00	1,666.66	533.33	2,500.00	1,500.00	9,900.00
9	2,500.00	1,200.00	1,666.66	533.33	2,500.00	1,500.00	9,900.00
10	2,500.00	1,200.00	1,666.66	533.33	2,500.00	1,500.00	9,900.00
11	2,500.00	—	1,666.66	533.33	—	1,500.00	6,200.00
12	2,500.00	—	1,666.66	533.33	—	1,500.00	6,200.00
13	2,500.00	—	1,666.66	533.33	—	1,500.00	6,200.00
14	2,500.00	—	1,666.66	533.33	—	1,500.00	6,200.00
15	2,500.00	—	1,666.66	533.33	—	1,500.00	6,200.00
16	2,500.00	—	—	—	—	1,500.00	4,000.00
17	2,500.00	—	—	—	—	1,500.00	4,000.00
18	2,500.00	—	—	—	—	1,500.00	4,000.00
19	2,500.00	—	—	—	—	1,500.00	4,000.00
20	2,500.00	—	—	—	—	1,500.00	4,000.00
40	50,000.00	—	—	—	—	—	—
Accumulated depreciation	$100,000.00	$12,000.00	$25,000.00	$8,000.00	$25,000.00	$30,000.00	$200,000.00

115

TABLE 7-12. Component Method Using 150-Percent Declining Balance

					Component		
Year	Building	Roofing	Electricity	Plumbing	Heating & Air Conditioning	Interior Walls & Floor	Total
1	$ 3,750.00	$1,800.00	$ 2,500.00	$ 800.00	$ 3,750.00	$ 2,250.00	$ 14,850.00
2	3,609.38	1,530.00	2,250.00	720.00	3,187.50	2,081.25	13,378.13
3	3,474.02	1,300.50	2,025.00	648.00	2,709.38	1,925.16	12,082.06
4	3,343.75	1,105.43	1,822.50	583.20	2,302.97	1,780.77	10,938.62
5	3,218.36	939.61	1,640.25	524.88	1,957.52	1,647.21	9,927.83
6	3,097.67	798.67	1,476.22	472.39	1,663.89	1,523.67	9,032.51
7	2,981.51	678.87	1,328.68	425.15	1,414.31	1,409.40	8,237.84
8	2,869.70	577.04	1,195.74	385.64	1,202.16	1,303.69	7,533.97
9	2,762.09	490.48	1,076.17	344.07	1,021.84	1,205.91	6,900.56
10	2,658.51	416.91	968.55	309.67	868.56	1,115.47	6,337.67
11	2,558.81	—	871.70	278.70	—	1,031.81	4,741.02
12	2,462.86	—	784.53	250.83	—	954.42	4,452.64
13	2,370.50	—	706.07	225.75	—	882.84	4,185.16
14	2,281.61	—	635.47	203.17	—	816.63	3,936.88
15	2,196.05	—	571.92	182.85	—	755.38	3,706.20
16	2,113.69	—	—	—	—	698.73	2,812.42
17	2,034.43	—	—	—	—	646.32	2,680.75
18	1,958.14	—	—	—	—	597.85	2,555.99
19	1,884.71	—	—	—	—	553.01	2,437.72
20	1,814.03	—	—	—	—	511.54	2,325.57
Accumulated depreciation	$53,439.82	$9,637.51	$19,852.72	$6,354.30	$20,078.13	$23,691.06	$133,053.54

TABLE 7-13. Component Method Using 200-Percent Declining Balance

				Component			
Year	Building	Roofing	Electrical	Plumbing	Heating & Air Conditioning	Interior Walls & Floors	Total
1	$ 5,000.00	$ 2,400.00	$ 3,333.33	$1,066.67	$ 5,000.00	$ 3,000.00	$ 19,800.00
2	4,750.00	1,920.00	2,888.89	924.44	4,000.00	2,700.00	17,183.33
3	4,512.50	1,536.00	2,503.70	801.18	3,200.00	2,430.00	14,983.38
4	4,286.88	1,228.80	2,169.88	694.36	2,560.00	2,187.00	13,126.92
5	4,072.53	983.04	1,880.56	601.78	2,048.00	1,968.30	11,554.21
6	3,868.90	786.43	1,629.82	521.54	1,638.40	1,771.47	10,216.56
7	3,675.46	629.15	1,412.51	452.00	1,310.72	1,594.32	9,074.16
8	3,491.69	503.32	1,224.17	391.74	1,048.58	1,434.89	8,094.39
9	3,317.10	402.65	1,060.95	339.51	838.86	1,291.40	7,250.47
10	3,151.25	322.12	919.49	294.24	671.09	1,162.26	6,520.45
11	2,993.68	—	796.89	255.01	—	1,046.04	5,091.62
12	2,844.00	—	690.64	221.00	—	941.43	4,697.07
13	2,701.80	—	598.56	191.54	—	847.29	4,339.19
14	2,566.71	—	518.75	166.00	—	762.56	4,014.02
15	2,438.38	—	449.58	143.87	—	686.30	3,718.13
16	2,316.46	—	—	—	—	617.67	2,934.13
17	2,200.63	—	—	—	—	555.91	2,756.54
18	2,090.60	—	—	—	—	500.32	2,590.92
19	1,986.07	—	—	—	—	450.28	2,436.35
20	1,886.77	—	—	—	—	405.26	2,292.03
Accumulated depreciation	$64,151.41	$10,711.51	$22,077.72	$7,064.88	$22,315.65	$26,352.70	$152,673.87

Minimum Tax and Depreciation

The 1969 Tax Reform Act created the minimum tax on what are called preference tax items. The purpose of the minimum tax is to ensure that everyone, both individuals and corporations, pay at least some income from preference items. The minimum used to be 10 percent. This was raised to 15 percent by the 1976 Tax Reform Act. The 1978 Tax Reform Act kept this 15-percent rate on certain items and created an alternative minimum tax rate of 10 percent on the first $40,000 of taxable income from tax-preference items, 20 percent on the next $40,000, and 25 percent on income over $100,000 on certain preference items.

The following items are counted as tax-preference income:

1. Accelerated depreciation on real property in excess of straight-line.
2. Untaxed part of long-term capital gains for individuals. This portion is equal to 60 percent of the long-term gain under the 1978 Act. This 60 percent is subject to the alternative minimum tax.
3. The aggregate amount of itemized deductions in excess of 60 percent of adjusted gross income for individuals. These are subject to the alternative minimum tax.
4. Amortization of railroad rolling stock.
5. Amortization of certified pollution-controlled facilities.
6. The excess of fair market value of stock, in the case of specified stock and specified stock options, at the time of exercise of the option over the option price of the stock.
7. Reserve for bad debts of financial institutions.
8. Depletion deductions in excess of cost basis.
9. Excess investment interest with the exception of regular corporations.
10. Accelerated depreciation on personal property subject to any lease (except for regular corporations).
11. Intangible drilling cost deductions in excess of income from oil and gas production.

The major preference tax items of concern to the real estate investor are: (1) the excess of accelerated depreciation over straight-line, and (2) the excluded part (60 percent) of an individual's long-term capital gains. Thus, the investor may have some benefit from the accelerated depreciation but for certain taxpayers this benefit may be subject to taxation in the form of the minimum tax. Each year the investor has to calculate the accelerated depreciation amount as well as the straight-line amount. The excess of accelerated over straight-line becomes a tax-preference item and is possibly subject to a 15-percent tax rate under the ordinary minimum tax structure.

To calculate the taxable income from ordinary preference tax items, the taxpayer has certain deductions that may be taken from preference income before it is subject to the minimum tax. The exemptions are the greater of $10,000 or one-half of the regular income taxes in the case of noncorporate taxpayers. In the case of regular corporations the deduction is $10,000 or the full amount of regular income taxes.

The 1978 Tax Act added what is called the alternative minimum tax. The two tax-preference items that are subject to the alternative minimum tax are (1) the untaxed part (60 percent) of long-term capital gains for individuals, and (2) the aggregate amount of itemized deductions in excess of 60 percent of adjusted gross income.

The Senate Finance Committee decided that the present minimum tax structure was resulting in a large minimum tax on individuals who were already paying substantial regular taxes. This was particularly true in the case of large capital gains. The 1978 Act created an alternative minimum tax to correct these perceived inequities. As noted, this alternative tax was applicable only to the capital gains and excess itemized deduction preference items. This new minimum tax will apply only to the extent that it exceeds an individual's regular tax plus his or her regular minimum tax.

The alternative minimum tax rates are as follows:

Amount	Tax Rate (%)
First $20,000	0
Next $40,000	10
Next $40,000	20
Over $100,000	25

The following example shows the computation of an individual's tax under the alternate and regular minimum-tax structures.

Facts	
Taxable income:	$60,000
Capital gains preference plus excess itemized deductions:	$175,000
Other preference items:	$50,000
Regular tax:	$19,678
Normal Tax Liability	
Other preference items	$50,000
Less $10,000 exclusion	(10,000)
	$40,000
Regular minimum tax rate (15%)	X.15
	$6,000
Plus regular tax	19,678
Total normal tax	$25,678

Alternative Minimum Tax	
Taxable income	$60,000
Capital gains preference plus excess itemized deductions	175,000
Statutory exclusion	(20,000)
Alternative minimum tax base	$215,000
Alternative Minimum Tax	
First $40,000 at 10%	$4,000
Second $40,000 at 20%	8,000
Balance $135,000 at 25%	33,750
Total Alternative	$45,750

The taxpayer would pay the greater of the total normal tax or the total alternative tax. In this example the taxes due would be $45,750.

In summary, the two preference tax items for a real estate investment are the excess of accelerated depreciation over straight-line and the excluded (60-percent) portion of long-term capital gains. Each of these items could have an impact on the feasibility of a real estate investment.

Excess Depreciation Recapture

The three objectives of a tax shelter are to defer taxes, to create deductions from the use of borrowed funds, and to convert ordinary income into capital gains. The depreciation deduction creates a tax savings in that taxes are deferred until the sale of the investment (assuming no capital loss). The depreciation allowance also allows the conversion of ordinary income to capital gains which are taxed at a lower rate. The use of borrowed funds creates financial leverage (increasing the rate of return on equity) and the interest payment is deductible for tax purposes.

The use of accelerated depreciation prior to the 1969 Tax Act allowed investors to convert a large portion of ordinary income to capital gains. This was attractive since capital gains are taxed at a rate lower than the ordinary income tax rate.

However, this loophole was closed by the 1969 Act and shut off almost completely by the 1976 Act. These tax acts provided for all of the excess depreciation (the accelerated amount over the straight-line amount) to be "recaptured." This means that on the sale of an investment, all of the excess is taxed as ordinary income. The only exception is new low-income housing financed by the federal government and held for a specified time period (discussed in Chapter 8). Thus, the investor is no longer allowed to use the accelerated depreciation techniques to switch ordinary income to capital gains income. The accelerated method is still attractive since it allows the investor to defer taxes. The investor can, however, use the straight-line method to switch ordinary income to capital gains. This recapture of excess depreciation is discussed in greater detail in Chapter 8.

For the real estate investor, the excess of accelerated depreciation over the straight-line amount is possibly taxed twice: first, as a minimum tax item and, second, when recaptured at the time of sale. For most real estate investors who do not have a large amount of preference income, this minimum tax effect will probably not be important. The recapture effect, however, is extremely important and must be carefully considered as will be shown in the following chapter.

INCOME TAX RATES

There are two variables required to calculate the amount of taxes from the annual cash flow of a real estate investment: the taxable income and the tax rate. The preceding sections have discussed the calculation of the taxable income. This section discusses the federal tax rates on both personal and corporate income in the United States.

In making investment decisions, the marginal rate is the important rate. The marginal rate is simply the percentage of taxes that an investor would have to pay on additional income.

Personal Income Tax Rates

Tables 7-14 through 7-17 show the progressive personal income tax rates for 1979 taxable income. The reasoning behind the progressive structure is based on the idea that a taxpayer's ability to pay increases at a faster rate than his or

TABLE 7-14. Personal Income Tax Schedules, 1979 Income, Unmarried

Taxable Income		Tax	Marginal Rate Applied to Income in Excess of Column (a) Amount
(a) Over	(b) Not Over		
$ 2,300	$ 3,400	$ 0	14%
3,400	4,400	154	16
4,400	6,500	314	18
6,500	8,500	692	19
8,500	10,800	1,072	21
10,800	12,900	1,555	24
12,900	15,000	2,059	26
15,000	18,200	2,605	30
18,200	23,500	3,565	34
23,500	28,800	5,367	39
28,800	34,100	7,434	44
34,100	41,500	9,766	49
41,500	55,300	13,392	55
55,300	81,800	20,982	63
81,800	108,300	37,677	68
108,300	—	55,697+	70

TABLE 7-15. Personal Income Tax Schedules, 1979 Income,
Married—Joint Return or Surviving Spouse

Taxable Income			Marginal Rate Applied to Income in Excess of
(a) Over	(b) Not Over	Tax	Column (a) Amount
$ 3,400	$ 5,500	$ 0	14%
5,500	7,600	294	16
7,600	11,900	630	18
11,900	16,000	1,404	21
16,000	20,200	2,265	24
20,200	24,600	3,273	28
24,600	29,900	4,505	32
29,900	35,200	6,201	37
35,200	45,800	8,162	43
45,800	60,000	12,720	49
60,000	85,600	19,678	54
85,600	109,400	33,502	59
109,400	162,400	47,544	64
162,400	215,400	81,464	68
215,400	–	117,504+	70

her income. Marginal tax rates on personal income range from 14 percent to 70 percent. The taxpayer is categorized according to one of the following tax classifications: unmarried, married filing a joint return (or surviving spouse), head of household, or married filing a separate return.

To illustrate, suppose a taxpayer, married, filing a joint return, has a taxable income of $40,000. The taxes due are $10,228. Suppose the taxpayer makes a real estate investment that generates a taxable income of $3,000. The

TABLE 7-16. Personal Income Tax Schedules, 1979 Income, Head of Household

Taxable Income			Marginal Rate Applied to Income in Excess of
(a) Over	(b) Not Over	Tax	Column (a) Amount
$ 2,300	$ 4,400	$ 0	14%
4,400	6,500	294	16
6,500	8,700	630	18
8,700	11,800	1,026	22
11,800	15,000	1,708	24
15,000	18,200	2,476	26
18,200	23,500	3,308	31
23,500	28,800	4,951	36
28,800	34,100	6,859	42
34,100	44,700	9,085	46
44,700	60,600	13,961	54
60,600	81,800	22,547	59
81,800	108,300	35,055	63
108,300	161,300	51,750	68
161,300	–	87,790+	70

TABLE 7-17. Personal Income Tax Schedules, 1979 Income, Married—Separate Return

Taxable Income		Tax	Marginal Rate Applied to Income in Excess of Column (a) Amount
(a) Over	(b) Not Over		
$ 1,700	$ 2,750	$ 0	14%
2,750	3,800	147	16
3,800	5,950	315	18
5,950	8,000	702	21
8,000	10,100	1,133	24
10,100	12,300	1,637	28
12,300	14,950	2,253	32
14,950	17,600	3,101	37
17,600	22,900	4,081	43
22,900	30,000	6,360	49
30,000	42,800	9,839	54
42,800	54,700	16,751	59
54,700	81,200	23,772	64
81,200	107,700	40,732	68
107,700	–	58,752+	70

total taxable income is now $43,000 ($40,000 + $3,000) with taxes of $11,518 due.

The taxes have increased from $10,228 to $11,518 or $1,290 while the taxable income increased $3,000. This represents a 43-percent marginal tax rate ($1,290 ÷ $3,000). Thus, 43 cents out of every additional dollar goes to taxes.

Now suppose the real estate investment is generating a negative taxable income of $3,000. A negative taxable income does not mean that the investment is losing money. It simply means that the investment is generating a tax loss.

What impact does this negative taxable income have on the investor's tax liability? The negative taxable income from the investment reduces his or her total taxable income to $37,000 ($40,000 - $3,000). The taxes are now $8,894, a reduction of $1,334. This means that the investor has saved $1,334 in income that otherwise would have been paid in taxes.

Corporate Tax Rates

The 1978 Tax Act reduced the corporate tax rates. Effective at the beginning of 1979, the corporate rates were:

Taxable Income	New Rate (%)	Old Rate (%)
Up to $25,000	17	20
$25,001 to $50,000	20	22
$50,001 to $75,000	30	48
$75,001 to $100,000	40	48
Over $100,000	46	48

CALCULATING AFTER-TAX
CASH FLOWS: AN EXAMPLE

Using the discussion of the preceding chapters, it is now possible to illustrate the calculation of the after-tax cash flows from any real estate investment.

EXAMPLE 7-1

An investor has the opportunity to invest in a new warehouse. The warehouse has 12,000 square feet and is currently leased for twenty years with an annual rental of $1.50 per square foot. The lease calls for adjustments to be made in the rent at a rate of increase of 3 percent per year. The tenant pays all expenses of operation except property taxes and insurance which are estimated at $4,000 for the first year. These expenses are expected to increase at a rate of 5 percent per year. The selling price is $125,000 of which the investor can borrow 75 percent (93,750) at 10-percent interest with annual payments for twenty years. It is estimated that the investor can depreciate 85 percent of the total cost with a useful life of thirty years using the 150-percent declining balance method. The investor is in a 50-percent ordinary income tax bracket.

Problem: Set up the expected cash flow statement, using these inputs, for Years 1 through 10.

Table 7-18 contains the after-tax cash flow estimates for this example. The potential gross income (PGI) is $18,000 for the first year. This is the 12,000 square feet multiplied by the $1.50 rent per square foot per year. The potential gross income increases at a rate of 3 percent per year. At the end of the ten-year period, the rents would be approximately $1.96 per square foot. The building is 100-percent rented over the ten-year period. Thus vacancies and other losses are zero. There is no miscellaneous income; thus effective gross income is equal to potential gross income in each year.

The operating expenses are $4,000 for the first year and are estimated to increase at a rate of 5 percent per year. The operating expense ratio (OER) is 22 percent in the first year. This is the ratio of operating expenses to effective gross income ($4,000 ÷ $18,000). This ratio increases steadily over the ten years since expenses are rising at a faster rate than rents. In the fifth year, the OER is 24 percent ($4,862 ÷ $20,260); in the tenth year, the OER is 26 percent ($6,204 ÷ $23,487). The relationship between changes in operating expenses and changes in rents is of key concern for the investor. In this example, even though the operating expenses are rising at a faster rate (5 percent) than rents (3 percent), the net effect is to produce an increasing net operating income over the ten-year period. The NOI increases from $14,000 in the first year to an estimated $17,283 in the tenth year.

TABLE 7-18. Annual Operating Cash Flow Statement for a Real Estate Investment

					Year					
	1	2	3	4	5	6	7	8	9	10
Potential gross income (PGI)	$18,000	$18,540	$19,096	$19,669	$20,259	$20,867	$21,493	$22,138	$22,802	$23,486
Less vacancies and bad debts	—	—	—	—	—	—	—	—	—	—
Plus miscellaneous income	—	—	—	—	—	—	—	—	—	—
Effective gross income (EGI)	18,000	18,540	19,096	19,669	20,259	20,867	21,493	22,138	22,802	23,486
Less operating expenses	-4,000	-4,200	-4,410	-4,631	-4,862	-5,105	-5,360	-5,628	-5,910	-6,205
Net operating income (NOI)	14,000	14,340	14,686	15,038	15,398	15,762	16,133	16,510	16,892	17,281
Less debt service	-11,012	-11,012	-11,012	-11,012	-11,012	-11,012	-11,012	-11,012	-11,012	-11,012
Before-tax cash flow (BTCF)	2,988	3,328	3,674	4,026	4,386	4,750	5,121	5,498	5,880	6,269
Plus principal	+1,637	+1,801	+1,981	+2,179	+2,397	+2,636	+2,900	+3,190	+3,509	+3,860
Less depreciation	-5,313	-5,047	-4,795	-4,555	-4,327	-4,111	-3,905	-3,710	-3,524	-3,348
Plus replacement reserves	—	—	—	—	—	—	—	—	—	—
Less amortized costs	—	—	—	—	—	—	—	—	—	—
Taxable income (TI)	-688	-82	860	1,650	2,455	3,275	4,116	4,978	5,865	6,781
Multiplied by tax rate	.5	.5	.5	.5	.5	.5	.5	.5	.5	.5
Taxes	-344	-42	430	825	1,228	1,638	2,058	2,489	2,933	3,390
After-tax cash flow (ATCF) (BTCF minus Taxes)	3,332	3,370	3,244	3,201	3,158	3,113	3,063	3,009	2,948	2,879

The next step in setting up the cash flow statement is to deduct the payment on the mortgage (debt service). The investor was borrowing 75 percent of the total cost. This gives an amount borrowed of $93,750 as shown in Table 7-19. The interest rate is 10 percent per year with annual payments for twenty years. The mortgage constant is .11746. This is found by looking at Table A-3 in the Appendix, in the column labeled 10% interest for a 20-year term. Multiplying the mortgage constant (.11746) by the amount borrowed ($93,750) gives the debt service of $11,012.

Table 7-19 illustrates the amortization schedule for this mortgage. The split of debt service between interest and principal is necessary for calculating the taxable income from the project.

The taxable income is calculated by adding to BTCF the payment on principal for the mortgage each year and deducting the depreciation allowance. Table 7-20 illustrates the calculation of the depreciation schedule.

The investment has a total cost of $125,000 of which 85 percent is depreciable. The depreciable amount is $106,250. The nondepreciable (land) amount is equal to $18,750. The building is assumed to have a salvage value of zero and the useful life is estimated at thirty years. Since the asset is a new nonresidential property, the investor can use the 150-percent declining balance technique. The straight-line percent depreciation is $\frac{1}{30}$ or 3.333 percent. The 150-percent declining balance percentage is 5 percent (1.50 × 3.333%).

Table 7-20 illustrates the depreciation schedule for both the 150-percent method and the straight-line method. Also shown is the excess accelerated deduction over straight-line in Column 8. This excess represents a preference tax

TABLE 7-19. Mortgage Amortization Schedule

Amount borrowed: $93,750
Interest rate: 10%
Maturity term: 20 years
Payments: Annual
Loan-to-value ratio: 75%
Mortgage constant: 11746
Debt service: $11,012

Year	Portion Outstanding	Amount Outstanding	Debt Service	Interest Payment	Principal Payment
0	1.00000	$93,750	—	—	—
1	.98254	92,113	$11,012	$9,375	$1,637
2	.96333	90,312	11,012	9,211	1,801
3	.94220	88,331	11,012	9,031	1,981
4	.91895	86,152	11,012	8,833	2,179
5	.89339	83,755	11,012	8,615	2,397
6	.86527	81,119	11,012	8,376	2,636
7	.83434	78,219	11,012	8,112	2,900
8	.80031	75,029	11,012	7,822	3,190
9	.76288	71,520	11,012	7,503	3,509
10	.72171	67,660	11,012	7,152	3,860

TABLE 7-20. Depreciation Schedule

Total cost: **$125,000**
Depreciable amount: **$106,250**
Nondepreciable amount: **$18,750**
Useful life: **30 years**
Accelerated method: **150%**
Accelerated percent: **5%**
Straight-line method: **3.333%**

Year	Accelerated Method			Straight-line Method			Excess Depreciation
	Book Value	Amount	Cumulative	Book Value	Amount	Cumulative	
0	$106,250			$106,250			
1	100,937	$5,313	$ 5,313	102,708	$3,542	$ 3,542	$1,771
2	95,890	5,047	10,360	99,166	3,542	7,084	1,505
3	91,096	4,795	15,154	95,624	3,542	10,626	1,253
4	86,541	4,555	19,709	92,082	3,542	14,168	1,013
5	82,214	4,327	24,036	88,540	3,542	17,710	785
6	78,103	4,111	28,147	84,998	3,542	21,252	569
7	74,198	3,905	32,052	81,456	3,542	24,794	363
8	70,488	3,710	35,762	77,914	3,542	28,336	168
9	66,964	3,524	39,286	74,372	3,542	31,878	–18
10	63,616	3,348	42,634	70,830	3,542	35,420	–194

item and is subject to minimum tax under certain conditions as discussed in the preceding section of this chapter. In this example, this minimum tax is assumed to be not applicable.

The depreciation amount for each year using the 150-percent method is deducted from the BTCF plus the principal payment on the mortgage, as shown in Table 7-18, to arrive at the taxable income for each year.

Two other items, which were not applicable in this example, could affect the taxable income. The first is any allowance for replacements which might have been included in the operating expense. For example, an investment might include certain items of personal property, such as refrigerators, which have a shorter useful life than the real estate. While these are depreciable, just as the real estate, the investor should set aside an allowance for the replacement of these items. If this is done, it is not a deductible item for tax purposes even though it should be treated in the operating expense.

The second item that might affect the taxable income is amortized financing costs. Typically in taking out a mortgage, certain costs are incurred. These include such items as legal fees, appraisal fees, closing costs, and points on the mortgage. These costs must be amortized over the maturity term of the mortgage on a straight-line basis. The amount amortized each year is deductible from the BTCF in arriving at the taxable income.

In the example in Table 7-18, the taxable income in Years 1 and 2 is negative. This does not mean that the cash flow from the project is negative. Obviously the taxable income is negative because the depreciation allowance exceeds the BTCF plus the principal payment on the mortgage. This is an example of a tax shelter that shelters not only the cash flow from the project but that can also be used to shelter the other taxable income of the investor. Beginning in the third year, taxable income is positive and only part of the cash flow from the project is sheltered.

Notice that the taxable income increases steadily over the ten-year period. This is the result of several factors. First, the BTCF is increasing as a result of the rising rents. Second, the principal payment is increasing. In the early years of the mortgage, most of the debt service goes to interest with little going to principal. This relationship reverses itself over the life of the mortgage. Third, the depreciation deduction is decreasing. This is true for the accelerated methods of depreciation. The greatest depreciation amount is taken in the first year with the accelerated methods.

The investor can now calculate the amount of taxes due each year by multiplying the taxable income by the marginal tax rate of 50 percent. The after-tax cash flow (ATCF) is then calculated by subtracting the taxes from the BTCF. Notice that in Years 1 and 2 the taxes are negative. This results in ATCF's being greater than BTCF for these years.

As a result of the interaction between rent, operating expenses, principal payment, and depreciation changes, the ATCF rises between Years 1 and 2 and then steadily declines over the remainder of the ten-year period.

It should be noted that this cash flow statement is based on what the investor *expects* the investment to generate. Obviously, there is a lot of uncertainty in making a real estate or any other investment. Setting up the expected cash flow statement allows the investor to carefully formalize his or her expectations before making the final investment decision.

That, however, is only half of the problem. The investor also should formalize expectations of the disposition of the investment. How does the investor expect the value of the property to change over the holding period? Part 4 will discuss the calculation of the cash flow after taxes from the disposition of a real estate investment.

IV
Taxation
and Disposition

Taxation has two major impacts on the cash flow from a real estate investment. The first is the impact on the annual cash flow from the investment, discussed in Part 3. The second is the impact on the cash flow from the disposition of the real estate investment. Part 4 deals with this second impact.

Chapter 8 discusses the taxes due on the sale of a real estate investment. These taxes can be of three types: capital gains, excess depreciation recapture, and minimum taxes. Each of these potential forms of taxation must be carefully analyzed in planning a real estate investment. Chapter 9 outlines some alternative methods of disposition, primarily the deferred payment sale and exchanges, These methods of disposition involve different taxation impacts as compared to the disposition by sale.

8

The Sale
and the Taxes Due

INTRODUCTION

The previous sections in this book have dealt with how to minimize taxes on a
real estate investment by reducing the tax on the annual income from the rent
on income producing properties. It was shown that the proper handling of operating expenses, leverage, and depreciation had a significant impact on reducing
the taxable income for any type of real estate investment. At some point in time
the investor may want to sell the real estate. The selling of this property is a taxable event. A goal of any investor is to reduce the taxes due at the time of the
sale. Each investor wants the highest possible price but at the same time he or
she wants to pay the lowest possible tax. This chapter will be concerned with
taxes that apply to the sale of property.

THE AMOUNT REALIZED
FROM THE SALE

The first basic step in calculating the amount realized is to determine the gross
sale price of the property. The gross sale price of a real estate property is the
sum of (1) the cash paid; (2) any other accepted payment such as checks, bank
drafts, etc.; (3) the value of any other property received from the seller; and (4)
any liability against the property assumed by the buyer.

The amount realized from the sale of the real estate is the gross sale price minus any allowable deductions. The allowable deductions are selling expenses. The selling expenses are commissions, recording fees, legal fees, and any other expenses associated with the sale.

EXAMPLE 8-1

An investor sells an apartment building for $100,000 and receives $20,000 cash and the buyer takes an $80,000 mortgage. The gross sale price is computed as follows:

Cash received	$ 20,000
Mortgage against property	80,000
Gross sale price	$100,000

If the investor had received $10,000 cash and $20,000 in government bonds and the buyer had taken a $70,000 mortgage, the gross sale price would be computed as follows:

Cash received	$ 10,000
Government bonds	20,000
Mortgage against property	70,000
Gross sale price	$100,000

The amount realized from the sale would be the gross sale price less deductions.

EXAMPLE 8-2

An investor sells an apartment building and calculates a gross sale price of $100,000. The expenses are $8,000 for sales commission, $1,000 in legal fees, and a $100 recording fee. The amount realized would be:

Gross sale price		$100,000
Less:		
Sales commission	8,000.00	
Legal fees	1,000.00	
Recording fees	100.00	−9,100
Amount realized from sale		$ 90,900

The amount realized is often referred to as the net sale price and is used to compute the total gain from the sale. This total gain is the amount used to compute taxes.

The Timing of the Sale

The timing of the sale can be extremely important when considering in which taxable year to consummate the sale, the possibility of deferring taxes, and the holding period of the property. An investor may know that his or her personal income will be lower the year after the expected sale. In this case, the investor may be able to postpone the accepted date of the sale to the following year. Tax deferral is sensitive to the timing of the yearly payments. More will be said on tax deferrals in the next chapter. The holding period of property must be one year or more to qualify as a long-term capital gain. A mistake of even one day will lead to a short-term capital gain which is taxed at the much higher ordinary income rates.

The date of sale is usually considered the date on which the buyer takes title. This typically occurs on the closing date with the delivery of the deed. If the burden and risk of ownership is transferred before the closing date the Internal Revenue Service could decide to accept the earlier date as the time of sale. The holding period begins on the day after the property was accepted as sold to the present owner and ends on the day the property is sold to the new owner. For example, an investor buys a property on June 10, 1978, and sells it on June 12, 1979. The holding period is more than one year; thus, the sale qualifies for long-term capital gain. If the investor had sold the property on June 10, 1979, he would have realized a short-term capital gain because the holding period was not more than one year. An improvement must be based on the date of completion. In this case, the holding period of the property must be based on two separate dates, one for the original property and the other for the improvement. These examples illustrate the importance of properly timing the sale to obtain the best tax treatment.

THE TOTAL GAIN
FROM THE SALE

Having determined the amount realized from the sale, the next step is to determine the original basis. If the property was acquired by purchase, the original basis is the cost. In most cases this can be thought of as the amount the investor paid for the property. Of course, if the property was inherited or acquired by gift, the basis must be determined by other means, such as an appraisal of the property.

The original basis is adjusted to account for value of improvements made to the property and depreciation. This adjusted basis is used to compute the total gain or loss from the sale. Improvements would include any capital additions to the land such as buildings. Depreciation may be calculated on either a straightline or accelerated basis. The sum of the depreciation taken each year until the sale is used to calculate the total as discussed in Chapter 7.

EXAMPLE 8-3

An investor purchased an acre of land for $10,000 and built a warehouse worth $100,000 on the land. The original basis was $110,000. The property was held for ten years with a total depreciation of $50,000. The adjusted basis is calculated as follows:

Original basis for the land	$ 10,000
Improvement—Warehouse	100,000
	110,000
Less: Depreciation	−50,000
Adjusted basis	$60,000

The total gain is the amount realized less the adjusted basis. Using the above example with an amount realized of $200,000 the total gain is:

Amount realized	$200,000
Less adjusted basis	−60,000
Total gain	$140,000

The Right Strategy

As demonstrated in Example 8-3, the greater the depreciation, the smaller the adjusted basis. The smaller adjusted basis results in a larger total gain subject to tax. Is this the right strategy? The answer is yes. The reason is that the depreciation taken during the life of the real estate investment reduces the taxable income from the property. As was demonstrated in Chapter 7 depreciation reduces the amount of income subject to ordinary federal tax rates which are usually higher than the taxes on the total gain. The investor is able, using this procedure, to transfer income earned to a lower tax rate. The right strategy is to take as much depreciation as possible during the life of an investment. Property that qualifies for accelerated depreciation is of even more benefit. Accelerated depreciation provides more tax deferral but the IRS does not allow all the deferred income to be taxed at the lower capital gains rate. The IRS refers to the difference between accelerated and straight-line depreciation as excess depreciation, which must be "recaptured" and taxed as ordinary income.

RECAPTURE OF DEPRECIATION

Deductions for depreciation offset ordinary income and reduce the basis of the property. When the property is sold, the gain is the difference between the amount realized and the adjusted basis for depreciation. This may be subject to capital gain tax. Before the recapture rules enacted with 1969 Tax Act, the investor could use accelerated depreciation to convert ordinary income to capital gains. Now only straight-line depreciation can be used and the excess depreciation resulting from accelerated depreciation must be returned (recaptured) and taxed at the ordinary income rates.

The recapture rules on real property are designed to be limited to excess depreciation. This means that there will be no recapture where the amount of depreciation does not exceed what the depreciation would have been under the straight-line method. There is also a select set of properties where the amount of gain subject to ordinary income tax is reduced as the holding period of the property is extended. All property held for less than one year is subject to recapture of all depreciation.

Calculating the Recapture of Depreciation

The following example illustrates the recapture of depreciation under alternative methods.

EXAMPLE 8-4

Property type: New residential
Total cost: $250,000
Building: $200,000
Land: $50,000
Useful life: 25 years
Salvage value: None

The property is held for five years, then sold for $400,000. Tables 8-1 and 8-2 present the amount of recapture for alternative depreciation methods. As the depreciation method becomes more accelerated, the amount of recapture is greater. From 125 percent to 200 percent the amount recaptured goes from $5,243.81 to $28,183.70. The amount recaptured is calculated by subtracting the dollar amount of any particular accelerated method from the dollar amount of straight-line depreciation. For example in Table 8-1 the amount recaptured from a 150-percent accelerated method for the first year is the 150-percent depreciation of $12,000.00 less the straight-line depreciation of $8,000.00 which is equal to $4,000.00. The total recaptured is the 150-percent depreciation ($53,219.20) less the straight-line depreciation ($40,000) or $13,219.20. This total recaptured of $13,219.20 is referred to as excess depreciation.

The amount of recapture or excess depreciation can be reduced depending on the nature of the property over a specific period. The properties that qualify

TABLE 8-1. Recapture of Depreciation for 125-Percent and 150-Percent Declining Balance

Year	Method Straight-Line	125%	150%	Recapture 125%	150%
1	$ 8,000.00	$10,000.00	$12,000.00	$2,000.00	$ 4,000.00
2	8,000.00	9,500.00	11,280.00	1,500.00	3,280.00
3	8,000.00	9,025.00	10,603.20	1,025.00	2,603.20
4	8,000.00	8,573.75	9,967.01	573.75	1,967.01
5	8,000.00	8,145.06	9,368.99	145.06	1,368.99
Total Depreciation	$40,000.00	$45,243.81	$53,219.20	$5,243.81	$13,219.20

TABLE 8-2. Recapture of Depreciation for 200-Percent and Sum-of-the-Years' Digits

Year	Method Straight-Line	200%	Sum-of-the-Years' Digits	Recapture 200%	Sum-of-the-Years' Digits
1	$ 8,000.00	$16,000.00	$15,384.62	$ 8,000.00	$ 7,384.62
2	8,000.00	14,720.00	14,769.23	6,720.00	6,769.23
3	8,000.00	13,543.40	14,153.85	5,542.40	6,153.85
4	8,000.00	12,459.01	13,538.46	4,459.01	5,538.46
5	8,000.00	11,462.29	12,923.08	3,462.29	4,923.08
Total Depreciation	$40,000.00	$68,183.70	$70,769.24	$28,183.70	$30,769.24

are government-assisted projects constructed before 1975. For government-assisted projects constructed before 1975 the investor pays 100 percent of the recapture less 1 percent for each full month after twenty months. There is no re-capture after ten years. For post-1975 government-assisted rental housing the investor pays 100-percent recapture for the first 100 months with a 1-percent reduction each month of recapture over the next 100 months. All other properties must pay 100 percent of the recapture of excess depreciation regardless of the holding period.

Using Example 8-4 and Table 8-1 assume that the new residential apartment is a pre-1975 government-assisted project. The investor has used 150-percent declining balance as the depreciation method with a total depreciation after five years of $53,219.20. The amount of excess depreciation is $13,219.20. This investor qualifies for a reduction in the recapture equal to 40 percent (1 percent for each month after twenty, which is forty months). The new amount of excess depreciation is $7,931.52 ($13,219.20 - $5,287.68). Since excess depreciation is subject to ordinary tax rates this means that an additional $5,287.68 has been switched to capital gains. Once the excess depreciation has been calculated the next step is capital gains.

CAPITAL GAINS AND LOSSES

The gains and losses resulting from a sale of property will be treated either as capital gains and losses or as ordinary gains and losses. It is important to know in which category the sale belongs because long-term capital gains have lower tax liability, and losses can be taken from ordinary income. All real estate investment properties are capital assets. However, dealers in real estate holding property primarily for sales to customers cannot treat the property as a capital asset. Real estate held in the course of a business is also treated differently. Our primary attention will be on real estate assets held for investment.

Capital Gains of Investors

Capital assets are treated as long-term gains when the holding period exceeds one year. When the holding period is one year or less the gain is deemed short-term and taxed at the ordinary rates. The investor who has both long-term gains and losses must compute the net long-term gain. A loss is treated differently, as discussed below. If the investor has short-term gains and losses he or she must compute the net short-term gain. A net short-term gain is counted as ordinary income. A net short-term loss must be offset against a long-term gain. Only the excess net long-term gain is subject to the capital gain tax.

Assume that an investor has the following capital gains and losses for a given year:

Long-term capital gain	$20,000	
Long-term capital loss	−10,000	
Net long-term capital gain		$10,000
Short-term capital loss	$ 5,000	
Short-term capital gain	−2,000	
Net short-term capital loss		−3,000
Excess of net long-term capital gain over net short-term capital loss		$ 7,000

Capital Gains Tax

Only 40 percent of the net long-term capital gain over net short-term capital losses is subject to the ordinary income tax. In the above example the taxable gain for the noncorporate taxpayer would be:

Excess of net long-term capital gain over net short-term capital loss	$7,000
Taxable percentage	×40%
Taxable gain	$2,800

Capital Losses

Capital losses are deductible in a very limited way. As shown above all losses may be deducted from all gains. If the total losses exceed the total gain the excess may be deducted from ordinary income up to $3,000. Short-term capital loss leads to a $1,000 reduction in ordinary income. Net long-term losses may be deducted from ordinary income at a 50-percent rate; that is to say, a $1,000 long-term loss leads to a $500 reduction in ordinary income. In all cases, the total deduction is limited to $3,000.

Section 1231 Property

Most real estate investments are classified not as investment property, within the tax code's definition (see Chapter 1) but for use in a trade or business. Trade or business property is known as Section 1231 assets. Investment and trade or business properties are treated, for the most part, in a similar manner for tax purposes on the sale. The key difference is that the net gain from all sales of Section 1231 property is taxed as a long-term capital gain (if the holding period is for more than one year), and a net loss from such sales is fully deductible against other income without the limitations on the deductibility of losses on "investment" property.

THE MINIMUM TAX

The minimum tax was designed to force everyone to pay some tax. What the minimum tax actually does is to impose a 15-percent tax on tax-preference items and an alternative minimum tax on capital gains. There are only two tax-preference items relevant for real estate: (1) the accelerated depreciation on real estate property in excess of straight-line depreciation, and (2) the untaxed portion of an investor's long-term capital gains.

The minimum tax on excess depreciation is calculated for each year the property is held. The sale of the property does not directly effect the minimum excess depreciation tax; that is, there is no excess depreciation minimum tax resulting from the sale. The minimum tax on all tax-preference items other than capital gains is only for the amount of the tax preference during the year of the sale, not the sum of tax preferences for all the years the property was held. To calculate the minimum tax on capital gains it is necessary to know the minimum tax on excess depreciation (and all other tax-preference items) for the year of the sale.

The Minimum Tax on Excess Depreciation

Before any tax is applied, the excess depreciation is offset by a $10,000 exemption or one-half of the regular tax, whichever is greater. If any excess depreciation remains after the exemptions it is subject to a 15-percent tax. Assume an investor has other property that resulted in an excess depreciation of $100,000 during the year of the sale, and has a regular tax of $60,000. The tax would be calculated as follows:

Excess depreciation	$100,000
Less exemptions (the greater of statutory exclusion	
[$10,000] or one-half the regular tax [$30,000])	30,000
Taxable excess depreciation	$ 70,000
Tax rate	×15%
Minimum tax	$ 10,500

The Minimum Tax on Capital Gains

A new alternative minimum tax on capital gains was adopted in 1978. This new tax is on 60 percent of the capital gains and is paid only if it exceeds the investor's regular tax plus the regular minimum tax. The tax base for the new alternative minimum tax is the investor's taxable income plus the capital gain and excess itemized-deduction tax preferences less $20,000. The itemized tax preference is equal to the amount of qualified itemized deductions that exceed 60 percent of adjusted gross income. The amount of tax is calculated as follows:

Tax base subject to alternative minimum tax	Tax Rate (%)
0 to $40,000	10
$40,001 to $80,000	20
$80,001 and over	25

Assume an investor has sold a property that had in the year of the sale an excess depreciation of $10,000 with a minimum tax of zero and a recaptured depreciation of $100,000 with a tax of $60,250. The investor has a regular tax of $19,768 with a taxable income of $60,000 and no other tax-preference items except a net long-term capital gain of $1,000,000. The tax preference on the capital gain is 60 percent of $1,000,000 or $600,000. The investor has $10,000 excess itemized-deduction preference. The minimum capital gain tax is computed as follows:

Alternative minimum tax base:	
Regular taxable income	$ 560,000
Capital gain tax preference	600,000
Excess itemized deduction tax preference	10,000
Less exclusion	(20,000)
Total	$1,150,000

A. Alternative minimum tax:		
First $40,000 at 10%	$	4,000
Second $40,000 at 20%		8,000
Balance of $630,000 at 25%	$	267,500
Total	$	279,500
B. Regular tax liability (1979):		
Regular tax	$	358,724
Regular minimum tax		—
Total	$	358,724

If A is greater than B, the investor pays the difference between A and B. In this example B is greater, therefore the investor pays the regular tax of $358,724. The computation of the regular tax liability will be explained in Example 8-5.

In analyzing the alternative minimum tax it is clear that it changes the thrust of the minimum tax on capital gains. It is apparent that, since the first $80,000 is taxed at less than a 25-percent tax rate, it will take a very large amount of capital gains to approach an effective rate of 25 percent. Since the highest regular tax rate on capital gains is 28 percent it means that the alternative minimum tax rate will generally be lower and thus not applied to the typical investor.

THE TAXES ON SALE:
A SUMMARY

There are three basic taxes involved in the sale of investment real estate: (1) capital gains, (2) excess depreciation, and (3) minimum tax on capital gains. The previous sections discussed each tax separately. In this section an example will be given including all three taxes. The tax rate varies as the income increases; as an investor is moved up the income scale the tax rate increase must be taken into account. In the following example there is a different tax rate for the earned income, the income from capital gains, and the income from excess depreciation. In this example the tax rate is based on filing a married joint return (Table 7-15). Of course a negative sum amounts to zero tax due.

EXAMPLE 8-5

Facts

Taxable earned income: $60,000
Tax rate on earned income: 32.8%
Tax on earned income: $19,678
Excess depreciation from sale of real estate: $100,000
Net long-term capital gains: $1,000,000
Excess itemized deductions: $10,000
Excess depreciation on real estate not sold: $50,000

Now we can compute the tax on excess depreciation from the sale:

Excess depreciation	$ 100,000
Excess depreciation tax rate	X 60.25%
Tax on excess depreciation	$ 60,250

The tax rate of 60.25 percent is the effective marginal rate for the excess depreciation income level and is computed as follows on the $100,000 excess depreciation:

The first $25,000 at 54%	$ 13,824
$25,001 to $49,400 at 59%	14,042
$49,401 to $100,000 at 64%	32,384
Total excess depreciation tax	$ 60,250

The tax on capital gain is computed as follows:

Net long-term capital gain	$1,000,000
Taxable percentage	X 40%
Taxable gain	$ 400,000
Tax rate	X 68.7%
Tax on capital gain	$ 278,796

The tax rate of 68.7 percent is the effective marginal rate for the capital gains income level and is computed as follows on the $400,000 capital gain:

The first $2,400 at 64%	$ 1,536
$2,401.00 to $54,000 at 68%	36,048
$54,001.00 to $400,000 at 70%	241,220
Total capital gains tax	$ 278,796

Next we compute minimum tax on other preference items:

Excess depreciation	$ 50,000
Less one-half the regular tax on:	
Earned income ($19,678 × .50)	(9,839)
Excess depreciation ($60,250 × .50)	(30,125)
Capital gain ($278,796 × .50)	(139,388)
	$ (179,352)

Now applying the regular minimum tax of 15 percent we compute minimum tax on capital gains:

A. Normal tax liability	
Regular minimum tax	0
Plus	
Regular tax	358,724
Total normal tax	$ 358,724

B. Alternative minimum tax

Taxable income	$ 560,000
Capital gains preference plus	
excess itemized deductions	610,000
Statutory exclusion	(20,000)
Alternative minimum tax base	$1,150,000
First $40,000 at 10%	$ 4,000
Second $40,000 at 20%	8,000
Balance ($1,070,000) at 25%	267,500
Alternative minimum tax:	$ 295,500

When the normal tax liability is greater than the alternative minimum tax, the alternative minimum tax does not apply. When the alternative minimum tax is greater, the investor pays the difference between the alternative minimum tax and the normal tax as the minimum tax on capital gains.

The sum of the taxes due on this sale is as follows:

Tax on excess depreciation	$ 60,250
Tax on capital gain	278,796
Total tax on sale	$339,046

BEFORE-TAX EQUITY REVERSION

Remember that our goal is to calculate after-tax equity reversion. In other words, we want to find how much money the investor made on the sale of the property after taxes. To do this the investor must step backwards to the computation of the amount realized. In Example 8-2 an investor sells an apartment building and receives a sale price of $100,000. The expenses are $8,000 for the sales commission, $1,000 for legal fees and $100 for a recording fee. The amount realized is the sale price less the expenses, or $90,900.

Assume the above investor had an unpaid mortgage on the apartment building of $50,000. To calculate the before-tax equity reversion (BTER) all that is necessary is to subtract the unpaid mortgage from the amount realized. In the above example the amount realized was $90,900 and the unpaid mortgage balance of $50,000. The BTER would be $90,900 less $50,000 which is $40,900. In summary, BTER is:

Amount realized on sale	$90,900
Less unpaid mortgage balance	−50,000
Before-tax equity reversion	$40,900

The amount realized, not the before-tax equity reversion, is used to calculate the taxes on a reversion. This means that the investor pays taxes on the unpaid mortgage balance of a sold property. Under the current tax laws the return is usually greater with leverage—that is, with a substantial mortgage. The tax benefits during the period of ownership outweigh the increase in taxes when the property is sold. In some cases it may not be wise to refinance a real estate investment. Refinancing increases the unpaid mortgage which will increase taxes on the reversion. Thus, selling a building soon after refinancing may lead to a reduction in the overall rate of return.

AFTER-TAX EQUITY REVERSION

The after-tax equity reversion is simply the before-tax equity reversion less taxes. Assume an investor has an after-tax equity reversion of $100,000 with taxes of $90,000. The after-tax equity reversion is:

Before-tax equity reversion	$100,000
Taxes	−90,000
After-tax equity reversion	$ 10,000

The after-tax equity reversion is then used to compute an overall rate of return for the investment.

AN OUTLINE OF THE PROCEDURES TO CALCULATE CASH FLOW FROM A SALE

Sale Price
 minus Sale Expenses
 _____
Amount Realized (Net Sale Price)

 Amount Realized
  minus Adjusted Basis
  _____
 Total Gain or Loss
  minus Excess Depreciation
  _____
 Capital Gain or Loss

 Tax on Capital Gain
  plus
 Tax on Excess Depreciation
  plus
 Minimum Tax
  _____
 Total Taxes

Amount Realized
  minus Unpaid Mortgage Balance
  _____
Before-Tax Equity Reversion
  minus Total Taxes

  _____
After-Tax Equity Reversion

AN EXAMPLE OF THE CALCULATION OF THE AFTER-TAX EQUITY REVERSION

Assume an investor has taxable income of $50,000 (other than property sold) at an average tax rate of 28.96 percent. The tax is $14,778. The facts from the sale of the real estate are as follows:

Excess depreciation (recaptured): $20,000
Net long-term capital gain: $98,000
Adjusted basis: $20,000
Unpaid mortgage balance: $30,000
Excess depreciation during the year
  of the sale on other real estate
  (other preference items): $10,000

Step 1. Calculation of the amount realized:

Sale price	$150,000
Less: sale expenses	(12,000)
Amount realized	$138,000

Step 2. Calculation of total gain or loss:

Amount realized	$138,000
Less: adjusted basis	(20,000)
Total gain	$118,000

Step 3: Calculation of Capital gain:

Total gain	$118,000
Less excess depreciation recapture	(20,000)
Capital gain	$ 98,000

Step 4. Calculation of the tax on Capital gain:

Capital gain	$ 98,000
Taxable percentage	×40%
Taxable gain	$ 39,200
Marginal tax rate	×53.18%
Tax on capital gain	$ 20,848

The effective marginal tax rate on $39,200 capital gain is calculated as follows:

The first $10,000 at 49%	$ 4,900
$10,001 to $35,600 at 54%	13,824
$35,601 to $39,200 at 59%	2,124
Total tax on capital gain	$ 20,848

Step 5. Calculation of tax on excess depreciation:

Excess depreciation	$ 20,000
Marginal tax rate	×59%
Tax on excess depreciation	$ 11,800

Step 6. Calculation of minimum tax on other preference items:

Excess depreciation	$ 10,000
Less: one-half regular tax on	
Regular income ($14,778 × .50)	(7,389)
Excess depreciation ($11,800 × .50)	(5,900)
Capital gains ($20,848 × .50)	(10,424)
	(23,713)

A negative taxable excess depreciation is considered to be zero. Therefore the minimum tax on excess depreciation is also zero.

Step 7. Minimum tax on capital gains:

Alternative A:	
Normal tax liability	
Other tax preference items	$ 10,000
Less one-half regular tax	(23,713)
Regular minimum tax rate	×15%
	—
Regular tax	47,426
Total ordinary tax liability	$ 47,426

Alternative B:	
Alternative minimum tax	
Taxable income	$109,200
Capital gains preference	
Excess itemized deduction	58,800
Less statutory exclusion	(20,000)
Alternative minimum tax base	$148,000
Alternative minimum tax	
First $40,000 at 10%	$ 4,000
Second $40,000 at 20%	8,000
Balance $109,200 at 25%	17,000
	$ 29,000

If B is greater than A, the minimum tax is the difference between A and B. In this case B is less than A; therefore the minimum tax is zero.

Step 8. Calculation of the before-tax equity reversion:

Amount realized	$138,000
Less unpaid mortgage balance	(30,000)
Before-tax equity reversion	$108,000

Step 9. Calculation of the after-tax equity reversion:

Before-tax equity reversion	$108,000
Less: Capital gains tax	(20,848)
Tax on excess depreciation	(11,800)
Minimum taxes	—
After-tax equity reversion	$ 75,352

THE USE OF OPTIONS

An option on a property gives the buyer the right to purchase the property within a specified time period. If the buyer does not exercise the option, the seller receives compensation for having taken the property off the market during the option period. The purchase of the property occurs only if the option is exercised. The initial payment by the buyer for the option is not a taxable event. If the option is exercised the seller treats the proceeds from the option as part of the sale price. The amount paid by the buyer is added to his or her basis.

    As noted, the option itself does not generate a taxable event until it is exercised. It is, therefore, very important that the investor does not write an option that appears to be a sale. The agreement should clearly express the fact that it is an option. The evidence that is most often used to prove that it is not a sale is the length and price. The price of the option to the buyer should not even be close to the market price of the property. In fact, the option price should be lower than a reasonable down payment. The title should remain in the seller's name.

The property specified in the option determines the type of loss or gain. For real estate, the gain or losses resulting from an option are considered capital gain and losses and are taxed accordingly. The holding period of the option determines whether it is a short- or long-term gain or loss. If the holding period is less than one year it is a short-term gain or loss.

If the holder of the option takes ownership of the property, it increases the original basis of the property. The seller will then add it to the selling price. If the holder of the option fails to exercise it, the option is deemed to have been sold to the seller of the property. The buyer will then have a short- or long-term gain or loss, depending on the holding period of the option. The seller will have an increase in ordinary income equal to the value of the option.

VOLUNTARY AND INVOLUNTARY DISPOSITIONS

The tax rules vary with the type of disposition. The preceding sections have concentrated on disposition by voluntary sale. Other forms of disposition include abandonments, casualties, and easements. The tax rules vary with each type of disposition.

Casualty Losses

Casualty losses are generally deductible in the year they occur but for never more than the adjusted basis less any insurance coverage. The damage must be a sudden, unexpected event which damages or destroys the investor's property. The proof that damages occurred rests on the investor. The investor should take photographs and record all repair bills. In some cases an independent appraisal is useful in proving damages.

The rules for deducting casualty losses are different for business and nonbusiness properties. Business properties include all real estate held for income, trade, or business. Nonbusiness properties include all other types of property. The loss for business properties must be caused by an external force to be allowed as a current deduction. If the property is totally destroyed the deduction is equal to the adjusted basis less any insurance or salvage. If the property is partially destroyed the deduction is equal to the lesser of (1) the loss by destruction or (2) the adjusted basis of the assets.

Abandonments

In some situations obsolescence will increase to the point where it pays to abandon the property. An investor who sees that the real estate property is becoming obsolete at a faster rate than the depreciation rate has the option to increase the rate of depreciation. This increase in the rate of depreciation will provide additional deductions representing the loss due to obsolescence.

When the property is abandoned the deduction covers both the land and the improvement. A gradual reduction in the value of the property does not qualify the property for abandonment. The courts have required that (1) the property value be zero, and (2) that a particular event have caused this destruction of value. The courts accept many types of evidence for the worthlessness of property, for example: (1) operating expenses exceed income, (2) attempts to sell result in no offers, (3) no real estate taxes paid, and (4) any other evidence concerning the value of the property. The loss allowed will be limited to the adjusted basis of the property. Most business losses are deductible from ordinary income.

Voluntary Disposition

Whether or not a voluntary disposition qualifies for a tax deduction depends on the intent of the buyer. If at the time of purchase the investor intended on demolishing the building, no deduction will be allowed. The basis of the building and the cost or benefit of demolition must be added to the cost of the land. If the owner had no intention of demolishing the building the loss is deductible up to the basis of the building less any profit or plus any loss from the demolition of the building. The IRS sometimes disputes the intention of the buyer at the time of purchase. This occurs when the length of time between purchase and demolition is short. Evidence of no intention to demolish would be a city regulation affecting the value, poor information on the income-earning potential of the building, expenditure to improve the building, and loss of value due to damage after purchase.

Easements

Easements are an interest in a specific real estate property for special purposes. The effect on the owner is the single most important criterion for determining the tax outcome. If the easement is not beneficial to the owner it is treated as a sale of land; otherwise if the owner retains use of the land it is considered a sale of easement. For tax purposes, the sale of land is recognized as a gain whereas the sale of an easement reduces the basis of the land.

The next chapter will consider the tax advantages of deferred-payment sales and exchanges.

9

Deferred-Payment
Sales and Exchanges

INTRODUCTION

The sale of real estate may lead to substantial gain. Taxes have to be paid on that gain independent of the cash received for the property. An investor may pay out more in taxes than he or she receives in income. For example, an investor receives $1,000,000 for a real estate property and must pay $200,000 capital gains tax. The investor accepted a $100,000 down payment with future yearly payments. The taxes the investor must pay are larger than the cash received. The solution to this problem is deferred payment sales. This allows the investor the privilege of reporting gains and paying the tax over a period of years rather than paying the entire tax in the year of the sale. There are specific rules that allow investors to spread their tax payments.

INSTALLMENT SALES

It is advisable to spread the taxes over a number of years. First, it postpones the taxes. Second, with the U.S. graduated income tax a large gain in one year may lead to higher taxes. The spread of the taxes may also reduce the amount subject to minimum tax because of the $10,000 minimum tax exemption. Third, spreading the taxes may reduce the impact of tax preferences in the calculation of maximum tax on earned income. Installment sales allow for the possibility of the capital gains earning a reasonable interest. Also, the deferral of capital gains over a number of years allows the investor to generate capital losses to offset the capital gains.

To qualify for installment sales, the sale price must be payable over two or more years and the payment in the year of the sale must not exceed 30 percent of the selling price. The investor must make a declaration on his or her tax forms the year the installment sale is adopted. The tax returns should describe the sale, the sale price, the basis, and the total gain from the sale.

The 30-Percent
Down Payment Rule

The installment method of sale is not available unless payment, if any, in the year of the sale does not exceed 30 percent of the selling price. The sale price is the total amount the purchaser paid for the property. The unpaid mortgage is considered part of the sale price. The selling price cannot be reduced by selling expenses and commission charges.

The 30-percent down payment includes any property as a payment to the extent of its market value. The indebtedness of the buyer is excluded as part of the payment. Any other forms of payment that are payable on demand such as bonds or stocks are considered part of the initial payment. Any tangibles or intangibles that are exchanged or any debt of the seller that is reduced are all included in the initial payment. There are some important exceptions. They include (1) mortgage, (2) purchaser debt, (3) money in escrow, and (4) seller liabilities. The amount of mortgage on the property is not included in the initial payment. This means that the seller can increase his or her cash by mortgaging the property before the sale.

There is one serious problem with cashing out the mortgage before an installment sale. The extent to which the mortgage exceeds the basis of the property is counted as part of the initial payment. Thus, if the mortgage exceeds the seller basis by an amount greater than 30 percent of the selling price, the installment sale procedure is not possible. This means that the buyer cannot assume or take title to the property subject to the mortgage. A technique referred to as a wraparound mortgage is used to get around this problem. The seller takes a new mortgage from the buyer and continues to hold the old mortgage on the property. The buyer then makes payment to the seller and the seller makes payments on the old mortgage.

The purchaser's notes, whether secured or not, are not included in computing the initial payment. If the note is made payable on demand it will then be considered a part of the initial payment.

The reasons for an escrow should be clearly stated. The reasons should be based on business such as compliance with the seller's covenants or to clear title. The earnings on the funds in the escrow account should be given to the purchaser. If the reasons for the escrow are for business, the funds in escrow will not count towards the seller's initial payment. There have been cases where the buyer wanted to pay cash but the seller refused. They agreed instead to let the buyer place the money in escrow and have the escrow account make installment payments to the seller. The Internal Revenue Service has disallowed this use of escrow deposits.

The fact that a buyer liquidates a portion of the mortgage after the date of sale but within the same year is not counted as part of the initial payment. This same rule applies to any of the seller's unsecured debts that are assumed by the buyer. They are not counted toward the initial payment.

Many investors have lost their right to installment payments by forgetting that the installment payments along with the down payment during the initial year are included as part of the initial payment in the 30-percent rule. Another problem occurs even when the seller carefully plans the initial payment to be below 30 percent and then the buyer decides to make additional payments or to pay off the loan ahead of time. The sellers must protect themselves from unplanned early prepayments. These early payments, which are not part of the contract are counted by the IRS as part of the initial 30 percent of payment. Also sellers cannot protect themselves by refusing to accept the payment. It still counts, even if the seller refuses it. The seller can protect the installment sale by specifying in the contract that there is no prepayment in the year of sale.

The Taxable Gain of Installment Sales

The procedures used to compute taxable gain on installment sales are similar to those used to compute taxable gain on regular sales. The first step is to establish the sale price. The sale price less the expenses of the sale will give the amount realized. The amount realized less the adjusted basis provides the total gain on the sale. As a separate computation, the unpaid mortgage debt subtracted from the sale price gives the contract price. If the existing mortgage is greater than the seller's basis of the property, the excess is included in the contract price regardless of whether the mortgage is assumed by the purchaser. The contract price is generally the actual proceeds or amount received by the seller. It is in many cases the seller's equity in the property. The ratio of gain to contract price gives the percentage of initial payment taxable.

EXAMPLE 9-1

A purchaser buys a building for $100,000 subject to a mortgage of $5,000 with a $10,000 equity payment and a $90,000 mortgage with 10 percent interest for twenty years. The sale expenses are $2,000. The seller's basis is $20,000. The taxable gain is calculated in four steps.

Step 1. Calculation of total gain:

Sale price	$100,000
Less sale expenses	(2,000)
Amount realized	$ 98,000
Less adjusted basis	(20,000)
Total gain	$ 78,000

Step 2. Calculation of contract price:

Sale price	$100,000
Less mortgage debt	(5,000)
Contract price	$ 95,000

The ratio of the gain to the contract price is equal to 82 percent ($78,000 ÷ $95,000).

Step 3. Calculation of payments received during the year of the sale:

Down payment	$10,000
Installment payments	—
Total payments	$10,000

Step 4. Calculation of gain taxable in the year of the sale:

Total payment	$10,000
Gain-to-price ratio	×82%
Taxable gain	$ 8,200

The percentage of installment payments in the year of the sale to the selling price is 10 percent ($10,000 ÷ $100,000). This is within the 30-percent restriction.

The Selling of Installment Obligations

The sale of an installment obligation will result in a gain or loss. The gain or loss is calculated as the difference between the amount realized on the sale of the installment obligations and the basis of the obligation which is the face value of the obligation. The entire gain will be taxed in the year of the sale. The sale of an installment obligation doesn't affect the 30-percent qualification requirement for installment sales. The seller can dispose of all or part of the obligation in the year of the sale. None of the proceeds from such disposition is included in the calculation of the initial payment. This allows the seller to increase by a substantial proportion the cash derived from the sale in the same year without an increase in taxes.

EXAMPLE 9-2

An individual sells a building for $50,000 with a $10,000 down payment and a $40,000 installment note at 15-percent interest with a two-year term. The basis of the property was $5,000. In the same year the individual sold the installment obligation for $35,000. The gain for the year is calculated as follows:

Sale Price	$50,000
Less the basis	(5,000)
Total gain	$45,000

The contract price is $50,000, the same as the sale price, since there is no mortgage. The ratio of the gain to the contract price is 90 percent. The payments for the first year were $10,000. Therefore the taxable gain is $9,000. The gain on the notes is the sale price ($35,000) less the basis of the notes ($3,500), which is $32,500. The total cash received is $42,500 but the $32,500 does not disqualify the sale from the installment method under the 30-percent rule.

A seller may pledge the installment notes as collateral to borrow money. As long as the pledges are to a third party it will not change the status of the deferred installment gain. Care must be taken to ensure that the pledge is for collateral on a personal loan. If the IRS decides that the installment payments have been sold, the seller may be subject to taxes on the gains.

Installment Sales and Repossession

As a general rule the seller does not have any gain or loss on a repossession that is recognized by the IRS. There is no claim allowed even for bad debt. However, there is an exception to the rule. If the seller receives some payments prior to repossession and these payments exceed the amount of gain reported by the seller, then a tax occurs at the time of repossession. Fortunately there is a limitation to the amount of tax. In no case is the gain from payments received before repossession to exceed the gain attributable to the sale less the sum of the amounts already reported by income and the amount of money paid by the seller to repossess the property.

EXAMPLE 9-3

An investor sells a real estate property for $80,000 with a basis of $40,000. The purchaser pays $20,000 down and agrees to pay $12,000 a year for five years plus 10 percent on the unpaid balance. The investor elects installment reporting. After the first three $12,000 payments the purchaser defaults and the seller repossesses the property. This repossession costs the seller $10,000. The seller has received a total payment of $56,000 and has reported a gain of $14,000. The seller has a potential gain upon repossession of $42,000. The limitations restrict the taxable gain to $16,000. This is calculated as follows:

Sale price	$80,000
Less: Basis of property	(40,000)
Previous gain	(14,000)
Repossession cost	(10,000)
Limitation on gain	$16,000

In Example 9-3 the seller must readjust the basis so that the gain not reported is recognized on the future sale of the property. The repossessed property must take the basis on the purchase money obligation. This basis is then increased by the previously reported gain and by any cost of repossession. In Example 9-3 the seller has a basis in the purchaser obligation of $25,500 ($34,000 unpaid balance multiplied by 75, the percentage borrowed). This is increased by the $14,000 gain upon repossession and by the $10,000 cost of reacquiring the property. This new basis is $48,000.

Other Deferred Payment Sales

In many cases the seller cannot meet the requirement of installment sales. For example, the initial payment may be more than 30 percent of the sale price. The taxes on such a sale depend on whether the sale is considered an open or closed transaction.

An open transaction means that the buyer's promise to pay has no market value. The seller is then allowed to report the gain on a cost recovery method. The seller is allowed to first recover the basis of the property before any tax may be collected. Also, once the basis is paid, all other payments and gains qualify for capital gain treatment.

The closed transaction occurs when the debt of the purchaser has a fair market value. In this case a taxable event has occurred in the year of the sale. The seller, if selling a capital asset, pays at the capital gains rate for any amount received above the basis of the property. The calculation of the amount received includes all payments plus the debt obligation from the buyer. The seller has a basis for the buyer's obligation equal to its fair market value in the year of the sale. Each future payment is prorated between the return of basis and taxable gain. These taxable gains must be reported as ordinary income since the repayment of the obligation does not qualify as a sale or exchange.

In general it is to the advantage of the seller to establish an open transaction. This is usually very difficult to do, as the IRS has stated that only in rare cases will there be no fair market value. However, if the sale price is uncertain then the buyer's promise to pay has no market value. An open transaction can be accomplished by stating that the sale price is based on the future income produced by the property.

IMPUTED INTEREST ON SELLING PRICE

A strategy for reducing ordinary income into capital gain is to increase the sale price and reduce the interest rate. For example an investor sells a building for $150,000 and receives a $30,000 down payment with a note for annual installments of $10,000 with an interest on the unpaid balance of 10 percent. The investor has decided to use the installment method to report the capital gains. The income from the interest over the twelve-year period would amount to $78,000. If the interest had been 5 percent, the income generated would be $39,000 which is $39,000 lower. The seller could increase the sales price by $39,000, thus converting ordinary income gain into capital gain.

The IRS has decided that this procedure must be changed. Therefore, under present law all contracts with payments due after the year of the sale must charge an imputed 7-percent interest rate when no interest charge is stated in the terms or when the interest rate is less than 6 percent. If the interest rate is less than 6 percent the following steps must be taken:

1. The actual interest agreed to by the buyer and seller is used to compute the interest income payable to the buyer. In some cases the total interest cost is agreed to in terms of a fixed dollar amount. Implicit in this fixed cost is an imputed interest rate.

2. A 6-percent rate is then applied to the agreement. A total interest cost is calculated using the 6-percent rate. This cost or income to the seller is compared to the agreed interest cost (Step 1). If the 6-percent interest cost is greater than the imputed cost in Step 1, the seller must apply a 7-percent interest to the agreement.

EXAMPLE 9-4

Assume an investor sells a property for $50,000 payable in five $10,000 annual installments. The agreement stated an interest payment for the sale of $1,000. At 6-percent interest on the unpaid balance the agreement would produce an interest cost of $3,000. As the $1,000 is less than this 6-percent amount, therefore a 7-percent interest must be applied to the loan. This would result in an interest cost of $3,500. The seller would then increase the interest charge from $1,000 to $3,500. This would increase the income of the seller subject to ordinary income tax and reduce the seller's capital gains by $2,500. The increased interest charge is allocated by five $700 payments over the life of the loan.

This procedure reduces the sale price and increases the interest payments. It is important that the decrease in the sale price does not result in a violation of the 30-percent rule for installment payments.

EXAMPLE 9-5

Assume an investor sells a real estate property for $60,000, receiving an equity payment of $18,000 and a promised balloon payment at the end of five years of $42,000. The investor's basis is $30,000. The percentage of payment in the year of sale is 30 percent, calculated by dividing the payment received in the year of the sale ($18,000) by the seller's price ($60,000).

The 30-percent payment is within the 30-percent rule; therefore the sale qualifies for the installment method. The IRS states that the agreement has an imputed interest rate of $5,000. This reduces the sale price to $55,000 and the percentage of payment increases to 32.7 percent. This disqualifies the sale for installment payments and the seller must pay taxes on the full gain of $25,000.

TAX-FREE EXCHANGES

An investor holding property for investment has the right of deferring the possible taxes on a sale by exchanging it for another real estate property of a like kind. An owner of an apartment building can exchange it for a different apartment building without paying taxes. For example an investor buys a building for $300,000. The building appreciates to $1,000,000. If the investor sells the building the potential taxable gain is very large, probably $500,000 to $550,000, depending on the sale cost and depreciation. The investor can defer the tax payments by exchanging the building for one of like kind. If the investor finds a $1,000,000 building for exchange he or she will pay no taxes. This holds true for farms, apartment buildings, and most other real estate properties.

The rules governing exchange are not voluntary—if the exchange qualifies, the procedure must be applied to the investor's property. The first step is to determine how a property of like kind is defined.

The IRS is very liberal in defining the term "like kind." They state that like kind refers to the character or nature of the property and not to the quality or grade. This statement that grade and quality is unimportant means that improved and unimproved land are the same kind of property. Therefore, an investor can exchange farmland for an apartment building, or a leasehold for fee simple, or improved land for unimproved land with no gain or loss recognized by the IRS. If ten investors own ten different real estate properties of like kind such as five apartment buildings and five vacant lots, they can combine the properties to form one parcel of land for investment and no gain or loss will be recognized. The property must not only be of like kind, it also must not be combined with property held primarily for sale.

The Basis of Tax-Free Exchange

The property acquired through tax-free exchange must adopt the old basis of the transferred property. If one investor trades an apartment worth $100,000 with a basis of $10,000 for a vacant lot worth $100,000 with a basis of $50,000, the new basis for the land will be $10,000 and for the apartment, $50,000. The holding period for the apartment owner and the landowner is the sum of the two holding periods. The holding period does not have to be extended. In summary, the basis of the property received is equal to the basis of the property transferred.

If an investor trades an apartment building for two separate properties the old basis is allocated between them proportionately. The basis is calculated as follows:

Value of the apartment building	$100,000
Basis of the apartment building	$ 20,000
Value of Property A	$ 40,000
Value of Property B	$ 60,000
Basis of Property A for the new owner ($20,000 × .40)	$ 8,000
Basis of Property B for the new owner ($20,000 × .60)	$ 12,000

The Boot

The value of the properties exchanged is often not exactly equal. One of the investors most likely will have to provide some extra cash or property to make the exchange equal. This extra payment is called a boot. If this boot is of property of like kind it will not affect the tax treatment of the exchange. If the boot is cash or property not of like kind it will affect the taxes of the exchange. The tax effect of the exchange is recognized when the boot is received. There is no recognized gain or loss to the giver when the boot is paid in cash. If the boot is paid by property of unlike kind there is a recognized gain or loss. There is no recognized loss when receiving a boot. The tax effects vary with the type of transfer. The procedure can be broken down into four steps: (1) calculating the realized gain or loss, (2) determining the amount of gain recognized, (3) deriving the basis of the received asset, and (4) including the impact of the mortgage. A boot that affects the status of the tax treatment converts a part of the exchange into a taxable gain.

EXAMPLE 9-6:
A BOOT PAID IN CASH

An investor exchanges real estate with a basis of $30,000 and a value of $100,000, plus $20,000 cash for a $155,000 building. The gain is calculated as follows:

Value of property received	$155,000
Less: Basis of property transferred	(30,000)
Cash paid (boot)	(30,000)
Total gain	$ 95,000
Total gain recognized	0
Amount of tax on the gain	0

No gain or loss is recognized from a boot when paid in cash. The boot will be recognized when paid in unlike property.

EXAMPLE 9-7:
A BOOT PAID IN UNLIKE PROPERTY

An investor exchanges real estate with a basis of $30,000 and a value of $100,000, plus $20,000 in bonds with a basis of $10,000 for a $155,000 building. The recognized gain is calculated as follows:

Value of property received	$155,000
Less: Basis of property transferred	(30,000)
Basis of bonds	(10,000)
Potential gain realized	$115,000

The taxable gain is calculated as follows:

Value of bonds (boot) paid	$ 20,000
Less the basis of the bonds	(10,000)
Taxable gain	$ 10,000

EXAMPLE 9-8:
A BOOT RECEIVED

An investor exchanges land valued at $30,000 with a basis of $15,000 for land valued at $5,000 plus $25,000 in cash. The investor has received $25,000 as a boot with a total gain of $15,000. The total gain is exceeded by the boot; therefore, the entire gain is taxed and the excess boot ($10,000) is tax free as part of the basis of the former property.

The amount realized on the exchange is calculated as follows:

Value of the land received	$ 5,000
Value of the cash (boot)	25,000
Less the basis	(15,000)
Total gain	$15,000

The taxable amount of the total gain is:

Total gain	$15,000
Cash received (boot)	$25,000
Taxable gain (lesser of the gain or boot)	$15,000

If the value of the land received was $20,000 and the boot $10,000 the taxable gain would be:

Value of the land received	$20,000
Value of the cash (boot)	10,000
Less the basis	(15,000)
Total gain	$15,000

The taxable amount would be:

Total gain	$15,000
Cash received (boot)	$10,000
Taxable gain (lesser of the gain or boot)	$10,000

The boot is taxed if smaller than or equal to the gain. The amount of the boot greater than the gain is not taxed.

If the boot is combined with an exchange loss the investor is not entitled to a deduction. The loss or potential loss is not recognized as a taxable event and cannot be declared. The basis of the new property is equal to the basis of the exchanged property minus the loss.

The Basis with a Boot

The tax basis of the property is necessary to calculate depreciation and any future gain or loss on the exchanged property. As stated above, with no boot, the basis of the received property is equal to the basis of the transferred property plus the cash. If a property of unlike kind is paid, the basis of the received property is equal to the basis of the transferred property plus the market value of the unlike property.

EXAMPLE 9-9:
THE BASIS WITH A BOOT PAID IN CASH

An investor exchanges real estate with a basis of $30,000 and a value of $100,000 plus $20,000 cash for a $155,000 building. To determine the basis of the received property, the first step is to calculate the recognized gain:

Value of property received	$155,000
Less: Basis of property transferred	(30,000)
Cash paid	(30,000)
Recognized gain	$ 95,000

The boot is paid in cash; therefore there is no recognized gain.

The basis of received property is now determined as:

Basis of transferred property	$ 30,000
Cash paid	30,000
Gain recognized	—
Basis of received property	$ 60,000

EXAMPLE 9-10:
THE BASIS WITH A BOOT PAID IN UNLIKE PROPERTY

An investor exchanges real estate with a basis of $30,000 and a value of $100,000 plus $20,000 in bonds with a basis of $10,000 for a $155,000 building. The potential gain is calculated as follows:

Value of property received	$155,000
Less: Basis of transferred property	(30,000)
Basis of bonds	(10,000)
Potential gain realized	$115,000

The next step is to calculate the amount of taxable gain:

Value of the bonds paid	$ 20,000
Less the basis of the bond	(10,000)
Taxable gain	$ 10,000

Now we can determine the basis of the received property:

Basis of the transferred property	$ 30,000
Bond's basis	10,000
Gain recognized	10,000
Basis of the received property	$ 50,000

EXAMPLE 9-11:
THE BASIS WITH A BOOT RECEIVED IN CASH

An investor exchanges land valued at $30,000 with a basis of $15,000 for land valued at $5,000 plus $25,000 in cash. The investor receives a $25,000 boot with a total gain of $15,000. The total gain is exceeded by the boot; therefore the entire gain is taxed and the excess boot ($10,000) is tax free. The basis change is calculated in the following way:

Value of the land	$ 5,000
Value of the boot	25,000
Amount realized on the exchange	
Less the basis of transferred land	(15,000)
Total gain on the exchange	$15,000
Basis of the transferred land	$15,000
Less cash received	(25,000)
Plus the gain taxes on exchange	15,000
Basis of the received land	$ 5,000

EXAMPLE 9-12:
THE BASIS OF THE BOOT RECEIVED IN UNLIKE PROPERTY

An investor exchanges land valued at $30,000 with a basis of $15,000 for land valued at $5,000 plus $25,000 boot in unlike property with a total gain of $15,000. The total gain is exceeded by the boot; therefore, the entire gain is taxed.

Value of the land	$ 5,000
Value of the diamonds (boot)	25,000
Amount realized on the exchange	$30,000
Less the basis of transferred land	(15,000)
Total taxable gain	$15,000
Basis of the transferred land	$15,000
Less the boot received	(25,000)
Plus taxes	15,000
Basis of received land	$ 5,000

In summary, if a boot is received in cash and there is a recognized gain in the exchange, the received property has the basis of the transferred property less the cash boot plus the amount of gain recognized. If the boot is other than cash the basis of the transferred property is decreased by the market value of the boot plus the recognized gain.

THE MORTGAGE AND
THE BOOT

The exchange of property often occurs with both or at least one of the properties having an existing mortgage. When an investor is relieved of debt by an exchange and the new debt is less than the old, the difference is treated as a boot. The difference is often referred to as the net liability or net debt.

EXAMPLE 9-13

Two investors, X and Y, exchange properties with X's property valued at $20,000 and Y's property worth $30,000. The mortgages on X's and Y's properties are $5,000 and $10,000 respectively. The net equities would be $15,000 and $20,000 for X and Y respectively. X has given up a mortgage of $5,000 and Y a mortgage of $10,000. Y is deemed to have received a boot of $5,000. If Y realizes a gain it will be taxable up to $5,000.

In Example 9-13 Y received an excess liability of $5,000 (a boot) which may be taxable. This excess liability can be offset by cash and other like properties paid to X. The reverse is not true; if Y had received cash or other like property it could not be offset by excess liability. This complicated set of rules means that certain forms of tax planning may be possible.

EXAMPLE 9-14

Assume that X and Y agree to exchange real estate with the following mortgages and values:

	X's Property	Y's Property
Value	$100,000	$80,000
Mortgage	80,000	20,000
Net equity	$ 20,000	$60,000

In this exchange X has a boot of $40,000 which is the excess of X's mortgage over Y's ($60,000) less the $20,000 boot X will pay to Y to equalize the exchange. The results are different if Y borrows an additional $20,000 before the exchange. In this case X has a boot of $40,000 which is the excess of X's mortgage over Y's ($40,000). X would have to give Y no cash and Y would have received no boot.

The Basis with a Boot and a Mortgage

As stated above an owner exchanges a property with debt for a property with no debt. This means that the owner is credited with receiving a boot equal to the debt. What happens to the basis of the new property received by the owner? It (the basis) must be reduced by the amount of debt transferred with the owner's previous property.

EXAMPLE 9-15

An investor exchanges a building worth $100,000 with a basis of $10,000 and a mortgage of $20,000 for a property worth $90,000 with a basis of $20,000 and a mortgage debt of $10,000. The investor has received a boot of $10,000 (the difference in mortgage debt). This means that out of the gain of $90,000 only $10,000 is taxable. This is calculated as follows:

Value of building received	$ 90,000
The amount of mortgage reduction	10,000
Amount realized on exchange	$100,000
Less the basis of the transferred building	(10,000)
Amount of gain	$ 90,000
Taxable gain is the lesser of (a) the amount of gain ($90,000 in this case), or (b) the amount of mortgage reduction; in this case it is the latter, amounting to	$ 10,000
The transferred basis	$ 10,000
Less the boot (mortgage reduction)	(10,000)
Plus the gain taxed	$ 10,000
The basis of the received building	$ 10,000

If the investor exchanges a debt-free property for a property with debt this is a giving of boot which does not affect the exchange.

EXAMPLE 9-16

An investor exchanges a building worth $100,000 with a basis of $10,000 and a mortgage of $20,000 for a property worth $90,000 with a basis of $20,000 and a mortgage of $40,000. The investor has given a boot of $30,000. No gain would be taxed to the investor. However, the new debt of $20,000 may be added to the transferred basis.

165

Value of the building received	$90,000
Less the additional mortgage debt	(20,000)
Amount realized on exchange	$70,000
Less transferred basis	(10,000)
Amount of gain	$60,000
Recognized gain	-0-
The transferred basis	$10,000
Additional debt (boot paid)	$20,000
Basis on the building received	$30,000

EXCHANGE AND RECAPTURE
OF DEPRECIATION

Depreciation may be subject to recapture in a tax-free exchange. If the received property has a market value less than the depreciation recapture of the transferred property, the exchange is subject to ordinary income tax. If an apartment building on which the investors had taken accelerated depreciation was exchanged for land, the recaptured depreciation would be taxable at the time of the exchange. The recapture potential of the transferred property that is not recognized upon the exchange is applied to the received property. This recaptured depreciation will be recognized at the time the property is sold.

Tax-free exchange can be used to increase the amount of depreciation. If an investor exchanges property and the received property has a shorter useful life than the original property, this could lead to more depreciation. Another possibility is to change the basis of the property.

EXAMPLE 9-17

An investor has an apartment building valued at $20,000 with a basis of $20,000, with no mortgage. He exchanges it for a property worth $100,000 with a basis of $60,000 and a mortgage of $50,000. The new basis for the investor is the old basis ($20,000) plus the mortgage assumed ($50,000), less the mortgage he gave up (zero, in this case), plus the cash he gave up to equalize the exchange ($30,000). The new basis is $100,000. This new high basis will allow the investor to increase his depreciation deductions in future years.

Exchanges can be useful in many areas of real estate planning. For example, when different investors have different time horizons they may find an exchange to be quite useful. Other possibilities include the offsetting of gains and losses in prior years and in the year of the sale, and various possible tax deferrals and reductions.

THREE-PARTY EXCHANGES

Three-party exchanges occur when an investor wants to purchase a property from a second investor who wants the transaction to be an exchange for tax reasons. The first investor has no property to exchange; therefore, he or she will seek out a third investor and either buy the property from the third investor and exchange it with the first, or have the third investor exchange with the first and then buy from the third. These transactions will qualify as a tax-free exchange provided the regulations are followed.

When a three-party exchange involves the purchase of one of the properties with cash, care must be taken to avoid the loss of the tax-free status. If an investor is under obligation for a sale and instead arranges an exchange, the investor may be considered an agent which would result in a taxable exchange. The critical distinction seems to be whether the investor buys a property to exchange with a second investor using the second investor's money. Three-party exchanges are useful but are difficult to arrange. Care must be taken to avoid being taxed.

V

Applying the After-Tax Investment Process

The purpose of Part 5 is to demonstrate the application of the principles discussed in the preceding chapters. The after-tax investment process is applied to an apartment-investment example. This case has been developed to demonstrate the aspects of decision making on an after-tax basis. While any case analysis represents an abstraction of reality, the underlying principles should aid the investor in making real estate investment decisions.

10

The
Investment Process:
An Apartment-Building
Example

INTRODUCTION

The preceding chapters have discussed the impact of taxation on real estate investments. The purpose of this chapter is to lead the investor through the real estate investment process by illustrating an apartment-building investment. The taxation effects are probably the most complicated. The investor, however, should commit equity to an investment only after careful consideration of the tax consequences. While it is impossible to build an example that will illustrate all the problems faced by an investor, this example provides an illustration of the principles taught in the preceding chapters. The reader is encouraged to work through the numbers to make certain the process is understood.

STEP 1: IDENTIFYING INVESTOR OBJECTIVES

As was pointed out in Figure 1-1, the first step in the investment process is to identify the objectives of the investor.

The Investors

Two investors, Mr. X and Ms. Y, are considering forming a partnership to invest in a new apartment building. The asking price is $225,000. Table 10-1

TABLE 10-1. The Investors

Financial Data	Mr. X	Ms. Y
Other taxable income	$100,000	$40,000
Tax status	Married, filing joint return	Married, filing joint return
Share in equity	65%	35%
Share in profit and loss	65%	35%
Share in reversion	65%	35%

outlines some of the characteristics of the two investors. Both have a substantial amount of wealth in the form of savings. Mr. X currently has other taxable income (OTI) of $100,000, while Ms. Y has $40,000; both investors are married and file joint returns. Table 10-2 shows the income tax rates for 1979 taxable income. Mr. X is going to provide 65 percent of the necessary equity, while Ms. Y is providing 35 percent. The equity is the difference between the total cost and the amount borrowed. They are going to share in the annual cash flow and reversion cash flow at a rate of 65 percent to Mr. X and 35 percent to Ms. Y.

As can be seen in Table 10-2, Mr. X's taxable income of $100,000 puts him in a 59-percent marginal tax bracket. This means that for every additional dollar of increased taxable income he earns, taxes will take 59 cents of that dollar. Likewise, for every additional dollar of decrease, he would have a tax savings of 59 cents. Ms. Y is in a 43-percent marginal tax bracket.

Mr. X and Ms. Y want to earn 12 percent per year on an after-tax basis on the investment over the expected period of ten years. This desired rate of return reflects not only a "real" rate of return but also the risks and inflation, which must be taken into account when investing in the project.

TABLE 10-2. Federal Income Tax Rates, 1979 Income, Married—Filing Joint Return

Taxable Income		Tax	Marginal Rate Applied to Income in Excess of Column (a) Amount
(a) Over	(b) Not Over		
$ 3,400	$ 5,500	$ 0	14%
5,500	7,600	294	16
7,600	11,000	630	18
11,900	16,000	1,404	21
16,000	20,200	2,265	24
20,200	24,600	3,273	28
24,600	29,900	4,505	32
29,900	35,200	6,201	37
35,200	45,800	8,162	43
45,800	60,000	12,720	49
60,000	85,600	19,678	54
85,600	109,400	33,502	59
109,400	162,400	47,544	64
162,400	215,400	81,464	68
215,400	–	117,504+	70

STEP 2: ANALYZING THE INVESTMENT MARKET

The second step in the investment process is a detailed examination of the investment climate and the market conditions influencing the investment. Mr. X and Ms. Y have made a detailed study of the apartment market and have arrived at the conclusion that there is a demand for more housing units.

Market and Legal Analysis

The process of determining the feasibility of an investment requires two basic steps: market study and financial analysis. This section outlines the basic factors to be considered in a market study. Steps 3 and 4 will discuss the financial analysis part of a feasibility study.

To conduct a market study, the investors must analyze supply and demand factors. The market study is used to determine whether or not a particular investment is marketable. A market study for a proposed project is somewhat more detailed than a market study for an existing project.

The basic steps in a market study include:

1. Definition and delineation of the market area for an investment.
2. Analysis of the demand factors. Demand for housing is dependent on number of households, income levels, and other demographic aspects, such as sex, age, and education.
3. Analysis of supply factors. This includes the existing competition in the market area, a survey of projects currently under construction, and an understanding of projects under consideration. This later category is the most difficult to obtain information about. However, real estate lenders, appraisers, brokers, developers, and other real estate professionals can provide this type of information. Vacancy rates for existing competition should be carefully analyzed along with rent levels and operating expenses.
4. The physical and legal aspects of any proposed or existing project must be carefully reviewed. Such factors as the compatibility with existing uses, size, shape, topography, zoning regulations, density requirements, deed restrictions, and others must be analyzed.

The goal of the market study is to provide information for the real estate investor with respect to such items as anticipated rent levels, vacancy rates, and forecasts of future property values. The market study informs the investor about the degree of demand associated with the investment. Typically the market study will result in a range of expected rent levels and other factors. While the investor can estimate a most probable rent or vacancy level, there is always some variation from the most probable estimate. Careful market study should, however, help the investor to minimize this range in these key factors which are the foundation of the financial analysis.

Another key area to be analyzed is the legal environment. Particularly important is the partnership agreement. Example 10-1 gives the partnership agreement between Mr. X and Ms. Y. Their agreement follows the suggested outline of the Uniform Partnership Act discussed in Chapter 4. This agreement outlines the terms of the investment between the two partners. It lays the ground rules for the partnership. Obviously, those entering into any partnership should consult their own attorney in writing such an agreement.

EXAMPLE 10-1:
PARTNERSHIP AGREEMENT BETWEEN MR. X AND MS. Y

This agreement is executed as of the first day of July 1979 by and among Mr. X and Ms. Y both of Anywhere, USA (both parties hereinafter are sometimes referred to as the "Partners").

The Partners desire to form a Partnership for the purpose of acquiring that certain tract of land and the structure erected thereon consisting of approximately one acre commonly known as 109 Roman Drive (hereinafter referred to as the "Premises").

The Partners hereto desire to define the respective rights and obligations of their association.

Now, therefore, intending to be legally bound hereby, the parties hereto form this Partnership in accordance with the laws of the State of Anywhere, under the following terms and conditions:

Article 1. Name of Business

The name of the Partnership shall be the XY Partnership.

Article 2. Place of Business

The business office of the Partnership shall be located on the Premises. The mailing address for this office shall be 109 Roman Drive, Anywhere, USA.

Article 3. Purpose of the Business

The sole purpose of this Partnership shall be the acquisition, ownership, and operation of the Premises. The operation of the Premises shall include only such activities deemed necessary by the Partners to maintain the Premises and lease any part or all of the Premises.

Article 4. Initial Contribution to Capital

A. There shall be individual capital accounts established and maintained for the Partners. The initial balance of said accounts shall be equivalent to the respective contribution of the Partners.

B. The initial capital of the Partnership shall be equivalent to the amount necessary to complete the purchase of the Premises and to establish an operating fund of $2,000. Each of the Partners shall contribute funds from his or her personal resources on a pro rata basis as follows.

    Mr. X—65%
    Ms. Y—35%

Article 5. Additional Contributions to Capital

A. In the event that additional capital funds in excess of the initial contributions are required by the Partnership, each of the Partners shall be obligated to contribute on a pro rata basis (see Article 6). Regardless of their proportionate interests in the Partnership, each of the Partners shall have an equivalent position in the determination of need for additional capital. Thus, mutual agreement is the only condition sufficient for this determination.

B. Upon a determination of a need for additional funds, if either Partner should not desire to contribute according to his obligation or not be able to contribute then there shall be the following consequences.

(a) The Partner not in default may elect to advance to the Partnership the amount required of the defaulting Partner as a loan to the defaulting Partner. A note shall be prepared for the amount of the loan, due and payable upon demand, with interest accruing at the prime rate for short-term loans at Merchant's Bank of Anywhere. This note shall be secured by the defaulting Partner's interest in the Partnership. The nondefaulting Partner shall also have the right to deduct funds from the defaulting Partner's share of the earnings of the Partnership to the extent of the interest and principal.

(b) If no loan agreement is executed, the nondefaulting Partner may elect to advance to the Partnership the amount required of the defaulting Partner. In that event, the nondefaulting Partner has the right to acquire that fraction of the defaulting Partner's interest in the Partnership represented by the amount obligated by the defaulting Partner but paid by the nondefaulting Partner. The defaulting Partner may "reacquire" such a fractional interest at any time for a period of one year from the date that the nondefaulting Partner fulfilled the obligation by payment of the principal amount plus interest at the prime rate for short-term loans at Merchant's Bank of Anywhere.

Article 6. Partnership Participation

The fractional interests of each Partner shall be based upon his or her individual capital account balance. The proportion of his or her individual account balance to the total capital of the Partnership shall determine his or her pro rata share of any given date for all purposes other than annual profit and loss distribution (Article 8, Section A).

Article 7.

A. An independent certified public accountant shall be engaged to maintain appropriate books and records such as necessary for the determination of profits and losses, and the preparation of state and federal income tax returns.

B. The Partnership books shall be maintained in accordance with generally accepted accounting principles on an accrual basis with the exception of those procedures outlined in Article 8, Section B.

C. The fiscal year shall be the calendar year.

D. All company books and records shall remain at the business office available for inspection by the Partners.

Article 8. Profit and Losses

A. The average individual capital account balance shall be determined each year in order to establish each Partner's fractional interest in the Partnership for annual profit and loss distributions. In the event of circumstances described in Article 5, Section B, Paragraph (b), the nondefaulting Partner's individual capital account shall reflect the increase of his or her fractional interest from the date of the advance.

B. In the determination of the share of net profits attributable to each Partner no deduction for depreciation shall be included. The depreciation shall be apportioned for tax purposes in a like manner to profits and losses.

C. Net profits or losses attributable to each Partner shall be credited to his or her individual capital account.

D. Distributions of profits in the form of cash or assets shall be only by mutual agreement of the Partners. Each Partner shall have an equivalent position in this determination.

Article 9. Management

A. Responsibility for routine management of the Premises shall rest equally with both partners. All major decisions or those involving expenditures of $1,000.00 or greater shall be subject to consultation of both Partners. In the event of disagreement, the Partner holding a majority interest shall have final determination.

B. Any loans, contracts, or lease agreements entered into on behalf of the Partnership shall require the signature of both Partners. All checks drawn on the operating fund to be established in Merchant's Bank of Athens, shall require the signature of both Partners.

C. Each Partner shall contribute equally such time as necessary for the management and operation of the business. There shall be no compensation to the Partners other than the profit accruing to them.

Article 10. Involuntary Dissolution

A. The death of a Partner shall not serve to immediately dissolve the Partnership. The executors, administrators, heirs legatees, devises, and distributors of a deceased partner shall have all the rights and responsibilities of the deceased Partner. In the event that the Partnership shall be dissolved within two years of the death of a Partner, the surviving Partner shall have the right to continue the business under the present name.

B. In the event that any Partner should file or have filed against him or her a petition of bankruptcy, or is subject to an application to a competent court by a judgment creditor to charge that Partner's interest in the Partnership or to appoint a receiver for the Partner, the following shall apply:

(a) The other Partner shall have the right to purchase the insolvent Partner's interest in the Partnership. He or she should give written notice of intent to purchase within fifteen days of the date he or she received notice of the occurrence of such a filing or application as described above.

(b) The purchase price shall be the selling Partner's fractional interest of the fair market value of the Partnership. If it is necessary to secure an appraiser, the appraisal fee shall be paid one-half by each Partner. Any other selling expenses shall be divided equally. Any amounts due to the Partnership shall be deducted from the selling price.

Article 11. Voluntary Dissolutions

A. This article is superseded by circumstances described in Article 10, Sections A and B.

B. In the event that either Partner desires to sell his or her interest in the Partnership he or she may do so with the following stipulations:

(a) The remaining Partner shall have the right to purchase the selling Partner's interest at terms equivalent to the most favorable terms offered to any potential purchaser. The remaining Partner shall have thirty days written notice before a sales agreement is executed during which he or she may exercise this right to purchase the selling Partner's interest.

(b) The remaining Partner shall be considered the majority Partner for management authority such as described in Article 9, Section A.

(c) The purchasing party must agree in writing to abide by this Partnership Agreement in its entirety.

C. In the event that a Partner transfers his or her interest in the Partnership by gift, the donee must agree in writing to abide by this Partnership Agreement in its entirety.

D. In the event that the Premises are sold by the Partnership, any remaining assets of the Partnership shall be liquidated and the Partnership shall be dissolved. The proceeds from the liquidation shall be distributed in the following order:

(a) All debts of the Partnership owed to creditors other than the Partners,

(b) All debts of the Partnership owed to the Partners other than capital,

(c) Amounts accruing to the Partner's in respect of capital,

(d) Any remainder shall be distributed to the Partners on a pro rata basis according to their fractional interests.

Article 12. Notices

Any notices required by this Agreement shall be in writing and delivered by registered or certified United States mail to the party entitled to receive some at his or her address written into this Agreement. This address may be changed by notice as described in this article.

Article 13. Miscellaneous

A. This Agreement contains the entire agreement of the Partners with respect to the subject matter hereof. There exist no additional understanding, promises, or warranties either oral or written. This Agreement is not subject to amendment or termination orally.

B. In the event that any provisions of this Agreement are determined by competent legal authority to be invalid, such a ruling shall not affect the validity or enforceability of the remaining provisions of the Agreement.

C. This Agreement shall be terminated by agreement of the Partners or upon disposition of the Premises. The procedure for liquidation and distribution is stated in Article 11, Section C.

The Investment Assumptions

The investment under consideration is an apartment investment containing twenty two-bedroom units. Comparable properties, with similar characteristics, are currently renting in a range of $190 to $220 per month per unit. Thus, it is concluded that the rents on this property will most probably be $200 per month

TABLE 10-3. First-Year Operating Expenses

Expense		Amount
Real estate taxes		$ 8,000
Management fees		2,400
Insurance		1,600
Repairs and maintenance		2,500
Resident manager's apartment		2,400
Utilities		1,500
Advertising and legal fees		1,200
Replacements[a]		
Dishwashers ($200/10 × 20)	$400	
Refrigerator ($350/10 × 20)	700	
Disposals ($125/10 × 20)	250	
Stoves ($350/10 × 20)	700	
		2,050
Total operating expenses		$21,650

[a]Cost of each item is divided by 10 (the expected useful life in years) and multiplied by 20 (the number of rental units).

per unit. Market analysis indicates that rents will probably increase at the rate of 3 percent per year. Vacancies in competing properties are 5 percent per year.

Table 10-3 shows the projected operating expenses in the first year. Total expenses are estimated at $21,650 and are also expected to increase at a rate of 3 percent per year.

Mr. X and Ms. Y have also analyzed the mortgage market. Lenders are willing to loan 70 percent of the total value at an interest rate of 11 percent with annual payments for twenty-five years. There are no prepayment penalties for paying the loan off early. There are, however, closing costs and fees of 4 percent of the mortgage amount.

Mr. X and Ms. Y estimate that the project will increase in value over the ten-year holding period by 20 percent to 40 percent. They expect that selling expenses will be 5 percent of the selling price at the end of the ten-year period.

Summary of Inputs

Table 10-4 gives a summary of the input data concerning the investment. It should be remembered that these are the expected inputs. The investors must carefully analyze the investment market to be relatively certain that these are correct. Obviously, the investors cannot remove all of the uncertainty about the inputs since the future is unknown. However, the investors must make commitments based on this uncertain future. The goal of the investment analyses process is to reduce the uncertainty, and hence, risk, of investing to a minimum.

TABLE 10-4. Summary of Inputs

Input	Assumption
Asking price	$225,000.
Number of units	Twenty two-bedroom units.
Rents	Range of $190 to $220 per month per unit; expected to increase at 3 percent per year.
Vacancies	5 percent per year.
Operating expenses	$21,650 first year; expected to increase 3 percent per year.
Financing	70 percent of total value; 11-percent interest rate; annual payments for twenty-five years; no prepayment penalties; 4 percent fees and closing costs.
Depreciation	200-percent method; useful life of thirty years; 80 percent of total value is depreciable.
Holding period	Ten years.
Reversion	Selling price expected to increase 20 percent to 40 percent over the ten-year period.
Investors	Share in profits and losses at 65 percent for Mr. X and 35 percent for Ms. Y. Mr. X is in a 59-percent tax bracket. Ms. Y is in a 43-percent tax bracket.
Equity	$67,500 plus $6,300 financing costs; total of $73,800.

STEP 3: FORECASTING THE CASH FLOWS

The third step in the investment process is to forecast the expected cash flows for the expected holding period. The cash flows are derived from two sources: (1) the annual cash flows from rental collections less all expenses, and (2) the cash flow from the disposition (normally sale) of the investment. The investors are interested in the after-tax cash flow. This represents the amount of cash that the project is expected to generate after all obligations have been met, including income taxes.

It should be pointed out that the cash flows are those which the project is *expected* to generate. The investor will not know the *actual* cash flows until the project has been bought, operated, and then sold. This is what investing is all about—sacrificing certain outflows for expected inflows. There is always the possibility that a project will generate more or less than the investor expected when he or she bought the investment.

The Annual Cash-Flow Statement

Table 10-5 uses the input information and shows the expected annual cash-flow statement.

TABLE 10-5. Annual Operating Cash-Flow Statement for an Apartment-Building Investment

	Year									
	1	2	3	4	5	6	7	8	9	10
Potential gross income (PGI)	48,000	49,440	50,923	52,451	54,024	55,645	57,315	59,034	60,805	62,629
Less vacancies and bad debts	-2,400	-2,472	-2,546	-2,623	-2,701	-2,782	-2,866	-2,952	-3,040	-3,131
Plus miscellaneous income	—	—	—	—	—	—	—	—	—	—
Effective gross income (EGI)	45,600	46,968	48,377	49,828	51,323	52,863	54,449	56,082	57,765	59,498
Less operating expenses	-21,650	-22,300	-22,968	-23,658	-24,367	-25,098	-25,851	-26,627	-27,426	-28,248
Net operating income (NOI)	23,950	24,668	25,409	26,170	26,956	27,765	28,598	29,455	30,339	31,250
Less debt service	-18,702	-18,702	-18,702	-18,702	-18,702	-18,702	-18,702	-18,702	-18,702	-18,702
Before-tax cash flow (BTCF)	5,248	5,966	6,707	7,468	8,254	9,063	9,896	10,753	11,637	12,548
Plus principal	+1,377	+1,528	+1,697	+1,883	+2,090	+2,320	+2,575	+2,859	+3,173	+3,522
Less depreciation	-12,000	-11,200	-10,453	-9,756	-9,106	-8,499	-7,932	-7,404	-6,910	-6,449
Plus replacement reserves	+2,050	+2,050	+2,050	+2,050	+2,050	+2,050	+2,050	+2,050	+2,050	+2,050
Less amortized financing costs	-252	-252	-252	-252	-252	-252	-252	-252	-252	-4,032
Taxable income (TI)	-3,577	-1,908	-251	1,393	3,036	4,682	6,337	8,006	9,698	7,639

Net Operating Income. The first year's potential gross income is $48,000. This is calculated by multiplying the number of units (20) times the expected rent per unit ($200 per month) times twelve months. The PGI increases at a rate of 3 percent per year. The PGI in the tenth year is projected to be $62,629 which equals a rent of $261 per month per unit. Rents are thus projected to increase from $200 per month to $261 per month over the ten-year period.

The next step is to subtract the vacancy and bad debt losses which were estimated at 5 percent of PGI each year. Thus vacancy losses are estimated at $2,400 in Year 1 and increase to $3,131 in Year 10. There is no expected miscellaneous income.

Effective gross income (EGI) is the difference between PGI and vacancy losses. EGI in the first year is estimated at $45,600 and increases to $59,498 in Year 10.

The operating expenses, shown in Table 10-4 were estimated at $21,650 in Year 1. These were assumed to increase at a rate of 3 percent per year. Thus in Year 10, the operating expenses are $28,248.

EGI less operating expenses yields the net operating income (NOI) from the project. The NOI in Year 1 is estimated at $23,950 and increases to $31,250 in Year 10.

Before-Tax Cash Flow. The next item to be subtracted in setting up the cash flow statement is the payment on the mortgage debt. This payment is referred to as debt service in a real estate investment.

The mortgage indebtedness is $157,500 since it was assumed that the investors could borrow 70 percent of the value ($225,000). The interest rate was 11 percent for twenty-five years with annual payments. This results in mortgage constant of .11874 which, when multiplied by the amount borrowed, results in a payment of $18,702 per year.

This $18,702 payment includes both repayment of the mortgage debt and the interest on the debt. The investors must separate this total payment into the interest payment and the principal amortization payment. The interest portion is deductible for tax purposes and the principal payment is not. Table 10-6 shows these calculations for Years 1 through 10.

The original amount outstanding is $157,500. The interest payment in the first year is $17,325 ($157,500 × .11). The difference between the total payment, $18,702, and the interest portion, $17,325, results in the principal payment of $1,377. The balance at the end of the first year is thus $156,123 ($157,500 − $1,377). The interest payment in the second year is $17,174 ($156,123 × .11). The principal payment in the second year is $1,528 ($18,702 − $17,174). The amount outstanding at the end of the second year is thus $154,595 ($156,123 − $1,528). This process is continued for each of the ten years. At the end of ten years, the amount outstanding is $134,476.

The NOI minus the debt service payment results in the before-tax cash flow (BTCF) for each year.

TABLE 10-6. Mortgage Amortization Schedule

Amount borrowed: $157,500.00
Interest rate: 11%
Maturity term: 25 years
Payments: Annual
Loan-to-value ratio: 70%
Mortgage constant: .11874
Debt service: $18,702.00

Year	Amount Outstanding	Debt Service	Interest Payment	Principal Payment
0	$157,500			
1	156,123	$18,702	$17,325	$1,377
2	154,595	18,702	17,174	1,528
3	152,898	18,702	17,005	1,697
4	151,015	18,702	16,819	1,883
5	148,925	18,702	16,612	2,090
6	146,605	18,702	16,382	2,320
7	144,030	18,702	16,127	2,575
8	141,171	18,702	15,843	2,859
9	137,998	18,702	15,529	3,173
10	134,476	18,702	15,180	3,522

After-Tax Cash Flow. The final step in estimating the annual cash flow statement is the calculation of income taxes. To calculate the taxes, the investors must calculate the taxable income and the tax rate. The taxable income (TI) from a real estate investment is different from the cash flow from the investment; it is calculated as follows:

$$TI = BTCF + \text{Principal payments} - \text{Depreciation deduction} + \text{Replacement reserves} - \text{Amortized financing costs}$$

The principal payment each year on the mortgage is calculated in Table 10-7. These must be added back since only the interest payment is deductible for tax purposes. The replacement reserves must be added back because for tax purposes they are not operating expenses.

TABLE 10-7. Allowed Depreciation Techniques for Alternative Types of Real Estate

Type of Real Estate	Straight-Line	Depreciation Method			Sum-of-the-Years' Digits
		200%	150%	125%	
New Residential	Yes	Yes	Yes	Yes	Yes
Used Residential[a]	Yes	No	No	Yes	No
New Nonresidential	Yes	No	Yes	Yes	No
Used Nonresidential	Yes	No	No	No	No

[a]Must have a useful life of at least 20 years. If less than 20, 125% method is not allowed.

The replacement reserves are the amount set aside to replace the items of personal property. The costs of financing, such as legal fees and points on the mortgage, must be amortized over the life of the mortgage. In this example, these fees were $6,300 (4 percent of the $157,500). The costs are not deductible at the beginning but can be amortized over the twenty-five-year life of the mortgage or $252 per year ($6300 ÷ 25). It should be remembered that these costs add to the total cost of the investment. In essence, the cost has increased from $225,000 to $231,300 for the investors. This results in an increase in their equity investment of $6,300. The unamortized balance is deductible in the year of sale.

The final step in calculating the taxable income is the deduction of the depreciation allowance. The depreciation allowance is simply a deduction against taxable income without any cash outlay. The idea behind depreciation is that the building part of a real estate investment is a wasting asset and the investor should be allowed to recover the cost of the investment over its useful life.

To determine the depreciation deduction in any year, the investor must estimate:

1. *The amount to be depreciated.* This is typically the cost of the investment. Land is not depreciable. Thus the investor must allocate the total cost between the value of the building and the value of the land. In this example, the value of the building is assumed to be 80 percent of the total $225,000 cost. Thus the amount to be depreciated is $180,000.

2. *The useful life.* The useful life of an asset is the period of time over which it is expected to be useful to the investor in producing income. In most real estate investments, the useful life has little to do with the physical life. The useful life in this example is estimated to be thirty years. The shorter the useful life, the larger the depreciation deduction.

3. *The depreciation method must be determined.* Table 10-7 outlines the various depreciation methods that are allowed with alternative real estate investments. For tax purposes, real estate is classified as either new or used, and either residential or nonresidential. New residential property enjoys the greatest flexibility with respect to depreciation methods, as can be seen in Table 10-8. The depreciation method used in this example is the 200-percent declining balance technique.

Table 10-8 illustrates the depreciation schedules for this example. The depreciation deduction in each year is calculated using a depreciable basis of $180,000 (80 percent of total value, $225,000) a thirty-year useful life, and the 200-percent declining balance method. The beginning book value is $180,000. The straight-line percentage is $\frac{1}{30}$ or 3.333 percent each year. As the name implies, the 200-percent declining balance method is calculated at double the straight-line percentage on the declining balance. The 200-percent declining balance percentage is thus 6.666 percent. Thus the first-year deduction is $12,000

TABLE 10-8. Depreciation Schedule

Total cost: $225,000
Depreciable amount: $180,000
Nondepreciable amount: $45,000
Useful life: 30 years
Depreciation method: 200%
Straight-line percent: 3.333%
Accelerated percent: 6.666%

Year	Accelerated Method			Straight-Line Method			Excess Depreciation
	Book Value	Amount	Cumulative	Book Value	Amount	Cumulative	
0	$180,000	—	—	$180,000	—	—	—
1	168,000	$12,000	$12,000	174,000	$6,000	$ 6,000	$6,000
2	156,800	11,200	23,200	168,000	6,000	12,000	5,120
3	146,347	10,453	33,653	162,000	6,000	18,000	4,453
4	136,591	9,756	43,409	156,000	6,000	24,000	3,756
5	127,485	9,106	52,515	150,000	6,000	30,000	3,106
6	118,986	8,499	61,014	144,000	6,000	36,000	2,499
7	111,054	7,932	68,946	138,000	6,000	42,000	1,932
8	103,650	7,404	76,350	132,000	6,000	48,000	1,404
9	96,740	6,910	83,260	126,000	6,000	54,000	910
10	90,291	6,449	89,709	120,000	6,000	60,000	449

TABLE 10-9. Distribution of After-Tax Cash Flow

After-Tax Cash Flow to Mr. X (65% of the Total Given in Table 10-5)

	Year									
	1	2	3	4	5	6	7	8	9	10
BTCF	$3,411	$3,878	$4,360	$4,854	$5,365	$5,891	$6,432	$6,989	$7,564	$8,156
Taxable income	-2,325	-1,240	-163	905	1,973	3,043	4,119	5,204	6,304	4,965
Tax rate	.59	.59	.59	.59	.59	.59	.59	.59	.59	.59
Taxes	-1,372	-732	-96	534	1,164	1,795	2,430	3,070	3,719	2,930
ATCF	4,783	4,610	4,456	4,320	4,201	4,096	4,002	3,919	3,845	5,226

After-Tax Cash Flow to Ms. Y (35% of the Total Given in Table 10-5)

	Year									
	1	2	3	4	5	6	7	8	9	10
BTCF	$1,837	$2,088	$2,347	$2,614	$2,889	$3,172	$3,464	$3,764	$4,073	$4,392
Taxable income	-1,252	-668	-88	488	1,063	1,639	2,218	2,802	3,394	2,674
Tax rate	.43	.43	.43	.43	.43	.43	.43	.43	.43	.43
Taxes	-538	-287	-38	210	457	705	954	1,205	1,459	1,150
ATCF	2,375	2,375	2,385	2,404	2,432	2,467	2,510	2,559	2,614	3,242

($180,000 × .0666). Deducting this from the original $180,000 gives a book value at the end of Year 1 of $168,000. The depreciation deduction in the second year is $11,200 ($168,000 × .0666). This process is continued for each year. The book value of the building at the end of ten years is $90,303.

As was discussed in Chapter 7, the excess depreciation *each year* is a preference-tax item and thus potentially subject to regular minimum taxation. For example, the excess depreciation in the first year of $6,000, as shown in Table 10-9, could possibly be taxed as a preference income.

To determine whether or not there are any taxes owed on the excess depreciation each year, the investors must first calculate their taxes on other taxable income. Mr. X's other taxable income was assumed to be $100,000. His normal tax liability would be $41,998 (using the tax rates in Table 10-2). His share of the excess depreciation in the first year would be 65 percent of $6,000, or $3,900.

Under the tax rules for the regular minimum tax, Mr. X gets a deduction of the larger of $10,000 or one-half of his regular tax liability. In this example, Mr. X would get a deduction of one-half of $41,998 or $20,999. This is obviously larger than his tax-preference income of $3,900. Thus he owes no minimum tax.

If, however, the tax-preference income was larger than the deduction, Mr. X would have to pay at a tax rate of 15 percent. For example, if Mr. X had tax-preference items of $25,000 deducting the $20,999 amount would give $4,001. In this case, his minimum tax liability would be 15 percent of $4,001, or $600. Thus the excess depreciation would not be "free" since the investor must pay a minimum tax as a result of the excess depreciation being considered a tax-preference item.

Now the total taxable income can be calculated. This is shown in Table 10-5. To estimate the amount of taxes due in each year, this taxable income is multiplied by the tax rate. However, the tax rate differs for the two investors. Thus, Table 10-9 has been constructed.

Table 10-9 (page 185) shows the distribution of the total cash flow between the two investors. The cash flows are distributed, according to the partnership agreement, at 65 percent to Mr. X and 35 percent to Ms. Y.

Notice that in the first three years of operation the project is creating a negative taxable income. This does not mean that the investment is losing money! It simply means that for tax purposes, the taxable income is negative. The investors can use this tax loss to offset their other taxable income, thereby reducing their taxes. Using the marginal tax rates of 59 percent for Mr. X and 43 percent for Ms. Y, the taxes are calculated by multiplying these rates by the taxable income.

The after-tax cash flow is calculated by subtracting the taxes from the before-tax cash flow. Since the taxes are negative in the Years 1 through 3, the ATCF is larger than the BTCF. In the first year for Mr. X, the ATCF is $4,783. This is found by taking the BTCF ($3,411) and subtracting the taxes (-$1,372).

But subtracting a negative number yields

$$ATCF = \$3,411 - (-1,373)$$
$$= \$4,783$$

The ATCF is largest in the first year of operation for Mr. X. In the fourth year, the investment begins generating a positive taxable income. Thus it loses its tax advantage of sheltering the investor's other taxable income but it still shelters part of the cash flow from the project. This can be seen by observing that the taxable income is less than the BTCF. The loss of tax shelter is the result of several factors: The BTCF is increasing, the principal payment on the mortgage is increasing, and the depreciation deduction is decreasing. The net effect is to increase the taxable income from the investment in each year of the operation of the investment.

The Cash Flow from Sale (Reversion)

The second form of cash flow from a real estate investment comes at the time of sale of the investment. In real estate investing, this is referred to as the reversion. In this example, the investors are assumed to sell the investment at the end of the tenth year.

The Before-Tax Equity Reversion (BTER). Table 10-10 illustrates the calculation of the before-tax equity reversion (BTER). It is called the equity reversion since it is the amount of cash flow to the equity investor after all expenses have been paid except income taxes (see Chapter 8). The investors anticipate that the investment will increase in value at least 20 percent but not more than 40 percent over the ten-year holding period. Thus, if the investors pay $225,000 they expect to sell the property for at least 20 percent more than they paid for it at the end of the ten years, giving an estimated selling price of $270,000.

The costs of selling the investment are estimated to be 5 percent of the expected selling price or $13,000 ($270,000 X .05). Another expense that many investors might face on the sale is prepayment penalties on the mortgage. In this example the investors can pay the mortgage off early without any penalties. However, prepayment penalties are typical in most real estate mortgages.

TABLE 10-10. Before-Tax Equity Reversion

Selling price	$270,000
Less selling expenses	−13,500
Amount realized on sale	$256,500
Less unpaid mortgage balance	−134,476
Before-tax equity reversion	$122,024

TABLE 10-11. Taxable Income from Sale

Taxable Income from Sale	
Amount realized	$256,500
Less adjusted basis	–135,291
Total gain	$121,209
Less excess depreciation	–29,709
Capital gain	$ 91,500
Total Taxable Income from Sale	
1. Capital gain (40% of $91,500)	$ 36,600
2. Excess depreciation recapture	$ 29,709
3. Preference tax income (60% of $91,500)	$ 54,900

These expenses are subtracted from the estimated selling price of the property to arrive at the amount realized from the sale, or $256,500. From the amount realized the unpaid mortgage balance ($134,476) is deducted to arrive at the before-tax equity reversion (BTER). This represents the amount of cash that the investors expect to have from the sale of the project before the taxes are paid.

Table 10-11 illustrates the taxable income from the sale. Taxes due on the sale are of three possible types: (1) taxes from capital gains, (2) taxes on the recapture of excess depreciation, and (3) minimum taxes on preference income.

To calculate the taxes due on sale, the amount realized on the sale less the unamortized financing costs and the adjusted basis of the property results in the total gain on the sale. The adjusted basis of the property is the total original cost ($225,000) less the cumulative depreciation ($89,709). The total gain is $121,209. This total gain is composed of two parts which must be separated: (1) the capital gain, and (2) the excess depreciation.

The total excess depreciation can be found in Table 10-12. The cumulative depreciation deduction using the accelerated method is $89,709. The cumulative deductions which would have been taken had the straight-line method been used are $60,000. The difference between these two numbers is the excess depreciation, $29,709. The total excess depreciation is taxed as ordinary income to the investors. All the investors are doing by using the accelerated method is postponing the taxes until the time of sale.

It should also be noted that the excess depreciation *each* year is a preference tax item and possibly subject to the minimum tax. At the time of sale, the *total* excess depreciation is taxed as ordinary income. The excess depreciation is thus potentially taxed twice: on an annual basis as preference income and at the time of sale as ordinary income.

The total gain ($121,209) less the excess depreciation ($29,703) yields the capital gain ($91,500). The current capital gains tax laws allow for an exclusion of 60 percent of the capital gain. Thus the capital gain that is taxed is $36,600 ($91,500 × .40). This is taxed at the investors' ordinary income tax rates. The

TABLE 10-12. After-Tax Equity Reversion for Mr. X

Taxable Income		
1. Share of capital gain		$23,790
2. Share of depreciation recapture		$19,311
3. Share of preference income		$35,685
Taxes		
1. Capital gains ⎱	taxed as ordinary income	$27,118
2. Depreciation recapture ⎰		
3. Preference income		–
Total taxes on sale		$27,118
After-Tax Equity Reversion		
Before-tax equity reversion (65% of $122,024)		$79,316
Less taxes on sale		–27,118
After-tax equity reversion (ATER)		$52,198

excluded 60-percent part of the capital gain is a tax-preference item and is possibly subject to the alternative minimum tax. As was discussed in Chapter 8, the tax on this 60-percent excluded part of the capital gain will be negligible for most real estate investors.

Tables 10-12 and 10-13 show the calculation of the after-tax equity reversion (ATER) for Mr. X and Ms. Y. Their share in the taxable income from the sale of the project is based on the 65-35 split in the partnership agreement. To illustrate, Mr. X's share in the taxable income from the capital gain is $23,790. This is 65 percent of the total taxable capital gain (from Table 10-11) of $36,600.

Mr. X has other taxable income of $100,000 (see Table 10-1). If you use the tax rates in Table 10-2, his regular tax liability would be $41,998. His share

TABLE 10-13. After-Tax Equity Reversion for Ms. Y

Taxable Income		
1. Share of capital gain		$12,810
2. Share of depreciation recapture		$10,398
3. Share of preference income		$19,215
Taxes		
1. Capital gains ⎱	taxed as ordinary income	$11,184
2. Depreciation recapture ⎰		
3. Preference income		–
Total taxes on sale		$11,184
After-Tax Equity Reversion		
Before-tax equity reversion (35% of $122,024)		$42,708
Less taxes on sale		–11,184
After-tax equity reversion (ATER)		$31,524

of the taxable capital gain is $23,790. His share of the taxable depreciation recapture is $19,311. This increases his total taxable income to $143,101 as a result of the sale. Using the tax table (Table 10-2), his total taxes are now $69,113. Thus his taxes have increased from $41,995 to $69,113, or by $27,118, as a result of the sale of the project.

The third type of tax which might be owed is the minimum tax on the excluded 60 percent of the capital gain. This is classified as a tax-preference item. Under the 1978 Tax Act, it could be subject to the alternative minimum tax.

As illustrated in Chapter 8, the alternative minimum tax is calculated as follows: First, the investor calculates the tax on the sum of his or her other taxable income, the capital gain, and depreciation recapture. This was calculated at $69,113. Second, the investor finds the alternative minimum tax base by adding to his or her other taxable income: (1) the 40-percent portion of the capital gain, (2) the excess depreciation recapture, and (3) the 60-percent excluded portion of the capital gain. The investor deducts $20,000 as an exclusion. This results in the alternative minimum tax base which is taxed at a rate of 10 percent on the first $40,000, 20 percent on the second $40,000, and 25 percent on the balance.

In this example, Mr. X would make the following calculation:

Other taxable income	$100,000
Plus taxable portion of capital gain	23,790
Plus excess depreciation recapture	19,311
Plus excluded portion of capital gain	35,685
Less $20,000 exclusion	(20,000)
Alternative minimum tax base	$158,786

The tax on this amount is:

First $40,000 at 10%	$ 4,000
Next $40,000 at 20%	8,000
Remainder ($78,786) at 25%	19,697
Total taxes	$31,697

Under the tax law, the investor would pay the *larger* of the taxes on the alternative minimum tax base or the regular taxes. In this example, the taxes on the regular tax base are $69,113 while the taxes on the alternative are $31,697. Mr. X must may $69,113 in taxes. Thus, the investor owes no tax on the 60 percent excluded portion of the capital gain.

For Mr. X, the after-tax equity reversion (ATER) from the sale of the investment is the difference between his share in the before tax equity reversion ($79,316) and the increase in the amount of taxes ($27,118). This results in an ATER for Mr. X of $52,198.

For Ms. Y, the ATER is $31,524. This was calculated using her taxable income of $40,000 and following the procedures outlined in the calculation of Mr. X's ATER.

The investors have now forecast the expected after-tax cash flow from the investment. Should they invest? To answer this question it is ncesssary to apply some investment criteria to the cost and expected benefits of investing.

STEP 4: APPLYING THE INVESTMENT CRITERIA

The investors have forecast the expected cash flows from the investment on an after-tax basis. To make the investment decision, it is necessary to compare the cost of investing to the expected benefits of investing (the expected cash flows). The methods for comparing these costs and benefits are referred to as investment criteria.

There are many criteria for comparing the costs and benefits. Each criterion has some limitations. The criteria are divided into three major categories: rules of thumb, traditional appraisal techniques, and discounted cash flow techniques. The latter category is the most sophisticated and the most accurate.

Rule-of-Thumb Techniques

The two most common rule-of-thumb techniques for investment decisions are the gross income multiplier (GIM) and the cash-on-cash rate of return.

To estimate the value of an investment using the gross income multiplier (GIM), the investor simply multiplies the estimated first year's gross income (either potential gross or effective gross) times a constant amount. To illustrate, the asking price in this example is $225,000 and the estimated potential gross income in the first year is $48,000. Thus the GIM is $225,000 ÷ $48,000 which is equal to 4.7. In other words, the "value" ($225,000) of the investment is 4.7 times the gross income ($48,000).

To make the investment decision using the gross income multiplier, the investors must decide if they should pay 4.7 times the estimated gross income for the project. How do they decide? One method is to compare the gross income multiplier with the multiplier for other projects of the same type which have recently sold in the same neighborhood. The investors would calculate their GIM by dividing their selling price by the gross income of these investments. The investors would then compare these GIMs with the GIM for the investment under consideration. If the GIMs for the other projects were higher than the GIM for the investment under consideration, the investors *might* conclude that they should invest in the project.

The gross income multiplier is obviously a very aggregate measure of the investment value. It varies over time and by location. It might, however, provide the investors with a good first estimate of the feasibility of their investment. (For the reader acquainted with the stock market, the gross income multiplier is very similar to the price-earnings ratio used in stock analysis).

A second widely used rule of thumb is known as the cash-on-cash rate of return. To calculate the cash-on-cash rate of return the investors simply divide the expected first year before-tax cash flow by the amount of cash they plan to invest in the project (hence the name "cash-on-cash").

In the example, the estimated before-tax cash flow for the first year is $5,248 (see Table 10-5). The amount of total equity investment is $73,800. Thus the cash-on-cash return for the first year is $5,248 ÷ $73,800 which equals a 7-percent rate of return. Does this meet the investors' required rate of return? If it does, they *might* conclude that they should invest in the project; if not, they *might* conclude that they should not invest.

The obvious problem of the cash-on-cash criterion is that it takes into account only the cash flow in the first year. It ignores the tax benefits (or cost) from the investment. It also ignores the expected cash flow from the sale of the investment at the end of the holding period. It should only be used as a guideline— a rule of thumb which is not always correct.

Traditional Appraisal Techniques

A second major category of investment criteria includes the traditional appraisal techniques. The method most widely used by real estate appraisers for estimating the value of a parcel of real estate is the direct sales comparison approach.

As the name implies, value estimation by the direct sales comparison approach involves using comparable properties to estimate the value of the subject property. The investors would simply examine the selling price of similar properties in the area to arrive at a value for their investment.

For this approach to be accurate, the investors must find similar properties, particularly with respect to location, time of sale, financing conditions, and physical characteristics. No two parcels of real estate are exactly alike. The investors must be careful not to conclude that since another investment similar to theirs sold for a certain amount that they could pay that amount for their investment.

The sales comparison approach can, however, serve as a useful guideline for making investment decisions. The investors should be aware of the selling price for property similar to their investment. If their estimate of value varies widely from the selling price of similar properties, the investor would be well advised to re-examine their value estimate for potential errors.

Discounted Cash Flow Techniques

The best techniques for making investment decisions are what are known as discounted cash flow (DCF) models. As the name implies, discounted cash flow models estimate value or rate of return for an investment by "discounting" the expected cash flow.

The best measure of the expected cash flow is the after-tax estimate. To use the DCF model, the investors must (1) estimate the expected cash flow, and (2) find the present value of the estimates at some required rate of return.

The first nine chapters of this book dealt with how to estimate the expected after-tax cash flow. All that remains to be done is to find the present value of these estimates at the desired rate of return.

The investors in this case have fixed their required rate of return at 12 percent per year. Tables 10-9, 10-12, and 10-13 gave the estimated after-tax cash flows. Using the present value of $1.00 tables in the Appendix, the investors can calculate the present value of these estimates. These calculations are shown in Tables 10-14 and 10-15.

Tables 10-14 and 10-15 show the present value of the expected ATCF and the expected ATER using a required rate of return of 12 percent. This present value is found by multiplying the expected cash flow by the present value factor. The investment tables in the Appendix provide these factors at various rates of return. Looking in Table A-1 of the Appendix under the column labeled 12% the

TABLE 10-14. Present Value of After-Tax Cash Flows at 12% Rate of Return to Mr. X

Year	ATCF	ATER	Present Value Factor at 12%	Present Value
1	$4,783	—	0.892857	$ 4,271
2	4,610	—	0.797194	3,675
3	4,456	—	0.711780	3,172
4	4,320	—	0.635518	2,745
5	4,201	—	0.567427	2,384
6	4,096	—	0.506631	2,075
7	4,002	—	0.452349	1,810
8	3,919	—	0.403883	1,583
9	3,845	—	0.360610	1,387
10	5,226	$52,198	0.321973	18,489
Total present value				$41,591

TABLE 10-15. Present Value of After-Tax Cash Flows at 12% Rate of Return to Ms. Y

Year	ATCF	ATER	Present Value Factor at 12%	Present Value
1	$2,375	—	0.892857	$ 2,121
2	2,375	—	0.797194	1,893
3	2,385	—	0.711780	1,698
4	2,404	—	0.635518	1,528
5	2,432	—	0.567427	1,380
6	2,467	—	0.506631	1,250
7	2,510	—	0.452349	1,135
8	2,559	—	0.403883	1,034
9	2,614	—	0.360610	943
10	3,242	$31,524	0.321973	$11,194
Total present value				$24,176

investors can find these present value factors. These factors are then multiplied by the expected cash flows to find the present value.

The present values of the expected cash flows in each year are then summed to obtain the total present value. Notice that the total present value of the after-tax cash flows at the 12-percent rate of return is $41,591 for Mr. X and $24,176 for Ms. Y.

How do these values compare to the costs of investing? For Mr. X, the equity investment would be $47,970. This is his cost of investing. The cost of investing exceeds the present value of the expected cash flow at the 12-percent rate of return. Since the cost exceeds the present value of the cash flow, Mr. X should *not* invest in the project. If he does invest and the project generates the expected cash flow, Mr. X will not earn a 12-percent rate of return. He will earn less than a 12-percent rate of return.

For Ms. Y, the cost of her equity investment would be $25,830. The present value of the expected cash flow for her is $25,464. In her case, the present value of the expected benefits is also less than the cost. Thus, since the cost exceeds the present value of the investment, Ms. Y would *not* earn her required 12-percent rate of return if she invested in the project.

STEP 5: THE INVESTMENT DECISION

Mr. X should not invest, and Ms. Y should not invest. What should the partnership do? The investment should not be undertaken since the criteria result in a "don't invest" decision for Mr. X and Ms. Y.

The present value criterion illustrated in this example is the best criterion to use for the investment decision. Investors must explicitly formulate their expected cash flows from the investment. This requires a number of assumptions. But this is the "realism" of real estate investment decisions. Investors who are not overly confident about their forecasts of the expected cash flows can change their assumptions and work through the investment process using the new assumptions. This is called sensitivity analysis, that is, determining how sensitive their investment decision is in relation to the assumptions they have made. The next section illustrates sensitivity analysis.

A RE-EVALUATION OF THE INVESTMENT

In setting up the expected cash-flow statement in our example, the investors have obviously made a number of assumptions—the essence of investing. It is better that investors explicitly formulate their assumptions and examine the expected impact on the investment decision. All of the investment criteria discussed previously have implicit assumptions hidden in them.

TABLE 10-16. Annual Operating Cash-Flow Statement for an Apartment-Building Investment—Revised

	Year									
	1	2	3	4	5	6	7	8	9	10
Potential gross income (PGI)	$52,800	$54,384	$56,016	$57,696	$59,427	$61,210	$63,045	$64,937	$66,885	$68,892
Less vacancies and bad debts	-2,640	-2,719	-2,801	-2,885	-2,971	-3,961	-3,152	-3,247	-3,344	-3,445
Plus miscellaneous income	—	—	—	—	—	—	—	—	—	—
Effective gross income (EGI)	50,160	51,665	53,215	54,811	56,456	58,150	59,893	61,690	63,540	65,447
Less operating expenses	-21,650	-22,300	-22,968	-23,658	-24,367	-25,098	-25,851	-26,627	-27,426	-28,248
Net operating income (NOI)	28,510	29,365	30,247	31,153	32,089	33,052	34,042	35,063	36,114	37,199
Less debt service	-18,702	-18,702	-18,702	-18,702	-18,702	-18,702	-18,702	-18,702	-18,702	-18,702
Before-tax cash flow	9,808	10,663	11,545	12,451	13,387	14,350	15,304	16,361	17,412	18,497
Plus principal	+1,377	+1,528	+1,697	+1,883	+2,090	+2,320	+2,575	+2,859	+3,173	+3,522
Less depreciation	-12,000	-11,200	-10,453	-9,756	-9,106	-8,499	-7,932	-7,404	-6,910	-6,449
Plus replacement reserves	+2,050	+2,050	+2,050	+2,050	+2,050	+2,050	+2,050	+2,050	+2,050	+2,050
Less amortized financing costs	-252	-252	-252	-252	-252	-252	-252	-252	-252	-4,032
Taxable income (TI)	$ 983	$ 2,789	$ 4,587	$ 6,376	$ 8,169	$ 9,969	$11,781	$13,614	$15,473	$13,588

195

Investors who are not confident about their expectations can reexamine their assumptions and determine the impact on the investment decision. This is generally referred to as "sensitivity analysis," the process of changing one or more of the inputs in the investment process and examining the impact on the investment decision.

In this section, the apartment example is reworked changing two of the initial inputs: the expected rent per unit and the expected selling price.

From the market analysis, the investors had estimated initial rents to be in the range of $190 to $220 per month per unit. The above analysis used an expected initial rent of $200 per unit per month. What would be the impact on the annual cash-flow statement if the initial rent was $220 per month per unit?

The second input to be changed is the assumption of the selling price at the end of the holding period. The investors initially used an estimate of a 20-percent increase over purchase price. Suppose, however, that the change in value was 40 percent. What would the after-tax equity reversion be using this assumption?

Revised Annual Cash-Flow Statement

Table 10-16 shows the annual cash-flow statement assuming a rent of $220 per month per unit. The remainder of the inputs are the same as those used previously (see Table 10-5). One obvious change using this assumption is that the investment has a positive taxable income in the early years whereas previously the taxable income was negative. This positive taxable income means that the project is not sheltering all of the before-tax cash flow from the investment.

Table 10-17 gives the distribution of the BTCF, taxable income, and after-tax cash flow to Mr. X and Ms. Y. Comparing this table with Table 10-10 it can be seen that even though the investment is generating a higher taxable income, the ATCF for Mr. X and Ms. Y has increased in every year as a result of the higher estimated rent levels.

Revised After-Tax Equity Reversion

Tables 10-18 through 10-21 show the calculation of the after-tax equity reversion (ATER) using the assumption that the selling price will be 40 percent rather than 20 percent higher than the purchase price. The initial price is $225,000; thus, if the property is expected to increase in value by 40 percent, the expected selling price is $315,000 at the end of the holding period. It should be restated that if the investors are expecting this increase purely as a result of inflation, they should also increase their required rate of return to reflect this purchasing power risk. An investor would not pay more today for an investment simply because of expected general inflation.

TABLE 10-17. Distribution of After-Tax Cash Flow—Revised

After-Tax Cash Flow to Mr. X (65% of the Total Given in Table 10-16)

	Year									
	1	2	3	4	5	6	7	8	9	10
BTCF	$6,375	$6,931	$7,504	$8,093	$8,702	$9,328	$9,948	$10,635	$11,318	$12,023
Taxable income	639	1,813	2,982	4,144	5,310	6,480	7,658	8,849	10,057	8,832
Tax rate	.59	.59	.59	.59	.59	.59	.59	.59	.59	.59
Taxes	377	1,070	1,759	2,445	3,123	3,823	4,518	5,221	5,934	5,211
ATCF	5,998	5,861	5,745	5,648	5,569	5,505	5,430	5,414	5,384	6,812

After-Tax Cash Flow to Ms. Y (35% of the Total Given in Table 10-16)

	Year									
	1	2	3	4	5	6	7	8	9	10
BTCF	$3,433	$3,732	$4,041	$4,358	$4,685	$5,023	$5,356	$ 5,726	$ 6,094	$ 6,474
Taxable income	344	976	1,605	2,232	2,859	3,489	4,123	$ 4,765	5,416	4,756
Tax rate	.43	.43	.43	.43	.43	.43	.43	.43	.43	.43
Taxes	120	342	562	781	1,001	1,221	1,443	1,668	1,896	2,045
ATCF	3,313	3,390	3,479	3,579	3,684	3,802	3,913	4,058	4,198	4,429

TABLE 10-18. Before-Tax Equity Reversion—Revised

Selling price	$315,000
Less selling expenses	−15,750
Amount realized on sale	$299,250
Less unpaid mortgage balance	−134,476
Before-tax equity reversion	$165,774

TABLE 10-19. Taxable Income from Sale—Revised

Taxable Income from Sale	
Amount realized	$299,250
Less adjusted basis	−135,291
Total gain	$163,959
Less excess depreciation	−29,709
Capital gain	$134,250

Total Taxable Income from Sale	
1. Capital gain (40% of $134,250)	$ 53,700
2. Excess depreciation recapture	$ 29,709
3. Preference tax income (60% of $134,250)	$ 80,550

TABLE 10-20. After-Tax Equity Reversion for Mr. X—Revised
(65% of the Total Given in Table 10-19)

Taxable Income	
1. Share of capital gain	$ 34,905
2. Share of depreciation recapture	$ 19,311
3. Share of preference income	$ 52,358

Taxes		
1. Capital gains	taxed as ordinary income	$ 34,231
2. Depreciation recapture		
3. Preference taxes		—
Total taxes on sale		$ 34,231

After-Tax Equity Reversion	
Before-tax equity reversion (65% of $164,774)	$107,103
Less taxes on sale	34,231
After-tax equity reversion	$ 72,872

Tables 10-20 and 10-21 show the ATER for Mr. X and Ms. Y respectively. As expected, the ATERs have increased over those in Tables 10-12 and 10-13. The numbers in Tables 10-20 and 10-21 were calculated using the process outlined under the initial assumptions. The investors are now ready to reevaluate the investment decision using their new inputs and the expected after-tax cash flows.

TABLE 10-21.   After-Tax Equity Reversion for Ms. Y—Revised
(35% of the Total Given in Table 10-19)

Taxable Income	
1. Share of capital gain	$18,795
2. Share of depreciation recapture	$10,398
3. Share of preference income	$28,193

Taxes		
1. Capital gains		
2. Depreciation recapture	taxed as ordinary income	$14,416
3. Preference taxes		—
Total taxes on sale		$14,416

After-Tax Equity Reversion	
Before-tax equity reversion	
(35% of $164,774)	$57,671
Less taxes on sale	14,416
After-tax equity reversion	$43,255

The Revised Investment Decision

Tables 10-22 and 10-23 show the present value of the expected after-tax cash flows and the after-tax equity reversion for Mr. X and Ms. Y at the desired 12-percent rate of return. The present value factors are from Table A-1 in the Appendix. The total present value for Mr. X is $55,620 and $30,988 for Ms. Y. Comparing the present value of the expected cash flows to the costs of investing, the investors can now make an investment decision.

For Mr. X the cost of his equity investment is $47,970. The present value of the expected after-tax inflows is $55,620. The cost of investing is less than the present value of the expected inflows. Thus, Mr. X should invest in the project. If he did invest and if the cash flow was as expected, he would earn at least his 12-percent required return on an after-tax bases.

TABLE 10-22. Present Value of After-Tax Cash Flows at 12% Rate of Return to Mr. X

Year	ATCF	ATER	Present Value Factor at 12%	Present Value
1	$5,998	—	0.892857	$ 5,355
2	5,861	—	0.797194	4,672
3	5,745	—	0.711780	4,089
4	5,648	—	0.635518	3,589
5	5,569	—	0.567427	3,160
6	5,505	—	0.506631	2,789
7	5,430	—	0.452349	2,456
8	5,414	—	0.403883	2,187
9	5,384	—	0.360610	1,942
10	6,812	$72,872	0.321973	25,656
Total present value				$55,895

TABLE 10-23. Present Value of After-Tax Cash Flows at 12% Rate of Return to Ms. Y

Year	ATCF	ATER	Present Value Factor at 12%	Present Value
1	$3,313	—	0.892857	$ 2,958
2	3,390	—	0.797194	2,702
3	3,479	—	0.711780	2,476
4	3,579	—	0.635518	2,275
5	3,684	—	0.567427	2,090
6	3,802	—	0.506631	1,926
7	3,913	—	0.452349	1,770
8	4,058	—	0.403883	1,639
9	4,198	—	0.360610	1,514
10	4,429	$43,255	0.321973	15,353
Total present value				$34,703

For Ms. Y, the cost of her equity investment is $25,830 while the present value of the expected cash inflows is $34,703. In her case, the costs are also less than the expected benefits. She should also invest in the project.

Under this new set of assumptions about expected rents and expected selling price both Mr. X and Ms. Y should invest in the project. They know the expected outcome if their assumptions are correct. The question they must now answer is how confident are they in their expectations?

SUMMARY

The real estate investment process is complex and requires the careful consideration of many factors. This chapter has outlined an application of this process using an apartment investment example. As can be seen in this example, one of the key factors influencing the investment decision is taxation.

Every investment decision requires a number of assumptions regarding the expected cost and benefits from the investment. Investors should examine their expectations by formulating them and using the investment process to examine how these expectations influence the final decision. Almost all of the inputs in the investment process are uncertain. There always exists the risk that the actual outcome will not be the same as was expected. But this risk taking is the essence of investing. Although by examining the inputs carefully the investor can help reduce the risk of investing, the risk can never be completely eliminated—only reduced to an acceptable level.

Real estate investing can be very profitable. We hope that this book has helped make the investor more aware of the factors that can help make it so.

Bibliography

GENERAL REAL ESTATE INVESTMENT TEXTS

Beaton, William R., and T. D. Robertson. *Real Estate Investment*, 2nd ed. Englewood Cliffs, N.J.: Prentice-Hall, Inc., 1977.

Case, Fred E., *Investing in Real Estate*. Englewood Cliffs, N.J.: Prentice-Hall, Inc., 1978.

Kinnard, William N., *Income Property Valuation*. Lexington, Mass.: Heath, 1971.

Roulac, Stephen E., *Modern Real Estate Investment*. San Francisco: Property Press, 1976.

Wendt, P. F., and A. R. Cerf, *Real Estate Investment and Taxation*, 2nd. ed. New York: McGraw-Hill, 1979.

TAXATION AND REAL ESTATE INVESTMENTS

Anderson, Paul E., *Tax Factors in Real Estate Operations*, 5th ed. Englewood Cliffs, N.J.: Prentice-Hall, Inc., 1978.

Arnold, Alvin L., *Tax Shelters in Real Estate Under the Tax Reform Act of 1976*. Boston: Warren, Gorham, and Lamont, 1977.

201

Berman, Daniel S., and Sheldon Schwartz, *Tax Saving Opportunities in Real Estate Deals.* Englewood Cliffs, N.J.: Prentice-Hall, Inc., 1971.

Greer, Gaylon E., *The Real Estate Investor and the Federal Income Tax.* New York: Wiley-Interscience, 1978.

Levine, M. L., *Real Estate Tax Shelter Desk Book.* Englewood Cliffs, N.J.: Institute for Business Planning, Inc., 1978.

Morris, J. Scott, *Real Estate Tax Planning.* Boston: Little, Brown, 1977.

Prentice-Hall Federal Tax Handbook, 1979. Englewood Cliffs, N.J.: Prentice-Hall, Inc., 1979.

Robinson, Gerald J., *Federal Income Taxation of Real Estate.* Boston: Warren, Gorham, and Lamont, 1979.

Weiss, Robert M., *How to Maximize Tax Savings in Buying, Operating and Selling Real Property*, 2nd ed. Englewood Cliffs, N.J.: Prentice-Hall, Inc., 1977.

PARTNERSHIPS AND FORMS OF OWNERSHIP

Bellavance, Russell C., and Caroline S. Zaden, *Introduction to Real Estate Law.* The Institute for Paralegal Training. St. Paul, Minn.: West Publishing Company, 1978.

Klein, M. I., *The Bankrupt Real Estate Partnership: Practice and Procedure.* New York: Practicing Law Institute, 1977.

Kratovil, Robert, *Real Estate Law*, 7th ed. Englewood Cliffs, N.J.: Prentice-Hall, Inc., 1979.

Lynn, T. S., H. F. Goldberg, and D. S. Abrams, *Real Estate Limited Partnerships.* New York: Wiley-Interscience, 1977.

Volz, Marlin M., and Arthur L. Berges, *The Drafting of Partnership Agreements*, 6th ed. Philadelphia: American Law Institute, 1976.

FINANCING AND REAL ESTATE INVESTMENTS

Arnold, A. L., *Modern Real Estate and Mortgage Forms.* Boston: Warren, Gorham, and Lamont, 1978.

Bagby, Joseph R., *Real Estate Financing Desk Book*, 2nd ed. Englewood Cliffs, N.J.: Institute for Business Planning, Inc., 1977.

Brittan, J. A., and L. O. Kerwood, *Financing Income-Producing Real Estate.* New York: McGraw-Hill, 1976.

Cummings, J., *Complete Guide To Real Estate Financing*. Englewood Cliffs, N.J.: Prentice-Hall, Inc., 1978.

Hines, M. A., *Real Estate Finance*. Englewood Cliffs, N.J.: Prentice-Hall, Inc., 1978.

Hoagland, H. E., L. D. Stone, and W. B. Brueggeman, *Real Estate Finance*, 6th ed. Homewood, Ill.: Richard D. Irwin, 1977.

Maisel, S. J., and S. E. Roulac, *Real Estate Investment and Finance*. New York: McGraw-Hill, 1976.

PERIODICALS

The *Appraisal Journal*. American Institute of Real Estate Appraisers of the National Association of Realtors, 430 North Michigan Ave., Chicago, Ill., 60611.

Journal of Property Management. Institute of Real Estate Management of the National Association of Realtors, 430 North Michigan Ave., Chicago, Ill., 60611.

Mortgage Banker. Mortgage Bankers Association of America, 1125 Fifteenth St. N.W., Washington, D.C., 20005.

The *Real Estate Appraiser and Analyst*. Society of Real Estate Appraisers, 645 North Michigan Avenue., Chicago, Ill., 60611.

Real Estate Investing Letter. United Media International, Inc., 306 Dartmouth Street, Boston, Mass., 02116.

Real Estate Issues. American Society of Real Estate Counselors of the National Association of Realtors, 430 North Michigan Avenue., Chicago, Ill., 60611.

Real Estate Report. Real Estate Research Corporation, 72 W. Adams, Chicago, Ill., 60603.

Real Estate Review. Warren, Gorham, and Lamont, 210 South Street, Boston, Mass., 02111.

Real Estate Today. National Association of Realtors and the Realtors National Marketing Institute of National Association of Realtors, 430 North Michigan Ave., Chicago, Ill., 60611.

The *Tax Advisor*. American Institute of Certified Public Accountants, 1211 Avenue of the Americas, New York, N.Y., 10036.

Taxation for Accountants. The Journal of Taxation, Ltd., P.O. Box 318, Dover, N.J., 07801.

Taxes on Parade. Commerce Clearing House, Inc., P.O. Box 318, Dover, N.J., 07801.

Taxes: The Tax Magazine. Commerce Clearing House, Inc., 4025 W. Peterson Avenue, Chicago, Ill., 60646.

Appendix:
Real Estate
Investment Tables

The tables presented in this appendix are used in making real estate investment decisions. There are three sets of tables:

Table A-1—Present Value of $1.00
Table A-2—Mortgage Constant (Monthly Payments)
Table A-3—Mortgage Constant (Annual Payments)

Table A-1 provides the factors for finding the present value of a payment to be made in the future at various rates of discount. Tables A-2 and A-3 provide the mortgage constant factors for monthly and annual payments, respectively. The mortgage constant, when multiplied by the amount borrowed, tells the investor the payment necessary to repay the debt.

HOW TO USE TABLE A-1

Table A-1 is constructed using the following equation

$$V^n = \frac{1}{(1+i)^t}$$

where

$$V^n = \text{the present value of } \$1.00$$

$$i = \text{the rate of discount}$$

$$t = \text{the number of years}$$

EXAMPLE A-1

What is the present value of $1.00 to be received five years in the future, discounted at 10 percent per year?

$$V^n = \frac{1}{(1 + .1)^5} = \frac{1}{1.61051} = .62092$$

Thus, $1.00 to be received five years from now is worth 62 cents, at a discount rate of 10 percent. The factor .62092 for 10-percent interest for five years can be found in Table A-1 by looking under the column labeled "10% for 5 years."

Stated differently, an investor could pay 62 cents for an investment which would sell for $1.00 five years in the future and earn a rate of return of 10 percent.

Another way of saying the same thing is: If the investor deposited 62 cents in an account earning 10 percent per year, the 62 cents would be worth $1.00 at the end of five years. This can be seen as follows:

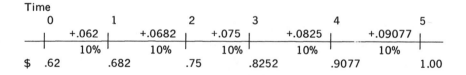

Time
0	1	2	3	4	5
+.062	+.0682	+.075	+.0825	+.09077	
10%	10%	10%	10%	10%	
$ .62	.682	.75	.8252	.9077	1.00

The investor invests 62 cents and earns 10 percent or .062 cents in interest the first year. This continues for five years, such that at the end of this period the 62 cents are worth $1.00. This is the same as saying that $1.00 five years in the future has a present value of 62 cents when discounted at the rate of 10 percent.

EXAMPLE A-2

A real estate investment is producing the following after-tax cash flow (ATCF):

Year	ATCF	Factor	Present Value
1	$3,332	.90909	$ 3,029.09
2	3,370	.82645	2,785.12
3	3,244	.75131	2,437.27
4	3,201	.68301	2,186.32
5	3,158	.62092	1,960.87
Total present value			$12,398.67

What is the present value of these cash flows at a rate of 10 percent? The present value factors from Table A-1 at 10 percent are shown in Column 3. Multiplying these factors by the ATCF yields the present value. Adding the present values results in a total present value of $12,398.67. What does this mean to the investor? It tells the investor that he or she can pay $12,398.67 for the investment and, assuming the investment generates the expected ATCF, earn a rate of return of 10 percent. If the investor pays more than $12,398.67, what would happen to his or her rate of return? It would be lower. If the investor paid less than $12,398.67, and assuming that the ATCFs were correct, the investor would earn greater than a 10-percent return on the investment.

HOW TO USE TABLES A-2 AND A-3

Tables A-2 and A-3 give the mortgage constant. The mortgage constant, when multiplied by the amount borrowed, results in the amount of debt service or payment to be made each period. Table A-2 is for payments made monthly while Table A-3 is for annual payments. If the mortgage calls for monthly payments do not use the annual table, and vice versa.

EXAMPLE A-3:
ANNUAL PAYMENTS

Problem 1. Mr. X borrows $100,000 from the XYZ bank. The loan is at 10-percent annual interest with payments to be made **annually** over a period of twenty-five years. What is the annual debt service?

Solution. Table 3 shows the mortgage constant factor for annual payments. Under "10% for 25 years," the factor is .11017. The debt service payment is thus:

$$\$100,000 \times .11017 = \$11,017.00$$

Mr. X must make a payment of $11,017.00 each year for twenty-five years. At the end of the twenty-five years he will have amortized (paid off) the loan.

Problem 2. What portion of the $11,017.00 payment is interest and what portion is principal payment for the Years 1 through 5?

Solution. The interest and principal are shown as follows:

Year	Amount Outstanding	Debt Service	Interest Payment	Principal Payment
0	$100,000.00	—	—	—
1	$ 98,983.00	$11,017.00	$10,000.00	$1,017.00
2	$ 97,864.30	$11,017.00	$ 9,898.30	$1,118.70
3	$ 96,633.73	$11,017.00	$ 9,786.43	$1,230.57
4	$ 95,280.00	$11,017.00	$ 9,663.37	$1,353.63
5	$ 93,791.11	$11,017.00	$ 9,528.01	$1,488.99

These numbers were calculated as follows: The original amount outstanding is $100,000.00. The debt service is a constant amount of $11,017.00 each year. Since the interest rate is 10 percent, the amount of interest in Year 1 is $10,000.00 ($100,000 × .10). The total payment is $11,017.00 and the interest payment is $10,000, thus the principal payment is $1,017.00 ($11,017.00 – $10,000.00). At the end of Year 1 the amount outstanding is $97,983.00. This is the original balance, $100,000.00, less the principal payment in Year 1, $1,017.00. Using this new balance, the interest payment in the second year is $9,898.30 ($98,983.00 × .10). The principal payment in the second year is $1,118.70 ($11,017.00 – $9,898.30). The amount outstanding at the end of the second year is $97,864.32. This process is continued for each year.

Notice that at the end of five years the amount outstanding is $93,791.11. Since the original amount was $100,000.00 the amount outstanding can be expressed as a percentage as follows

$$\text{Percent outstanding after 5 years} = \frac{\$93,791.11}{\$100,000.00} = 93.791\%$$

Problem 3. Suppose Mr. X decided to pay off the loan after five years. What amount of the loan would be still outstanding?

Solution. The answer is already known to be $93,791.11. There is another method of solving the problem without using the time-consuming process outlined in Problem 2.

To find the percent outstanding at the end of any year, the following equation can be used:

$$\text{Percent outstanding} = \frac{\text{Mortgage constant for total mortgage term}}{\text{Mortgage constant for remaining term}}$$

To illustrate, the mortgage constant for the total mortgage term of twenty-five years was .110168 (see Problem 1). Mr. X wants to pay the loan off after five years which gives a remaining term of twenty years. Using Table A-3 and the 10% for 20 years column, a mortgage constant of .117460 is obtained. Thus there is another way to find the percent outstanding:

$$\text{Percent outstanding after 5 years} = \frac{.11017}{.11746} = 93.794\%$$

Multiplying this percentage by the original loan amount of $100,000 yields

Amount outstanding = $100,000.00 × .93794 = $93,794.00

This is the same answer as in the solution used in Problem 2.

EXAMPLE A-4:
MONTHLY PAYMENTS

Problem 1. Ms. Y borrows $100,000 from the XYZ bank. The loan is at 10-percent interest with payments to be made **monthly** over a period of twenty-five years (300 monthly payments). What is the **annual** debt service?

Solution. The difference between this problem and Example A-3 is that the loan calls for monthly payments instead of annual payments. Table A-2 gives the mortgage constant under monthly payments. At 10-percent interest for twenty-five years, the monthly mortgage constant is .00909. The **monthly** payment is thus

$$100,000 \times .00909 = \$909.00$$

The annual payment is twelve times the monthly payment:

$$\$909.00 \times 12 = \$10,908.00$$

Notice that the annual payment when monthly amortization occurs ($10,908.00) is less than the annual payment in Example A-3 ($11,017.00). Why? Because with monthly payments, the total interest to be paid is less since the interest is paid on the amount outstanding.

If the loan calls for monthly payment, the monthly table must be used to calculate debt service.

Problem 2. What amount of the $100,000 would be outstanding after five years of monthly payments?

Solution. To find the percent outstanding, the procedure outlined in Problem 3 of Example A-3 can be used.

$$\text{Percent outstanding} = \frac{\text{Mortgage constant for total term}}{\text{Mortgage constant for remaining term}}$$

Using the 10% monthly Table A-2,

$$\text{Percent outstanding} = \frac{.00909}{= .00965} = 94.20\%$$

The percent outstanding after five years is found by dividing .00909, the mortgage constant for the total term (10% for 25 years, monthly payments), by .00965, the mortgage constant for the remaining term (10% for 20 years, monthly payments).

Multiplying the percent outstanding, 94.20 percent, by the original amount, $100,000, yields the amount outstanding after five years:

$$\$100,000.00 \times .9420 = \$94,200.00$$

TABLE 1:
Present Value of 1 (Annual)

Years	7.00%	7.25%	7.50%	7.75%	8.00%	8.25%	Years
			Interest Rate				
1	.93458	.93240	.93023	.92807	.92593	.92379	1
2	.87344	.86937	.86533	.86132	.85734	.85338	2
3	.81630	.81060	.80496	.79937	.79383	.78835	3
4	.76290	.75581	.74880	.74188	.73503	.72826	4
5	.71299	.70472	.69656	.68852	.68058	.67276	5
6	.66634	.65708	.64796	.63899	.63017	.62149	6
7	.62275	.61266	.60275	.59303	.58349	.57412	7
8	.58201	.57124	.56070	.55038	.54027	.53037	8
9	.54393	.53263	.52158	.51079	.50025	.48995	9
10	.50835	.49662	.48519	.47405	.46319	.45261	10
11	.47509	.46305	.45134	.43996	.42888	.41811	11
12	.44401	.43175	.41985	.40831	.39711	.38625	12
13	.41496	.40256	.39056	.37894	.36770	.35681	13
14	.38782	.37535	.36331	.35169	.34046	.32962	14
15	.36245	.34998	.33797	.32639	.31524	.30450	15
16	.33874	.32632	.31439	.30292	.29189	.28129	16
17	.31657	.30426	.29245	.28113	.27027	.25985	17
18	.29586	.28369	.27205	.26091	.25025	.24005	18
19	.27651	.26452	.23507	.24214	.23171	.22175	19
20	.25842	.24664	.23541	.22473	.21455	.20485	20
21	.24151	.22996	.21899	.20856	.19866	.18924	21
22	.22571	.21442	.20371	.19356	.18394	.17482	22
23	.21095	.19992	.18950	.17964	.17032	.16150	23
24	.19715	.18641	.17628	.16672	.15770	.14919	24
25	.18425	.17381	.16398	.15473	.14602	.13782	25
26	.17220	.16206	.15254	.14351	.13520	.12731	26
27	.16093	.15110	.14190	.13327	.12519	.11761	27
28	.15040	.14089	.13200	.12369	.11591	.10865	28
29	.14056	.13137	.12279	.11479	.10733	.10037	29
30	.13137	.12248	.11422	.10653	.09938	.09272	30
31	.12277	.11421	.10625	.09887	.09202	.08565	31
32	.11474	.10648	.09884	.09176	.08520	.07912	32
33	.10723	.09929	.09194	.08516	.07889	.07309	33
34	.10022	.09258	.08553	.07903	.07305	.06752	34
35	.09366	.08632	.07956	.07335	.06763	.06238	35
40	.06678	.06083	.05542	.05050	.04603	.04197	40
45	.04762	.04287	.03860	.03477	.03133	.02823	45
50	.03395	.03021	.02689	.02394	.02132	.01899	50

TABLE 1:
Present Value of 1 (Annual) [cont.]

			Interest Rate				
Years	8.50%	8.75%	9.00%	9.25%	9.50%	9.75%	Years
1	.92166	.91954	.91743	.91533	.91324	.91116	1
2	.84946	.84555	.84168	.83783	.83401	.83022	2
3	.78291	.77752	.77218	.76690	.76165	.75646	3
4	.72157	.71496	.70843	.70196	.69557	.68926	4
5	.66505	.65744	.64993	.64253	.63523	.62803	5
6	.61295	.60454	.59627	.58813	.58012	.57223	6
7	.56493	.55590	.54703	.53833	.52979	.52140	7
8	.52067	.51117	.50187	.49275	.48382	.47508	8
9	.47988	.47004	.46043	.45103	.44185	.43287	9
10	.44229	.43222	.42241	.41284	.40351	.39442	10
11	.40764	.39745	.38753	.37789	.36851	.35938	11
12	.37570	.36547	.35553	.34589	.33654	.32745	12
13	.34627	.33606	.32618	.31661	.30734	.29836	13
14	.31914	.30902	.29925	.28980	.28067	.27186	14
15	.29414	.28416	.27454	.26526	.25632	.24770	15
16	.27110	.26130	.25187	.24281	.23409	.22570	16
17	.24986	.24027	.23107	.22225	.21378	.20565	17
18	.23028	.22094	.21199	.20343	.19523	.18738	18
19	.21224	.20316	.19449	.18621	.17829	.17073	19
20	.19562	.18682	.17843	.17044	.16282	.15556	20
21	.18029	.17179	.16370	.15601	.14870	.14174	21
22	.16617	.15796	.15018	.14280	.13580	.12915	22
23	.15315	.14525	.13778	.13071	.12402	.11768	23
24	.14115	.13357	.12640	.11964	.11326	.10722	24
25	.13009	.12282	.11597	.10951	.10343	.09770	25
26	.11990	.11294	.10639	.10024	.09446	.08902	26
27	.11051	.10385	.09761	.09175	.08626	.08111	27
28	.10185	.09550	.08955	.08399	.07878	.07391	28
29	.09387	.08781	.08215	.07687	.07194	.06734	29
30	.08652	.08075	.07537	.07037	.06570	.06136	30
31	.07974	.07425	.06915	.06441	.06000	.05591	31
32	.07349	.06828	.06344	.05895	.05480	.05094	32
33	.06774	.06278	.05820	.05396	.05004	.04641	33
34	.06243	.05773	.05339	.04939	.04570	.04229	34
35	.05754	.05309	.04899	.04521	.04174	.03853	35
40	.03827	.03490	.03184	.02905	.02651	.02420	40
45	.02545	.02295	.02069	.01867	.01684	.01520	45
50	.01692	.01509	.01345	.01199	.01070	.00955	50

TABLE 1:
Present Value of 1 (Annual) [cont.]

			Interest Rate				
Years	10.00%	10.25%	10.50%	10.75%	11.00%	11.25%	Years
1	.90909	.90703	.90498	.90294	.90090	.89888	1
2	.82645	.82270	.81898	.81529	.81162	.80798	2
3	.75131	.74622	.74116	.73615	.73119	.72627	3
4	.68301	.67684	.67073	.66470	.65873	.65283	4
5	.62092	.61391	.60700	.60018	.59345	.58681	5
6	.56447	.55684	.54932	.54192	.53464	.52747	6
7	.51316	.50507	.49712	.48932	.48166	.47413	7
8	.46651	.45811	.44989	.44183	.43393	.42619	8
9	.42410	.41552	.40714	.39894	.39092	.38309	9
10	.38554	.37689	.36845	.36022	.35218	.34435	10
11	.35049	.34185	.33344	.32525	.31728	.30953	11
12	.31863	.31007	.30175	.29368	.28584	.27823	12
13	.28966	.28124	.27308	.26517	.25751	.25009	13
14	.26333	.25509	.24713	.23944	.23199	.22480	14
15	.23939	.23138	.22365	.21619	.20900	.20207	15
16	.21763	.20989	.20240	.19521	.18829	.18164	16
17	.19784	.19036	.18316	.17626	.16963	.16327	17
18	.17986	.17266	.16576	.15915	.15282	.14676	18
19	.16351	.15661	.15001	.14370	.13768	.13192	19
20	.14864	.14205	.13575	.12976	.12403	.11858	20
21	.13513	.12884	.12285	.11716	.11174	.10659	21
22	.12285	.11686	.11118	.10579	.10067	.09581	22
23	.11168	.10600	.10062	.09552	.09069	.08612	23
24	.10153	.09614	.09106	.08625	.08170	.07741	24
25	.09230	.08720	.08240	.07788	.07361	.06958	25
26	.08391	.07910	.07457	.07032	.06631	.06255	26
27	.07628	.07174	.06749	.06349	.05974	.05622	27
28	.06934	.06507	.06107	.05733	.05382	.05054	28
29	.06304	.05902	.05527	.05176	.04849	.04543	29
30	.05731	.05354	.05002	.04674	.04368	.04083	30
31	.05210	.04856	.04527	.04220	.03935	.03670	31
32	.04736	.04404	.04096	.03811	.03545	.03299	32
33	.04306	.03995	.03707	.03441	.03194	.02966	33
34	.03914	.03624	.03355	.03107	.02878	.02666	34
35	.03558	.03287	.03036	.02805	.02592	.02396	35
40	.02209	.02018	.01843	.01684	.01538	.01406	40
45	.01372	.01239	.01119	.01011	.00913	.00825	45
50	.00852	.00760	.00679	.00607	.00542	.00484	50

TABLE 1:
Present Value of 1 (Annual) [cont.]

Years	11.50%	11.75%	12.00%	12.50%	13.00%	13.50%	Years
			Interest Rate				
1	.89686	.89486	.89286	.88889	.88496	.88106	1
2	.80436	.80077	.79719	.79012	.78315	.77626	2
3	.72140	.71657	.71178	.70233	.69305	.68393	3
4	.64699	.64122	.63552	.62430	.61332	.60258	4
5	.58026	.57380	.56743	.55493	.54276	.53091	5
6	.52042	.51347	.50663	.49327	.48032	.46772	6
7	.46674	.45948	.45235	.43846	.42506	.41213	7
8	.41860	.41117	.40388	.38974	.37616	.36311	8
9	.37543	.36794	.36061	.34644	.33288	.31992	9
10	.33671	.32925	.32197	.30795	.29459	.28187	10
11	.30198	.29463	.28748	.27373	.26070	.24834	11
12	.27083	.26365	.25668	.24332	.23071	.21880	12
13	.24290	.23593	.22917	.21628	.20416	.19278	13
14	.21785	.21112	.20462	.19225	.18068	.16985	14
15	.19538	.18892	.18270	.17089	.15989	.14964	15
16	.17523	.16906	.16312	.15190	.14150	.13185	16
17	.15715	.15128	.14564	.13502	.12522	.11616	17
18	.14095	.13538	.13004	.12002	.11081	.10245	18
19	.12641	.12114	.11611	.10668	.09806	.09017	19
20	.11337	.10841	.10367	.09483	.08678	.07945	20
21	.10168	.09701	.09256	.08429	.07680	.07000	21
22	.09119	.08681	.08264	.07493	.06796	.06167	22
23	.08179	.07768	.07379	.06660	.06014	.05434	23
24	.07335	.06951	.06588	.05920	.05323	.04787	24
25	.06579	.06220	.05882	.05262	.04710	.04219	25
26	.05900	.05566	.05252	.04678	.04168	.03716	26
27	.05291	.04981	.04689	.04158	.03689	.03274	27
28	.04746	.04457	.04187	.03696	.03264	.02885	28
29	.04256	.03989	.03738	.03285	.02889	.02542	29
30	.03817	.03569	.03338	.02920	.02557	.02239	30
31	.03424	.03194	.02980	.02596	.02263	.01973	31
32	.03070	.02858	.02661	.02308	.02002	.01738	32
33	.02754	.02558	.02376	.02051	.01772	.01532	33
34	.02470	.02289	.02121	.01823	.01568	.01349	34
35	.02215	.02048	.01894	.01621	.01388	.01189	35
40	.01285	.01175	.01075	.00899	.00753	.00631	40
45	.00746	.00674	.00610	.00499	.00409	.00335	45
50	.00433	.00387	.00346	.00277	.00222	.00178	50

TABLE 1:
Present Value of 1 (Annual) [cont.]

			Interest Rate				
Years	14.00%	14.50%	15.00%	15.50%	16.00%	16.50%	Years
1	.87720	.87336	.86957	.86580	.86207	.85837	1
2	.76947	.76276	.75614	.74961	.74316	.73680	2
3	.67497	.66617	.65752	.64901	.64066	.63244	3
4	.59208	.58181	.57175	.56192	.55229	.54287	4
5	.51937	.50813	.49718	.48651	.47611	.46598	5
6	.45559	.44378	.43233	.42122	.41044	.39999	6
7	.39964	.38758	.37594	.36469	.35384	.34334	7
8	.35056	.33850	.32690	.31576	.30503	.29471	8
9	.30751	.29563	.28426	.27338	.26295	.25297	9
10	.26974	.25819	.24718	.23669	.22668	.21714	10
11	.23662	.22550	.21494	.20493	.19542	.18639	11
12	.20756	.19694	.18691	.17743	.16846	.15999	12
13	.18207	.17200	.16253	.15362	.14523	.13733	13
14	.15971	.15022	.14133	.13300	.12520	.11788	14
15	.14010	.13120	.12289	.11515	.10793	.10118	15
16	.12289	.11458	.10686	.09970	.09304	.08685	16
17	.10780	.10007	.09293	.08632	.08021	.07455	17
18	.09456	.08740	.08081	.07474	.06914	.06399	18
19	.08295	.07633	.07027	.06471	.05961	.05493	19
20	.07276	.06667	.06110	.05602	.05139	.04716	20
21	.06323	.05822	.05313	.04850	.04430	.04047	21
22	.05599	.05055	.04620	.04199	.03819	.03474	22
23	.04911	.04441	.04017	.03636	.03292	.02981	23
24	.04308	.03879	.03493	.03148	.02838	.02560	24
25	.03779	.03387	.03038	.02726	.02447	.02197	25
26	.03315	.02958	.02642	.02360	.02109	.01886	26
27	.02908	.02594	.02298	.02043	.01818	.01619	27
28	.02551	.02257	.01997	.01769	.01567	.01390	28
29	.02237	.01971	.01737	.01532	.01351	.01193	29
30	.01963	.01721	.01510	.01327	.01165	.01024	30
31	.01722	.01503	.01313	.01148	.01004	.00879	31
32	.01510	.01313	.01142	.00995	.00866	.00754	32
33	.01325	.01147	.00993	.00861	.00746	.00648	33
34	.01162	.01001	.00864	.00745	.00643	.00556	34
35	.01019	.00875	.00751	.00645	.00555	.00477	35
40	.00529	.00444	.00373	.00314	.00264	.00222	40
45	.00275	.00226	.00186	.00153	.00126	.00107	45
50	.00143	.00115	.00092	.00074	.00060	.00048	50

TABLE 1:
Present Value of 1 (Annual) [cont.]

				Interest Rate			
Years	17.00%	18.00%	19.00%	20.00%	21.00%	22.00%	Years
1	.85470	.84746	.84034	.83333	.82645	.81967	1
2	.73051	.71818	.70616	.69444	.68301	.67186	2
3	.62437	.60863	.59342	.57874	.56447	.55071	3
4	.53365	.51579	.49867	.48225	.46651	.45140	4
5	.45611	.43711	.41905	.40188	.38554	.37000	5
6	.38984	.37043	.35214	.33490	.31863	.30328	6
7	.33320	.31393	.29592	.27908	.26333	.24859	7
8	.28478	.26604	.24868	.23257	.21763	.20376	8
9	.24340	.22546	.20897	.19381	.17986	.16702	9
10	.20804	.19106	.17560	.16151	.14864	.13690	10
11	.17782	.16192	.14757	.13459	.12285	.11221	11
12	.15197	.13722	.12400	.11216	.10153	.09198	12
13	.12989	.11629	.10421	.09346	.08391	.07539	13
14	.11102	.09854	.08757	.07789	.06934	.06180	14
15	.09489	.08352	.07359	.06491	.05731	.05065	15
16	.08110	.07078	.06184	.05409	.04736	.04152	16
17	.06932	.05998	.05196	.04507	.03914	.03403	17
18	.05925	.05083	.04367	.03756	.03235	.02789	18
19	.05064	.04308	.03670	.03130	.02673	.02286	19
20	.04328	.03651	.03084	.02608	.02209	.01874	20
21	.03699	.03094	.02591	.02174	.01826	.01536	21
22	.03162	.02622	.02178	.01811	.01509	.01259	22
23	.02702	.02222	.01829	.01509	.01247	.01032	23
24	.02310	.01883	.01538	.01258	.01031	.00846	24
25	.01974	.01596	.01292	.01048	.00852	.00693	25
26	.01687	.01352	.01086	.00874	.00704	.00568	26
27	.01442	.01146	.00912	.00728	.00582	.00466	27
28	.01233	.00971	.00767	.00607	.00481	.00382	28
29	.01053	.00823	.00644	.00506	.00397	.00313	29
30	.00900	.00697	.00541	.00421	.00328	.00257	30
31	.00770	.00591	.00455	.00351	.00271	.00210	31
32	.00658	.00501	.00382	.00293	.00224	.00172	32
33	.00562	.00425	.00321	.00244	.00185	.00141	33
34	.00480	.00360	.00270	.00203	.00153	.00116	34
35	.00411	.00305	.00227	.00169	.00127	.00095	35
40	.00187	.00133	.00095	.00068	.00049	.00035	40
45	.00085	.00058	.00040	.00027	.00019	.00013	45
50	.00039	.00025	.00017	.00011	.00007	.00005	50

TABLE 1:
Present Value of 1 (Annual) [cont.]

| | | | Interest Rate | | | | |
Years	23.00%	24.00%	25.00%	26.00%	28.00%	30.00%	Years
1	.81301	.80645	.80000	.79365	.78125	.76923	1
2	.66098	.65036	.64000	.62988	.61035	.59172	2
3	.53738	.52449	.51200	.49991	.47684	.45517	3
4	.43690	.42297	.40960	.39675	.37253	.35013	4
5	.35520	.34111	.32768	.31488	.29104	.26933	5
6	.28878	.27509	.26214	.24991	.22737	.20718	6
7	.23478	.22184	.20972	.19834	.17764	.15937	7
8	.19088	.17890	.16777	.15741	.13878	.12259	8
9	.15519	.14228	.13422	.12493	.10842	.09480	9
10	.12617	.11635	.10737	.09915	.08470	.07254	10
11	.10258	.09383	.08590	.07869	.06617	.05580	11
12	.08339	.07567	.06872	.06245	.05170	.04292	12
13	.06781	.06103	.05498	.04957	.04039	.03302	13
14	.05512	.04921	.04398	.03934	.03155	.02540	14
15	.04481	.03969	.03518	.03122	.02465	.01954	15
16	.03643	.03201	.02815	.02478	.01926	.01503	16
17	.02962	.02581	.02252	.01967	.01505	.01156	17
18	.02408	.02082	.01801	.01561	.01175	.00889	18
19	.01958	.01679	.01441	.01239	.00918	.00684	19
20	.01592	.01354	.01153	.00983	.00717	.00526	20
21	.01294	.01092	.00922	.00780	.00561	.00405	21
22	.01052	.00880	.00738	.00619	.00438	.00311	22
23	.00855	.00710	.00590	.00491	.00342	.00239	23
24	.00695	.00573	.00472	.00390	.00267	.00184	24
25	.00565	.00462	.00378	.00310	.00209	.00142	25
26	.00460	.00372	.00302	.00246	.00163	.00109	26
27	.00374	.00300	.00242	.00195	.00127	.00084	27
28	.00304	.00242	.00193	.00155	.00100	.00065	28
29	.00247	.00195	.00155	.00123	.00078	.00050	29
30	.00201	.00158	.00124	.00097	.00061	.00038	30
31	.00163	.00127	.00099	.00077	.00047	.00029	31
32	.00133	.00102	.00079	.00061	.00037	.00023	32
33	.00108	.00083	.00063	.00049	.00028	.00017	33
34	.00088	.00067	.00051	.00039	.00023	.00013	34
35	.00071	.00054	.00041	.00031	.00018	.00010	35
40	.00025	.00018	.00013	.00010	.00005	.00003	40
45	.00009	.00006	.00004	.00003	.00001	.00001	45
50	.00003	.00002	.00001	.00001	.00000	.00000	50

TABLE 2:
Mortgage Constant (Monthly Payments)

			Interest Rate				
Years	7.00%	7.25%	7.50%	7.75%	8.00%	8.25%	Years
1	.08653	.08664	.08676	.08687	.08699	.08710	1
2	.04477	.04489	.04500	.04511	.04523	.04534	2
3	.03088	.03099	.03111	.03122	.03134	.03145	3
4	.02395	.02406	.02418	.02430	.02441	.02453	4
5	.01980	.01992	.02004	.02016	.02028	.02040	5
6	.01705	.01717	.01729	.01741	.01753	.01766	6
7	.01509	.01522	.01534	.01546	.01560	.01571	7
8	.01363	.01376	.01388	.01401	.01414	.01426	8
9	.01251	.01263	.01276	.01289	.01302	.01315	9
10	.01161	.01174	.01187	.01200	.01213	.01227	10
11	.01088	.01102	.01115	.01128	.01142	.01155	11
12	.01028	.01042	.01055	.01069	.01082	.01096	12
13	.00978	.00992	.01005	.01019	.01033	.01047	13
14	.00935	.00949	.00963	.00977	.00991	.01006	14
15	.00899	.00913	.00927	.00941	.00956	.00970	15
16	.00867	.00881	.00896	.00910	.00925	.00940	16
17	.00840	.00854	.00869	.00883	.00898	.00913	17
18	.00816	.00830	.00845	.00860	.00875	.00890	18
19	.00794	.00809	.00824	.00839	.00855	.00870	19
20	.00775	.00790	.00806	.00821	.00836	.00862	20
21	.00758	.00774	.00789	.00805	.00820	.00836	21
22	.00743	.00759	.00775	.00790	.00806	.00822	22
23	.00730	.00746	.00761	.00777	.00793	.00810	23
24	.00718	.00734	.00750	.00766	.00782	.00798	24
25	.00707	.00723	.00739	.00755	.00772	.00788	25
26	.00697	.00713	.00729	.00746	.00763	.00779	26
27	.00688	.00704	.00721	.00737	.00754	.00771	27
28	.00680	.00696	.00713	.00730	.00747	.00764	28
29	.00672	.00689	.00706	.00730	.00740	.00757	29
30	.00665	.00682	.00699	.00716	.00734	.00751	30
31	.00659	.00676	.00693	.00711	.00728	.00746	31
32	.00653	.00671	.00688	.00705	.00723	.00741	32
33	.00648	.00665	.00683	.00701	.00718	.00736	33
34	.00643	.00661	.00678	.00696	.00714	.00732	34
35	.00639	.00656	.00674	.00692	.00710	.00728	35
40	.00621	.00640	.00648	.00677	.00695	.00714	40
45	.00610	.00628	.00647	.00666	.00686	.00705	45
50	.00602	.00621	.00640	.00660	.00679	.00699	50

TABLE 2:
Mortgage Constant (Monthly Payments) [cont.]

			Interest Rate				
Years	8.50%	8.75%	9.00%	9.25%	9.50%	9.75%	Years
1	.08722	.08734	.08745	.08757	.08768	.08780	1
2	.04546	.04557	.04568	.04580	.04591	.04603	2
3	.03157	.03168	.03180	.03192	.03203	.03215	3
4	.02465	.02477	.02488	.02500	.02512	.02524	4
5	.02052	.02064	.02076	.02088	.02100	.02112	5
6	.01778	.01790	.01803	.01845	.01827	.01840	6
7	.01584	.01596	.01609	.01622	.01634	.01647	7
8	.01439	.01452	.01465	.01478	.01491	.01504	8
9	.01328	.01341	.01354	.01368	.01381	.01394	9
10	.01240	.01253	.01267	.01280	.01294	.01308	10
11	.01169	.01182	.01196	.01210	.01224	.01238	11
12	.01110	.01124	.01138	.01152	.01166	.01181	12
13	.01061	.01075	.01090	.01104	.01119	.01133	13
14	.01020	.01034	.01049	.01064	.01078	.01093	14
15	.00985	.00999	.01014	.01029	.01044	.01059	15
16	.00954	.00969	.00985	.01000	.01015	.01030	16
17	.00928	.00943	.00959	.00974	.00990	.01005	17
18	.00905	.00921	.00936	.00952	.00968	.00984	18
19	.00885	.00901	.00917	.00933	.00949	.00965	19
20	.00868	.00884	.00900	.00916	.00932	.00949	20
21	.00852	.00868	.00885	.00901	.00917	.00934	21
22	.00838	.00855	.00871	.00888	.00904	.00921	22
23	.00826	.00823	.00859	.00876	.00893	.00910	23
24	.00815	.00832	.00849	.00866	.00883	.00900	24
25	.00805	.00822	.00839	.00856	.00874	.00891	25
26	.00796	.00813	.00831	.00848	.00866	.00883	26
27	.00788	.00807	.00823	.00841	.00858	.00876	27
28	.00781	.00799	.00816	.00834	.00852	.00870	28
29	.00775	.00792	.00810	.00828	.00846	.00864	29
30	.00769	.00787	.00805	.00823	.00841	.00859	30
31	.00764	.00782	.00800	.00818	.00836	.00855	31
32	.00759	.00777	.00795	.00813	.00832	.00851	32
33	.00754	.00773	.00791	.00810	.00828	.00847	33
34	.00750	.00769	.00787	.00806	.00825	.00845	34
35	.00747	.00765	.00784	.00803	.00822	.00841	35
40	.00733	.00752	.00771	.00791	.00810	.00830	40
45	.00724	.00744	.00764	.00783	.00803	.00823	45
50	.00719	.00739	.00759	.00779	.00799	.00819	50

TABLE 2:
Mortgage Constant (Monthly Payments) [cont.]

			Interest Rate				
Years	10.00%	10.25%	10.50%	10.75%	11.00%	11.25%	Years
1	.08792	.08803	.08815	.08827	.08838	.08850	1
2	.04614	.04626	.04638	.04649	.04661	.04672	2
3	.03227	.03238	.03250	.03262	.03774	.03286	3
4	.02536	.02548	.02560	.02572	.02585	.02597	4
5	.02125	.02137	.02149	.02162	.02174	.02187	5
6	.01853	.01865	.01878	.01891	.01903	.01916	6
7	.01660	.01673	.01686	.01699	.01712	.01725	7
8	.01517	.01531	.01544	.01557	.01571	.01584	8
9	.01408	.01421	.01435	.01449	.01468	.01476	9
10	.01322	.01335	.01349	.01363	.01378	.01392	10
11	.01252	.01266	.01280	.01295	.01309	.01324	11
12	.01195	.01210	.01224	.01239	.01254	.01268	12
13	.01148	.01163	.01178	.01192	.01208	.01223	13
14	.01108	.01123	.01138	.01154	.01169	.01185	14
15	.01075	.01090	.01105	.01121	.01137	.01152	15
16	.01046	.01062	.01077	.01093	.01109	.01125	16
17	.01021	.01037	.01053	.01069	.01085	.01102	17
18	.01000	.01016	.01032	.01049	.01065	.01082	18
19	.00981	.00998	.01014	.01031	.01047	.01064	19
20	.00965	.00982	.00998	.01015	.01032	.01049	20
21	.00951	.00968	.00985	.01002	.01019	.01036	21
22	.00938	.00955	.00973	.00990	.01007	.01025	22
23	.00927	.00944	.00969	.00979	.00997	.01015	23
24	.00917	.00935	.00952	.00970	.00988	.01006	24
25	.00909	.00926	.00944	.00962	.00980	.00998	25
26	.00901	.00919	.00937	.00955	.00973	.00991	26
27	.00894	.00912	.00930	.00949	.00967	.00985	27
28	.00888	.00906	.00925	.00943	.00961	.00980	28
29	.00882	.00901	.00919	.00938	.00957	.00975	29
30	.00878	.00896	.00915	.00933	.00952	.00971	30
31	.00873	.00892	.00911	.00930	.00948	.00968	31
32	.00869	.00888	.00907	.00926	.00945	.00964	32
33	.00866	.00885	.00904	.00923	.00942	.00961	33
34	.00863	.00882	.00901	.00920	.00939	.00959	34
35	.00860	.00879	.00898	.00918	.00937	.00956	35
40	.00849	.00869	.00889	.00908	.00928	.00948	40
45	.00843	.00863	.00883	.00903	.00923	.00944	45
50	.00839	.00859	.00880	.00900	.00921	.00941	50

TABLE 2:
Mortgage Constant (Monthly Payments) [cont.]

			Interest Rate				
Years	11.50%	11.75%	12.00%	12.50%	13.00%	13.50%	Years
1	.08862	.08873	.08885	.08908	.08932	.08955	1
2	.04684	.04696	.04707	.04731	.04754	.04778	2
3	.03298	.03310	.03321	.03346	.03369	.03394	3
4	.02609	.02621	.02633	.02658	.02683	.02708	4
5	.02199	.02212	.02224	.02250	.02275	.02301	5
6	.01929	.01942	.01955	.01981	.02007	.02034	6
7	.01739	.01752	.01765	.01792	.01819	.01846	7
8	.01598	.01612	.01625	.01653	.01681	.01709	8
9	.01490	.01504	.01518	.01547	.01575	.01604	9
10	.01406	.01420	.01435	.01464	.01493	.01523	10
11	.01338	.01353	.01368	.01398	.01428	.01458	11
12	.01283	.01297	.01313	.01344	.01375	.01406	12
13	.01238	.01253	.01269	.01300	.01331	.01363	13
14	.01200	.01216	.01231	.01263	.01295	.01328	14
15	.01168	.01184	.01200	.01233	.01265	.01298	15
16	.01141	.01157	.01179	.01207	.01240	.01274	16
17	.01118	.01135	.01151	.01185	.01219	.01253	17
18	.01098	.01115	.01132	.01166	.01200	.01235	18
19	.01081	.01098	.01115	.01150	.01150	.01220	19
20	.01066	.01084	.01101	.01136	.01172	.01207	20
21	.01054	.01071	.01089	.01124	.01160	.01196	21
22	.01042	.01060	.01078	.01114	.01150	.01187	22
23	.01033	.01051	.01069	.01105	.01142	.01789	23
24	.01024	.01042	.01060	.01097	.01134	.01172	24
25	.01016	.01035	.01053	.01090	.01128	.01166	25
26	.01010	.01028	.01047	.01084	.01122	.01160	26
27	.01004	.01023	.01041	.01079	.01117	.01156	27
28	.00999	.01018	.01037	.01075	.01113	.01152	28
29	.00994	.01013	.01032	.01071	.01109	.01148	29
30	.00990	.01009	.01029	.01067	.01106	.01145	30
31	.00987	.01006	.01025	.01064	.01103	.01143	31
32	.00984	.01003	.01022	.01061	.01101	.01141	32
33	.00981	.01000	.01020	.01059	.01099	.01139	33
34	.00978	.00998	.01018	.01057	.01097	.01137	34
35	.00976	.00996	.01016	.01055	.01095	.01135	35
40	.00968	.00988	.01008	.01049	.01090	.01130	40
45	.00964	.00984	.01005	.01046	.01087	.01128	45
50	.00961	.00982	.01002	.01044	.01085	.01126	50

TABLE 2:
Mortgage Constant (Monthly Payments) [cont.]

			Interest Rate				
Years	14.00%	14.50%	15.00%	15.50%	16.00%	16.50%	Years
1	.08979	.09002	.09026	.09049	.09073	.09097	1
2	.04801	.04825	.04849	.04872	.04896	.04920	2
3	.03418	.03442	.03467	.03491	.03516	.03540	3
4	.02733	.02758	.02783	.02808	.02834	.02860	4
5	.02327	.02353	.02379	.02405	.02432	.02458	5
6	.02061	.02087	.02115	.02142	.02169	.02197	6
7	.01874	.01902	.01930	.01958	.01986	.02015	7
8	.01737	.01766	.01795	.01824	.01853	.01883	8
9	.01633	.01663	.01692	.01722	.01753	.01783	9
10	.01553	.01583	.01613	.01644	.01675	.01706	10
11	.01489	.01520	.01551	.01582	.01614	.01646	11
12	.01437	.01469	.01501	.01533	.01566	.01599	12
13	.01395	.01428	.01460	.01493	.01527	.01560	13
14	.01360	.01394	.01427	.01461	.01495	.01529	14
15	.01332	.01366	.01400	.01434	.01469	.01504	15
16	.01308	.01342	.01377	.01412	.01447	.01483	16
17	.01287	.01322	.01358	.01394	.01429	.01465	17
18	.01270	.01306	.01342	.01378	.01414	.01451	18
19	.01256	.01292	.01328	.01365	.01402	.01439	19
20	.01244	.01280	.01317	.01354	.01391	.01429	20
21	.01233	.01270	.01307	.01345	.01382	.01420	21
22	.01224	.01261	.01299	.01337	.01375	.01413	22
23	.01216	.01254	.01292	.01330	.01369	.01407	23
24	.01210	.01248	.01286	.01325	.01363	.01403	24
25	.01204	.01242	.01281	.01320	.01359	.01398	25
26	.01199	.01238	.01276	.01316	.01355	.01395	26
27	.01195	.01234	.01273	.01312	.01352	.01392	27
28	.01191	.01230	.01270	.01309	.01349	.01389	28
29	.01188	.01227	.01267	.01307	.01347	.01387	29
30	.01185	.01225	.01264	.01305	.01345	.01385	30
31	.01182	.01222	.01262	.01302	.01343	.01384	31
32	.01180	.01220	.01261	.01301	.01342	.01382	32
33	.01179	.01219	.01259	.01300	.01340	.01381	33
34	.01177	.01217	.01258	.01299	.01339	.01381	34
35	.01176	.01216	.01257	.01298	.01338	.01379	35
40	.01171	.01212	.01253	.01294	.01336	.01377	40
45	.01169	.01210	.01252	.01293	.01334	.01376	45
50	.01168	.01209	.01251	.01292	.01334	.01375	50

TABLE 2:
Mortgage Constant (Monthly Payments) [cont.]

Years	17.00%	17.50%	18.00%	18.50%	19.00%	19.50%	Years
			Interest Rate				
1	.09120	.09144	.09168	.09192	.09216	.09240	1
2	.04944	.04968	.04992	.05017	.05041	.05065	2
3	.03565	.03590	.03615	.03640	.03666	.03691	3
4	.02886	.02911	.02937	.02964	.02990	.03016	4
5	.02485	.02512	.02539	.02567	.02594	.02622	5
6	.02225	.02253	.02280	.02309	.02338	.02366	6
7	.02044	.02073	.02102	.02131	.02161	.02191	7
8	.01912	.01942	.01972	.02003	.02033	.02064	8
9	.01814	.01845	.01876	.01907	.01939	.01971	9
10	.01738	.01770	.01802	.01834	.01867	.01900	10
11	.01679	.01711	.01744	.01778	.01811	.01845	11
12	.01632	.01665	.01699	.01733	.01767	.01802	12
13	.01594	.01629	.01663	.01698	.01733	.01768	13
14	.01564	.01599	.01634	.01669	.01705	.01741	14
15	.01539	.01575	.01610	.01647	.01683	.01719	15
16	.01519	.01555	.01591	.01628	.01665	.01702	16
17	.01502	.01539	.01576	.01613	.01650	.01688	17
18	.01488	.01525	.01563	.01600	.01638	.01677	18
19	.01476	.01514	.01552	.01590	.01629	.01667	19
20	.01467	.01505	.01543	.01582	.01621	.01660	20
21	.01459	.01497	.01536	.01575	.01614	.01653	21
22	.01452	.01491	.01530	.01569	.01609	.01648	22
23	.01446	.01486	.01525	.01565	.01604	.01644	23
24	.01442	.01481	.01521	.01561	.01601	.01641	24
25	.01438	.01478	.01517	.01557	.01598	.01638	25
26	.01434	.01474	.01515	.01555	.01595	.01636	26
27	.01432	.01472	.01512	.01553	.01593	.01634	27
28	.01429	.01470	.01510	.01551	.01691	.01632	28
29	.01427	.01468	.01508	.01549	.01590	.01631	29
30	.01426	.01466	.01507	.01548	.01589	.01630	30
31	.01424	.01465	.01506	.01547	.01588	.01629	31
32	.01423	.01464	.01505	.01546	.01587	.01628	32
33	.01422	.01463	.01504	.01545	.01586	.01628	33
34	.01421	.01462	.01503	.01545	.01586	.01627	34
35	.01421	.01462	.01503	.01544	.01585	.01627	35
40	.01418	.01460	.01501	.01543	.01584	.01626	40
45	.01417	.01459	.01500	.01542	.01584	.01625	45
50	.01417	.01459	.01500	.01542	.01583	.01625	50

TABLE 2:
Mortgage Constant (Monthly Payments) [cont.]

Years	20.00%	20.50%	21.00%	21.50%	22.00%	22.50%	Years
			Interest Rate				
1	.09263	.09287	.09311	.09335	.09359	.09384	1
2	.05090	.05114	.05139	.05163	.05188	.05213	2
3	.03716	.03742	.03768	.03793	.03819	.03845	3
4	.03043	.03070	.03097	.03124	.03151	.03178	4
5	.02649	.02677	.02705	.02734	.02762	.02790	5
6	.02395	.02424	.02454	.02483	.02513	.02542	6
7	.02221	.02251	.02281	.02312	.02343	.02374	7
8	.02095	.02127	.02158	.02190	.02222	.02254	8
9	.02003	.02035	.02067	.02100	.02133	.02166	9
10	.01933	.01966	.01999	.02033	.02067	.02101	10
11	.01879	.01913	.01947	.01982	.02017	.02052	11
12	.01837	.01872	.01907	.01942	.01978	.02014	12
13	.01804	.01839	.01875	.01911	.01948	.01984	13
14	.01778	.01814	.01850	.01887	.01924	.01962	14
15	.01756	.01793	.01831	.01868	.01906	.01944	15
16	.01739	.01777	.01815	.01853	.01891	.01930	16
17	.01726	.01764	.01802	.01841	.01880	.01918	17
18	.01715	.01754	.01792	.01831	.01870	.01910	18
19	.01706	.01745	.01784	.01823	.01863	.01903	19
20	.01699	.01738	.01778	.01817	.01857	.01897	20
21	.01693	.01733	.01772	.01812	.01852	.01893	21
22	.01688	.01728	.01768	.01808	.01849	.01889	22
23	.01684	.01724	.01765	.01805	.01846	.01886	23
24	.01681	.01721	.01762	.01802	.01843	.01884	24
25	.01678	.01719	.01760	.01800	.01841	.01882	25
26	.01676	.01717	.01758	.01799	.01840	.01881	26
27	.01675	.01715	.01756	.01797	.01838	.01880	27
28	.01673	.01714	.01755	.01796	.01837	.01879	28
29	.01672	.01713	.01754	.01795	.01837	.01878	29
30	.01671	.01712	.01753	.01795	.01836	.01877	30
31	.01670	.01721	.01753	.01794	.01835	.01877	31
32	.01670	.01711	.01752	.01794	.01835	.01876	32
33	.01669	.01810	.01752	.01793	.01835	.01876	33
34	.01669	.01710	.01751	.01793	.01834	.01876	34
35	.01668	.01710	.01751	.01793	.01834	.01876	35
40	.01667	.01709	.01750	.01792	.01834	.01875	40
45	.01667	.01709	.01750	.01792	.01833	.01875	45
50	.01667	.01708	.01750	.01792	.01833	.01875	50

TABLE 3:
Mortgage Constant (Annual Payments)

Years	7.00%	7.25%	7.50%	7.75%	8.00%	8.25%	Years
			Interest Rate				
1	1.07000	1.07250	1.07500	1.07750	1.08000	1.08250	1
2	.55309	.55501	.55693	.55885	.56077	.56269	2
3	.38105	.38279	.38454	.38628	.38803	.38979	3
4	.29523	.29690	.29857	.30024	.30192	.30360	4
5	.24389	.24553	.24716	.24881	.25046	.25211	5
6	.20980	.21142	.21304	.21468	.21632	.21796	6
7	.18555	.18717	.18880	.19043	.19207	.19372	7
8	.16747	.16909	.17073	.17237	.17401	.17567	8
9	.15349	.15512	.15677	.15842	.16008	.16175	9
10	.14238	.14403	.14569	.14735	.14903	.15071	10
11	.13336	.13502	.13670	.13838	.14008	.14178	11
12	.12590	.12759	.12928	.13098	.13270	.13442	12
13	.11965	.12135	.12306	.12479	.12652	.12827	13
14	.11434	.11607	.11780	.11954	.12130	.12306	14
15	.10979	.11154	.11329	.11505	.11683	.11862	15
16	.10586	.10762	.10939	.11118	.11298	.11479	16
17	.10243	.10421	.10600	.10781	.10963	.11146	17
18	.09941	.10121	.10303	.10486	.10670	.10856	18
19	.09675	.09857	.10041	.10226	.10413	.10601	19
20	.09439	.09624	.09809	.09997	.10185	.10275	20
21	.09229	.09415	.09603	.09792	.09983	.10176	21
22	.09041	.09229	.09419	.09610	.09803	.09998	22
23	.08871	.09062	.09254	.09447	.09642	.09839	23
24	.08719	.08911	.09105	.09301	.09498	.09697	24
25	.08581	.08775	.08971	.09169	.08368	.09569	25
26	.08456	.08652	.08850	.09050	.09251	.09454	26
27	.08343	.08541	.08740	.08942	.09145	.09350	27
28	.08239	.08439	.08641	.08844	.09049	.09256	28
29	.08145	.08346	.08550	.08755	.08962	.09170	29
30	.08059	.08262	.08467	.08674	.08883	.09093	30
31	.07980	.08185	.08392	.08600	.08811	.09023	31
32	.07907	.08114	.08323	.08533	.08745	.08959	32
33	.07841	.08049	.08259	.08471	.08635	.08901	33
34	.07780	.07990	.08201	.08415	.08630	.08847	34
35	.07723	.07935	.08148	.08364	.08580	.08799	35
40	.07501	.07720	.07940	.08162	.08386	.08611	40
45	.07350	.07575	.07801	.08129	.08259	.08490	45
50	.08246	.07476	.07707	.07940	.08174	.08410	50

TABLE 3:
Mortgage Constant (Annual Payments) [cont.]

			Interest Rate				
Years	8.50%	8.75%	9.00%	9.25%	9.50%	9.75%	Years
1	1.08500	1.08750	1.09000	1.09250	1.09500	.09750	1
2	.56462	.56654	.56847	.57040	.57233	.57426	2
3	.39154	.39330	.39505	.39682	.39858	.40035	3
4	.30529	.30698	.30867	.31036	.31206	.31377	4
5	.25377	.25542	.25709	.25876	.26044	.26212	5
6	.21961	.22126	.22292	.22458	.22625	.22793	6
7	.19537	.19703	.19869	.20036	.20204	.20372	7
8	.17733	.17900	.18067	.18236	.18405	.18574	8
9	.16342	.16511	.16680	.16850	.17020	.17192	9
10	.15241	.15411	.15582	.15754	.15927	.16100	10
11	.14349	.14522	.14695	.14869	.15044	.15220	11
12	.13615	.13790	.13965	.14141	.14319	.14497	12
13	.13002	.13179	.13357	.13535	.13715	.13896	13
14	.12484	.12663	.12843	.13025	.13207	.13390	14
15	.12042	.12223	.12406	.12590	.12774	.12960	15
16	.11661	.11845	.12030	.12216	.12403	.12592	16
17	.11331	.11517	.11705	.11893	.12083	.12274	17
18	.11043	.11232	.11421	.11612	.11805	.11998	18
19	.10790	.10981	.11173	.11367	.11561	.11757	19
20	.10567	.10760	.10955	.11151	.11348	.11546	20
21	.10370	.10565	.10762	.10960	.11159	.11360	21
22	.10194	.10392	.10590	.10791	.10993	.11196	22
23	.10037	.10237	.10438	.10641	.10845	.11050	23
24	.09897	.10099	.10302	.10507	.10713	.10921	24
25	.09771	.09975	.10181	.10388	.10596	.10806	25
26	.09658	.09864	.10072	.10281	.10491	.10703	26
27	.09556	.09764	.09973	.10185	.10397	.10611	27
28	.09464	.09674	.09885	.10098	.10312	.10528	28
29	.09381	.09592	.09806	.10020	.10236	.10454	29
30	.09305	.09519	.09734	.09950	.10168	.10387	30
31	.09237	.09452	.09669	.09887	.10106	.10327	31
32	.09174	.09391	.09610	.09830	.10051	.10275	32
33	.09118	.09336	.09556	.09778	.10000	.10225	33
34	.09066	.09286	.09508	.09731	.09955	.10181	34
35	.09019	.09241	.09464	.09688	.09914	.10141	35
40	.08838	.09056	.09296	.09527	.09759	.09992	40
45	.08722	.08956	.09190	.09426	.09663	.09901	45
50	.08646	.08884	.09123	.09362	.09603	.09844	50

TABLE 3:
Mortgage Constant (Annual Payments) [cont.]

			Interest Rate				
Years	10.00%	10.25%	10.50%	10.75%	11.00%	11.25%	Years
1	1.10000	1.10250	.10500	1.10750	1.11000	1.11250	1
2	.57619	.57812	.58006	.58200	.58393	.58587	2
3	.40211	.40389	.40566	.40744	.40921	.41099	3
4	.31547	.31718	.31889	.32061	.32234	.32405	4
5	.26380	.26548	.26718	.26887	.27057	.27227	5
6	.22961	.23129	.23298	.23468	.23638	.23808	6
7	.20541	.20710	.20880	.21050	.21222	.21393	7
8	.18744	.18915	.19087	.19259	.19432	.19606	8
9	.17364	.17537	.17711	.17885	.18060	.18236	9
10	.16275	.16450	.16626	.16803	.16980	.17159	10
11	.15396	.15574	.15752	.15932	.16112	.16293	11
12	.14676	.14857	.15038	.15220	.15403	.15587	12
13	.14078	.14261	.14445	.14629	.14815	.15002	13
14	.13575	.13760	.13947	.14134	.14323	.14512	14
15	.13147	.13336	.13525	.13715	.13907	.14099	15
16	.12782	.12973	.13164	.13358	.13552	.13747	16
17	.12466	.12960	.12854	.13050	.13547	.13445	17
18	.12193	.12389	.12586	.12785	.12984	.13185	18
19	.11955	.12153	.12353	.12554	.12756	.12960	19
20	.11746	.11947	.12149	.12353	.12558	.12763	20
21	.11562	.11766	.11971	.12171	.12384	.12592	21
22	.11401	.11606	.11813	.12022	.12231	.12442	22
23	.11257	.11465	.11675	.11885	.12097	.12310	23
24	.11130	.11340	.11552	.11765	.11979	.12194	24
25	.11017	.11229	.11443	.11658	.11874	.12091	25
26	.10916	.11130	.11346	.11563	.11781	.12001	26
27	.10826	.11042	.11260	.11479	.11699	.11920	27
28	.10745	.10963	.11183	.11404	.11626	.11849	28
29	.10673	.10893	.11114	.11337	.11561	.11785	29
30	.10608	.10830	.11053	.11277	.11502	.11729	30
31	.10550	.10773	.10998	.11224	.11451	.11679	31
32	.10497	.10722	.10948	.11176	.11404	.11634	32
33	.10450	.10677	.10904	.11133	.11363	.11594	33
34	.10407	.10635	.10864	.11095	.11326	.11558	34
35	.10369	.10598	.10829	.11060	.11293	.11526	35
40	.10226	.10461	.10697	.10943	.11172	.11410	40
45	.10139	.10379	.10619	.10860	.11101	.11344	45
50	.10086	.10329	.10572	.10816	.11060	.11305	50

TABLE 3:
Mortgage Constant (Annual Payments) [cont.]

<table>
<tr><th colspan="8">Interest Rate</th></tr>
<tr><th>Years</th><th>11.50%</th><th>11.75%</th><th>12.00%</th><th>12.50%</th><th>13.00%</th><th>13.50%</th><th>Years</th></tr>
<tr><td>1</td><td>1.11500</td><td>1.11750</td><td>1.12000</td><td>1.12500</td><td>1.13000</td><td>1.13500</td><td>1</td></tr>
<tr><td>2</td><td>.58781</td><td>.58976</td><td>.59170</td><td>.59559</td><td>.59948</td><td>.60338</td><td>2</td></tr>
<tr><td>3</td><td>.41278</td><td>.41456</td><td>.41635</td><td>.41993</td><td>.42352</td><td>.42712</td><td>3</td></tr>
<tr><td>4</td><td>.32577</td><td>.32750</td><td>.32923</td><td>.33271</td><td>.33619</td><td>.33969</td><td>4</td></tr>
<tr><td>5</td><td>.27398</td><td>.27569</td><td>.27741</td><td>.28085</td><td>.28431</td><td>.28779</td><td>5</td></tr>
<tr><td>6</td><td>.23979</td><td>.24151</td><td>.24323</td><td>.24668</td><td>.25015</td><td>.25365</td><td>6</td></tr>
<tr><td>7</td><td>.21566</td><td>.21738</td><td>.21912</td><td>.22260</td><td>.22611</td><td>.22964</td><td>7</td></tr>
<tr><td>8</td><td>.19780</td><td>.19955</td><td>.20130</td><td>.20483</td><td>.20838</td><td>.21197</td><td>8</td></tr>
<tr><td>9</td><td>.18413</td><td>.18590</td><td>.18768</td><td>.19126</td><td>.19487</td><td>.19851</td><td>9</td></tr>
<tr><td>10</td><td>.17338</td><td>.17518</td><td>.17698</td><td>.18062</td><td>.18425</td><td>.18799</td><td>10</td></tr>
<tr><td>11</td><td>.16475</td><td>.16658</td><td>.16842</td><td>.17211</td><td>.17584</td><td>.17960</td><td>11</td></tr>
<tr><td>12</td><td>.15771</td><td>.15957</td><td>.16144</td><td>.16519</td><td>.16899</td><td>.17281</td><td>12</td></tr>
<tr><td>13</td><td>.15190</td><td>.15378</td><td>.15568</td><td>.15950</td><td>.16335</td><td>.16724</td><td>13</td></tr>
<tr><td>14</td><td>.14703</td><td>.14895</td><td>.15087</td><td>.15475</td><td>.14413</td><td>.16262</td><td>14</td></tr>
<tr><td>15</td><td>.14292</td><td>.14487</td><td>.14682</td><td>.15076</td><td>.15474</td><td>.15876</td><td>15</td></tr>
<tr><td>16</td><td>.13943</td><td>.14141</td><td>.14339</td><td>.14739</td><td>.15143</td><td>.15550</td><td>16</td></tr>
<tr><td>17</td><td>.13644</td><td>.13844</td><td>.14046</td><td>.14451</td><td>.14861</td><td>.15274</td><td>17</td></tr>
<tr><td>18</td><td>.13387</td><td>.13590</td><td>.13794</td><td>.14205</td><td>.14620</td><td>.15039</td><td>18</td></tr>
<tr><td>19</td><td>.13164</td><td>.13370</td><td>.13576</td><td>.13993</td><td>.14413</td><td>.14838</td><td>19</td></tr>
<tr><td>20</td><td>.12970</td><td>.13179</td><td>.13388</td><td>.13810</td><td>.14235</td><td>.14665</td><td>20</td></tr>
<tr><td>21</td><td>.12802</td><td>.13012</td><td>.13224</td><td>.13651</td><td>.14081</td><td>.14516</td><td>21</td></tr>
<tr><td>22</td><td>.12654</td><td>.12867</td><td>.13081</td><td>.13513</td><td>.13948</td><td>.14387</td><td>22</td></tr>
<tr><td>23</td><td>.12524</td><td>.12740</td><td>.12956</td><td>.13392</td><td>.13832</td><td>.14275</td><td>23</td></tr>
<tr><td>24</td><td>.12410</td><td>.12628</td><td>.12846</td><td>.13287</td><td>.13731</td><td>.14179</td><td>24</td></tr>
<tr><td>25</td><td>.12310</td><td>.12529</td><td>.12750</td><td>.13194</td><td>.13643</td><td>.14095</td><td>25</td></tr>
<tr><td>26</td><td>.12221</td><td>.12443</td><td>.12665</td><td>.13113</td><td>.13565</td><td>.14021</td><td>26</td></tr>
<tr><td>27</td><td>.12143</td><td>.12366</td><td>.12590</td><td>.13042</td><td>.13498</td><td>.13957</td><td>27</td></tr>
<tr><td>28</td><td>.12073</td><td>.12298</td><td>.12524</td><td>.12980</td><td>.13439</td><td>.13901</td><td>28</td></tr>
<tr><td>29</td><td>.12011</td><td>.12238</td><td>.12466</td><td>.12925</td><td>.13387</td><td>.13852</td><td>29</td></tr>
<tr><td>30</td><td>.11956</td><td>.12185</td><td>.12414</td><td>.12876</td><td>.13341</td><td>.13809</td><td>30</td></tr>
<tr><td>31</td><td>.11908</td><td>.12138</td><td>.12369</td><td>.12833</td><td>.13301</td><td>.13772</td><td>31</td></tr>
<tr><td>32</td><td>.11864</td><td>.12096</td><td>.12328</td><td>.12795</td><td>.13266</td><td>.13739</td><td>32</td></tr>
<tr><td>33</td><td>.11826</td><td>.12058</td><td>.12292</td><td>.12762</td><td>.13234</td><td>.13710</td><td>33</td></tr>
<tr><td>34</td><td>.11791</td><td>.12025</td><td>.12260</td><td>.12732</td><td>.13207</td><td>.13685</td><td>34</td></tr>
<tr><td>35</td><td>.11760</td><td>.11996</td><td>.12232</td><td>.12706</td><td>.13183</td><td>.13662</td><td>35</td></tr>
<tr><td>40</td><td>.11650</td><td>.11890</td><td>.12130</td><td>.12535</td><td>.13099</td><td>.13586</td><td>40</td></tr>
<tr><td>45</td><td>.11586</td><td>.11830</td><td>.12074</td><td>.12519</td><td>.13053</td><td>.13545</td><td>45</td></tr>
<tr><td>50</td><td>.11550</td><td>.11796</td><td>.12042</td><td>.12511</td><td>.13524</td><td>.13524</td><td>50</td></tr>
</table>

TABLE 3:
Mortgage Constant (Annual Payments) [cont.]

			Interest Rate				
Years	14.00%	14.50%	15.00%	15.50%	16.00%	16.50%	Years
1	1.14000	1.14500	1.15000	1.15500	1.16000	1.16500	1
2	.60729	.61120	.61512	.61904	.62296	.62689	2
3	.43073	.43435	.43798	.44161	.44526	.44891	3
4	.34320	.34673	.35027	.35381	.35738	.36095	4
5	.29128	.29479	.29842	.30185	.30541	.30898	5
6	.25716	.26069	.26424	.26780	.27138	.27499	6
7	.23319	.23677	.24036	.24398	.24761	.25128	7
8	.21557	.21920	.22285	.22653	.23022	.23395	8
9	.20217	.20586	.20957	.21332	.21708	.22087	9
10	.19171	.19547	.19925	.20306	.20690	.21077	10
11	.18339	.18722	.19107	.19495	.19886	.20280	11
12	.17667	.18056	.18448	.18844	.19241	.19648	12
13	.17116	.17512	.17911	.18313	.18718	.19127	13
14	.16661	.17063	.17469	.17878	.18290	.18705	14
15	.16281	.16690	.17102	.17517	.17936	.18357	15
16	.15962	.16376	.16795	.17216	.17641	.18069	16
17	.15692	.16112	.16537	.16964	.17395	.17829	17
18	.15462	.15889	.16319	.16752	.17188	.17628	18
19	.15266	.15698	.16134	.16572	.17014	.17459	19
20	.15099	.15536	.15976	.16420	.16867	.17316	20
21	.14954	.15396	.15842	.16290	.16742	.17196	21
22	.14830	.15277	.15727	.16179	.16636	.17094	22
23	.14723	.15174	.15628	.16085	.16545	.17007	23
24	.14630	.15085	.15543	.16004	.16467	.16933	24
25	.14550	.15008	.15470	.15934	.16401	.16871	25
26	.14480	.14942	.15407	.15875	.16345	.16817	26
27	.14419	.14885	.15353	.15823	.16296	.16772	27
28	.14366	.14834	.15306	.15779	.16255	.16733	28
29	.14320	.14792	.15265	.15741	.16219	.16699	29
30	.14280	.14754	.15230	.15708	.16189	.16671	30
31	.14245	.14721	.15200	.15680	.16162	.16646	31
32	.14215	.14693	.15173	.15656	.16140	.16625	32
33	.14188	.14668	.15150	.15635	.16120	.16608	33
34	.13165	.14647	.15131	.15616	.16104	.16592	34
35	.14144	.14628	.15113	.15601	.16089	.16579	35
40	.14075	.14565	.15056	.15549	.16042	.16537	40
45	.14039	.14533	.15028	.15524	.16020	.16517	45
50	.14020	.14517	.15014	.15512	.16010	.16508	50

TABLE 3:
Mortgage Constant (Annual Payments) [cont.]

			Interest Rate				
Years	17.00%	18.00%	19.00%	20.00%	21.00%	22.00%	Years
1	1.17000	1.18000	1.19000	.120000	1.21000	1.22000	1
2	.63083	.63872	.64662	.65455	.66249	.67045	2
3	.45257	.45992	.46731	.47473	.48218	.48966	3
4	.36453	.37174	.37899	.38629	.39363	.40102	4
5	.31256	.31978	.32705	.33438	.34177	.34921	5
6	.27861	.28591	.29327	.30071	.30820	.31576	6
7	.25495	.26236	.26985	.27742	.28507	.29278	7
8	.23769	.24524	.25289	.26061	.26841	.27630	8
9	.22469	.23239	.24019	.24808	.25605	.26411	9
10	.21466	.22251	.23047	.23852	.24667	.25489	10
11	.20676	.21478	.22289	.23110	.23941	.24781	11
12	.20047	.20863	.21690	.22526	.23372	.24228	12
13	.19538	.20369	.21210	.22062	.22923	.23794	13
14	.19123	.19968	.20823	.21689	.22565	.23449	14
15	.18782	.19640	.20509	.21388	.22277	.23174	15
16	.18500	.19371	.20252	.21144	.22044	.22953	16
17	.18266	.19149	.20041	.20944	.21855	.22775	17
18	.18071	.18964	.19868	.20781	.21702	.22631	18
19	.17907	.18810	.19724	.20646	.21577	.22515	19
20	.17769	.18682	.19605	.20536	.21474	.22420	20
21	.17653	.18575	.19505	.20444	.21391	.22343	21
22	.17555	.18485	.19423	.20369	.21322	.22281	22
23	.17472	.18409	.19354	.20307	.21265	.22229	23
24	.17402	.18345	.19297	.20255	.21219	.22188	24
25	.17342	.18292	.19249	.20212	.21180	.22154	25
26	.17292	.18247	.19209	.20176	.21149	.22126	26
27	.17249	.18209	.19175	.20147	.21123	.22103	27
28	.17212	.18177	.19147	.20122	.21101	.22084	28
29	.17180	.18150	.19123	.20102	.21084	.22069	29
30	.17154	.18126	.19103	.20085	.21069	.22057	30
31	.17132	.18107	.19087	.20070	.21057	.22046	31
32	.17113	.18091	.19073	.20059	.21047	.22038	32
33	.17096	.18077	.19061	.20049	.21039	.22031	33
34	.17082	.18065	.19051	.20041	.21032	.22026	34
35	.17070	.18055	.19043	.20034	.21027	.22021	35
40	.17032	.18024	.19018	.20014	.21010	.22008	40
45	.17015	.18010	.19008	.20005	.21004	.22003	45
50	.17007	.18005	.19003	.20002	.21002	.22001	50

TABLE 3:
Mortgage Constant (Annual Payments) [cont.]

			Interest Rate				
Years	23.00%	24.00%	25.00%	26.00%	28.00%	30.00%	Years
1	1.23000	1.24000	1.25000	1.26000	1.28000	1.30000	1
2	.67843	.68643	.69444	.70248	.71860	.73478	2
3	.49717	.50472	.51230	.51990	.53521	.55063	3
4	.40845	.41593	.42344	.43100	.44624	.46163	4
5	.35670	.36425	.37185	.37950	.39495	.41058	5
6	.32339	.33107	.33882	.34662	.36240	.37839	6
7	.30057	.30842	.31634	.32433	.34048	.35688	7
8	.28426	.29229	.30040	.30857	.32512	.34192	8
9	.27225	.28047	.28876	.29712	.31405	.33124	9
10	.26321	.26150	.28007	.28862	.30591	.32346	10
11	.25629	.26485	.27349	.28221	.29984	.31773	11
12	.25093	.25965	.26845	.27732	.29526	.31345	12
13	.24673	.25560	.26454	.27356	.29179	.31024	13
14	.24342	.25243	.26150	.27065	.28912	.30782	14
15	.24079	.24992	.25912	.26848	.28708	.30598	15
16	.23870	.24794	.25724	.26661	.28550	.30458	16
17	.23702	.24636	.25576	.26522	.28428	.30351	17
18	.23568	.24510	.25459	.26412	.28333	.30269	18
19	.23459	.24410	.25366	.26326	.28260	.30207	19
20	.23372	.24329	.25292	.26258	.28202	.30159	20
21	.23302	.24265	.25233	.26204	.28158	.30122	21
22	.23245	.24213	.25186	.26162	.28123	.30094	22
23	.23198	.24172	.25148	.26128	.28096	.30072	23
24	.23161	.24138	.25119	.26102	.28075	.30055	24
25	.23131	.24111	.25095	.26081	.28059	.30043	25
26	.23106	.24090	.25076	.26064	.28046	.30033	26
27	.23086	.24072	.25061	.26051	.28037	.30025	27
28	.23070	.24058	.25048	.26040	.28028	.30019	28
29	.23057	.24047	.25039	.26032	.28032	.30015	29
30	.23046	.24038	.25031	.26025	.28017	.30011	30
31	.23038	.24031	.25025	.26020	.28013	.30009	31
32	.23031	.24025	.25020	.26016	.28010	.30007	32
33	.23025	.24020	.25016	.26013	.28008	.30005	33
34	.23020	.24016	.25013	.26010	.28006	.30004	34
35	.23016	.24013	.25010	.26008	.28005	.30003	35
40	.23006	.24004	.25003	.26003	.28001	.30001	40
45	.23002	.24002	.25001	.26001	.28000	.30000	45
50	.27001	.24001	.25000	.26000	.28000	.30000	50

Index